T0401384

The political economy of Turkey's integration into Europe

Manchester University Press

PROGRESS IN POLITICAL ECONOMY

Series editors: Andreas Bieler (School of Politics and International Relations, University of Nottingham), Gareth Bryant (Department of Political Economy at the University of Sydney), Mònica Clua-Losada (Department of Political Science, University of Texas Rio Grande Valley), Adam David Morton (Department of Political Economy, University of Sydney), and Angela Wigger (Department of Political Science, Radboud University, The Netherlands).

Since its launch in 2014, the blog Progress in Political Economy (PPE) – available at www.ppesydney.net/ – has become a central forum for the dissemination and debate of political economy research published in book and journal article forms with crossover appeal to academic, activist and public policy related audiences.

Now the Progress in Political Economy book series with Manchester University Press provides a new space for innovative and radical thinking in political economy, covering interdisciplinary scholarship from the perspectives of critical political economy, historical materialism, feminism, political ecology, critical geography, heterodox economics, decolonialism and racial capitalism.

The PPE book series combines the reputations and reach of the PPE blog and MUP as a publisher to launch critical political economy research and debates. We welcome manuscripts that realise the very best new research from established scholars and early-career scholars alike.

To buy or to find out more about the books currently available in this series, please go to: https://manchesteruniversitypress.co.uk/series/progress-in-political-economy/

The political economy of Turkey's integration into Europe

Uneven development and hegemony

Elif Uzgören

MANCHESTER UNIVERSITY PRESS

Published by Manchester University Press
Oxford Road, Manchester, M13 9PL

www.manchesteruniversitypress.co.uk

British Library Cataloguing-in-Publication Data
A catalogue record for this book is available from the British Library

ISBN   978 1 5261 7253 2   hardback

First published 2025

EU authorised representative for GPSR:
Easy Access System Europe, Mustamäe tee 50, 10621 Tallinn, Estonia
gpsr.requests@easproject.com

Typeset
by New Best-set Typesetters Ltd

Contents

Tables

Abbreviations

AKP	Justice and Development Party
ANAP	Motherland Party
BDP	Peace and Democracy Party
Birleşik Kamu-İş	Confederation of United Public Workers' Unions
Birleşik Metal-İş	United Metalworkers' Union
BRICS	Brazil, Russia, India, China and South Africa
CEPS	Centre for European Policy Studies
CHP	Republican People's Party
ÇYDD	Association for the Support of Contemporary Life
DEVA	Democracy and Progress Party
DİSK	Confederation of Progressive Trade Unions of Turkey
DP	Democrat Party
DPT	State Planning Organisation
DSP	Democratic Left Party
DYP	True Path Party
EC	European Community
EEC	European Economic Community
ESDP	European Security and Defence Policy
ERT	European Roundtable of Industrialists
ETUC	European Trade Union Confederation
EU	European Union
FDI	foreign direct investment
GDP	gross domestic product
Hak-İş	Confederation of Turkish Real Trade Unions
ILO	International Labour Organization
IMF	International Monetary Fund
ISI	import substitution industrialisation
İHD	Human Rights Association

İKV	Economic Development Foundation
İSO	İstanbul Chamber of Commerce
Ka-der	Association for the Support and Training of Women Candidates
Kamer	Women's Centre, Education, Production, Consultation and Solidarity Foundation
Kesk	Confederation of Public Employees Trade Unions
KOSGEB	Small and Medium Enterprises Development Organization
Memur-Sen	Confederation of Public Servants Trade Unions
MHP	Nationalist Movement Party
MÜSİAD	Independent Industrialists and Businessmen Association
NATO	North Atlantic Treaty Organization
OECD	Organisation for Economic Cooperation and Development
OSD	Automotive Manufacturers Association
ÖDP	Freedom and Solidarity Party
Öz Tarım-İş	Real Trade Union for Workers in Agriculture, Land and the Water Industry
PKK	Kurdistan Workers' Party
SAK	Central Organization of Finnish Trade Unions
SMEs	small and medium-sized enterprises
Tarım Orman-İş	Agriculture and Forestry Union
Tarım-İş	Turkish Forestry, Soil, Water, Agriculture and Agricultural Workers Trade Union
Teksi	Textile, Knitting, Clothing, and Leather Industry Workers' Union of Turkey
Tekstil-İş	Textile Workers' Union
TEMA	Turkish Foundation for Combating Soil Erosion, Reforestation and the Protection of Natural Habitats
TESEV	Turkish Economic and Social Studies Foundation
TIAFI	Team International Assistance for Integration
TİM	Turkish Exporters Assembly
TİP	Workers' Party of Turkey
TİSK	Turkish Confederation of Employer Associations
TOBB	Union of Chambers and Commodity Exchanges of Turkey

Türk-İş	Confederation of Turkish Trade Unions
Türkiye Kamu-Sen	Confederation of Public Employees' Trade Unions
Türk Tarım-Orman-Sen	Union of Public Employees in Agriculture and Forestry of Turkey
TÜSİAD	Turkish Industry and Business Association
TZOB	Union of Turkish Agricultural Chambers
UNHCR	Office of the United Nations High Commissioner for Refugees
WB	World Bank
WTO	World Trade Organization

Introduction

The trajectory of Turkey's European Union (EU) membership question is puzzling and distinct from previous enlargement cases. Turkey's bid to join the European Economic Community (EEC) can be traced back to the Cold War when Turkey first formed an association partnership through the 1963 Ankara Treaty. Turkey's membership bid has lasted over half a century with various ups and downs. Indeed, scholars often describe Turkey–EU relations as 'cyclical with many ups and downs' (Eralp and Eralp, 2012: 164) or like a 'rollercoaster ride' (Yeşilada, 2013: 6). Historically, Turkey followed Greece in its application to form an association partnership, although it was not incorporated into the enlargement waves during the Cold War. When Turkey applied for full membership in 1987, the EEC found it eligible but not sufficiently ready to become a member and therefore suggested deepening integration with the European market through the Customs Union. Turkey is thus the only country to have participated in the Customs Union before attaining membership status. The EU also excluded Turkey from the Big Bang enlargement at the 1997 Luxembourg European Council, following which Turkey froze its political dialogue with the EU. The EU then officially declared Turkey as a candidate at the 1999 Helsinki European Council and started to implement a preaccession strategy.

The wavering character of Turkey–EU relations continued in the 2000s and 2010s. There was a pro-European conjuncture in the 2000s after accession talks opened in 2005 and Turkey's ruling Justice and Development Party (AKP) implemented the EU reform process. Turkey was described as a non-BRICS (Brazil, Russia, India, China and South Africa) emerging market with high growth rates following delocalisation of production globally. Under the AKP regime, Turkey was also presented as a model for Middle Eastern countries of a moderate form of Islam for 'Muslim democrats'. However, this pro-European atmosphere soon dissipated after negotiations were suspended in November 2006. Olli Rehn, then the EU Commissioner for Enlargement, described relations as a train crash due to Turkey's refusal to extend the Customs Union to all EU member states, including Cyprus.

The EU suspended negotiations in eight of thirty-five chapters (*Guardian*, 2006). Only one chapter, Science and Research, has been provisionally closed with six chapters suspended.

Relations deteriorated further in the 2010s within the historical conjuncture of crises of liberalism and the rise of populism. The AKP government was criticised for its authoritarian and majoritarian turn after the Gezi Park protests. Then, after the failed coup attempt on 15 July 2016 and Turkey's adoption of a presidential regime, the EU started to openly criticise its democratic backsliding (European Commission, 2018). Meanwhile, Turkey's future membership became the subject of populist demagogy in Europe (e.g. the Brexit campaign) while Turkish politicians accused the EU of unfair treatment or hypocrisy. Negotiations on a visa/readmission agreement failed to revitalise relations. İbrahim Kalın, senior foreign policy adviser of President Recep Tayyip Erdoğan, described Turkey's foreign policy as 'precious loneliness' (*Financial Times*, 2015). This reflected a non-aligned Turkey with regional ambitions that was decoupling from the West in its policies towards Syria, Libya, Qatar, China and Russia. In a populist move, Erdoğan even suggested that Turkey could join the Shanghai Cooperation Organisation (*Hürriyet Daily*, 2016). The EU has become increasingly critical of Turkey's backsliding from democracy, fundamental rights and freedoms, and its foreign policy related to Syria, Libya and the Eastern Mediterranean. Meanwhile, military tensions have escalated between Turkey and Greece related to conflicting claims over energy resources and maritime rights in the Eastern Mediterranean. In July 2023, President Erdoğan lifted Turkey's objection to Sweden's bid to join the North Atlantic Treaty Organisation (NATO) while calling on European leaders to revitalise Turkey's membership talks. However, EU enlargement has remained off the agenda.

Despite these fluctuations, Turkey–EU relations are generally discussed in the literature around the question of whether Turkey will become an EU member, particularly the future form of Turkey's integration with the EU (e.g. Buzan and Diez, 1999; Çarkoğlu and Rubin, 2003; Eralp and Eralp, 2012; Karakaş, 2013; Müftüler-Baç, 2017; Nas and Özer, 2017; Reiners and Turhan, 2021). However, this overlooks the socio-economic content and power relation of Turkey's ongoing relations with the EU, which pre-eminently relies on negative integration (market liberalisation) without the necessary instruments of positive integration (e.g. social policy, regional funds or free movement of workers). Moreover, Turkey has always been a part of Europe. For instance, during the collapse of the Ottoman Empire it was often referred to as 'the sick man of Europe' – 'sick', but in Europe. Turkey has always been integrated with European structures in various forms in a peripheral context in each historical period.

More importantly, the existing literature on Turkey–EU relations fails to incorporate structural dynamics and does not embed the EU membership question within globalisation. There is a compartmentalisation between literatures on global political economy and European studies in evaluating Turkey's European membership bid. Yet neither Turkey's integration with global political economy nor Turkey's integration into European structures is independent from each other. Turkey stands on the periphery of Europe so its integration into globalisation is not external to the processes surrounding its integration into European structures. Although some studies of Turkey–EU relations incorporate structure into their analyses, they consider international structure as a transformation from a bipolar to a multipolar international system. That is, they consider the Turkish case as a reinterpretation of Turkey–EU relations in the post-Cold War context (e.g. Buzan and Diez, 1999; Eralp and Eralp, 2012; Müftüler-Baç, 1997). This literature conceives of economics and politics as external phenomena, thereby ignoring the material transition and the transnational sphere. Another category of literature that incorporates 'structure' in explaining Turkey–EU relations is institutionalist political economy studies (e.g. Öniş, 2007). However, this literature ignores changes to the production structure and ongoing class struggles. It also discusses opposition in relation to nationalism, thereby constraining resistance to delegation of sovereignty from the national to the supranational level. This ignores labour movements and fails to question the power relations of Turkey's ongoing integration with Europe within the uneven and combined development of global capitalism.

While the bulk of literature on Turkey–EU relations lacks any theoretical perspective (Müftüler-Baç and McLaren, 2003: 19), studies based on specific European integration theories provide limited explanations of these relations. A group of studies has employed classical approaches, neo-functional and intergovernmental premises (e.g. Macmillan, 2009; Müftüler-Baç, 1997; Özen, 1998) to the Turkish enlargement case. Neo-functional logic assumes that countries with functional links join the EU earlier (Schmitter, 2005). Thus, it can hardly explain how functional links between Turkey and the EU has not resulted in Turkey's membership after almost half a century. The neo-functional assumption that Turkey is gradually moving closer to Europe behind an economic rationale (e.g. Macmillan, 2009) is highly problematic given the wavering relations with various ups and downs. Intergovernmentalism, which explains enlargement as the outcome of utility-maximising, rational choices of nation-states through interstate bargaining (e.g. Moravcsik, 1998; Moravcsik and Vachudova, 2003), cannot explain why Turkey agreed to open its market to the EU with the Customs Union while adapting its common external tariff without participating in EU decision making. Although neofunctionalism and intergovernmentalism develop counter-arguments about transcending the nation-state (Haas, 1958) or its endurance (Hoffman, 1966; Milward, 1992), they can be situated in the same neoliberal/neorealist paradigm within international relations. As such, they limit discussion around the transfer of sovereignty from the national to the international sphere, while their reflections on enlargement hardly extend beyond discussing the end-state of negotiations – the form of enlargement.

Especially following the 1999 Helsinki European Council, Turkey–EU relations are increasingly studied through Europeanisation, which proposes that the EU's capability to stimulate change in Turkey's politics increased through political conditionality after it was declared as a candidate country in 1999 (e.g. Aydın and Açıkmeşe, 2007; Aydın and Keyman, 2004; Diez et al., 2005; Müftüler-Baç, 2005; Öniş, 2003; Tocci, 2005). In the last decade, these studies have focused on de-Europeanisation (e.g. Aydın-Düzgit, 2016; Saatçioğlu, 2020; Yılmaz, 2016). However, this category of literature is Eurocentric on two grounds. First, it exaggerates Europe's role in stimulating change while ignoring structural factors. Second, it presents the EU as an ideal and superior type of democracy and economic development that candidate countries have to follow. As Anievas and Nişancıoğlu (2015: 5) argue, Eurocentrism is related to developing an 'internalist story of an autonomous and endogenous "rise of the West"… By positing a strong "inside-out" model of social causality (or methodological internalism) – whereby European development is conceptualised as endogenous and self-propelling – Europe is conceived as the permanent "core" and "prime mover" of history.' This presents non-Europe as 'exploited and passive', which in return erases or overlooks the agency of non-European societies (Anievas and Nişancıoğlu, 2015: 5). There is also a linear developmentalism, another dimension of Eurocentrism, behind the assumption that the European experience of modernity constitutes the universal path to development that non-European societies should follow (Anievas and Nişancıoğlu, 2015: 5).

A third category of literature is influenced by constructivist studies, mostly studying the normative dimension of European integration and the role of norms and rules in constructing identities (e.g. Checkel, 2001; Manners, 2002; Rumelili 2008 and 2011; Schimmelfennig et al., 2006). There is an emphasis on ideational factors in explicating enlargement, such as candidate countries' Europeanness and their contribution to a European identity. While helping to explain the role of ideational factors behind enlargement decisions, applying constructivism to Turkey's case limits discussion to a binary opposition between ideational factors and rational calculations while ignoring material content. That is, Turkey was unable to become a member because it failed to comply with certain European norms and standards (e.g. Schimmelfennig et al., 2006). Moreover, constructivism presents the EU as a civilian power as if there is no asymmetrical power relation between Europe's core and periphery in global capitalism. Here, Cox reminds us that 'imperialism is a rather loose concept which in practice has to be newly defined with reference to each historical period' (Cox, 1981: 142). For instance, Turkey is the main destination for Europe's waste, with Turkey taking 14.7 million tonnes in 2021, almost half of the EU's waste exports (Eurostat, 2022). Additionally, constructivist research presents the EU as a civilian power, thereby reducing imperialism to military intervention and abstracting imperialism from capitalist accumulation and economic strategies in the uneven and combined development of capitalism.

The Political Economy of Turkey's Integration into Europe: Uneven Development and Hegemony examines Turkey–EU relations from a critical political economy perspective by using a historical materialist theoretical lens. It thus considers Turkey–EU relations as an instance of class struggle within the uneven and combined geographical expansion of capitalist accumulation. There are four merits of adapting a historical materialist perspective. First, it situates Turkey–EU relations within the structural dynamics of globalisation and deglobalisation. It embeds the debate on Turkey's membership within the structural coordinates of core–periphery relations and discusses how uneven and combined capitalist development has reconfigured Turkey–EU relations at different historical conjunctures in the global political economy. Whereas global production was delocalising to the periphery – Global South – in the 2000s, with Turkey described as an emerging market, Turkey–EU relations are reconsidered in the 2010s according to the new coordinates of deindustrialisation, changes in global supply chain, populism and the COVID-19 pandemic. Second, rather than taking the future form of Turkey's membership bid at the centre of analysis, the book questions the power relations and socio-economic content of ongoing integration. Third, it unravels agency regarding who supports or contests membership, thereby opening a debate for alternatives. It investigates Turkey's membership question as an 'open-ended struggle' over hegemony, the outcome of which can only be determined by class struggle. Fourth, it analyses economics and politics (state/society relations) as integral for each period in its historical specificity.

More specifically, the book questions whether there was a hegemonic project in Turkey regarding membership in the 2000s. Was there an alternative counter-hegemonic project opposing membership? Which social forces, if any, supported an alternative and could they form a united front? How have deglobalisation, crises of liberalism and the COVID-19 pandemic impacted the coordinates of core–periphery relations? How do Turkey's social forces reconsider the membership project given the crises of liberalism and geostrategic rivalry? In the following chapters, I argue that there was not one pro-membership and one alternative counter-hegemonic project in the 2000s. The struggle was much more complex. The pro-membership was hegemonic in the 2000s supported by internationally and nationally oriented capital, as well as the AKP and state institutions related to the global economy. Social forces disadvantaged by globalisation contested the pro-membership perspective by developing two rival class strategies: Ha–vet (No to Capital's Europe, but yes to Social Europe) and neo-mercantilism. Yet none of them provided an overall alternative in the 2000s. The book then reconsiders the struggle among social forces in the 2010s and examines Turkey–EU relations in the new coordinates of global economy and core–periphery relations. Crises of liberalism, the COVID-19 pandemic, deindustrialisation on the periphery and wealth concentration in the global economy, as well as contradictions in the growth model of emerging markets in the Global South have widened the development gap between developed and developing countries. Accordingly, Turkey–EU relations is likely to return to the security perspective rather than being discussed within the context of membership. It is likely that the unevenness of Turkey–EU relations will further deepen through consolidating negative integration (market liberalisation and deregulation) without any mechanisms of positive integration (social protection or social policies to compensate market failures). The EU's official reports reveal that Turkey is discussed mostly in relation to bilateral cooperation on specific policies, such as migration management or strengthening resilience in the European neighbourhood. Turkey's representatives of capital aspire to modernise the Customs Union through further liberalising agriculture, services and/or public procurement. They defended the pro-membership perspective with two new arguments in the 2010s that EU membership would help Turkey comply with two transformations: the Green transition and digitalisation. Yet social forces disadvantaged by globalisation and liberalisation increased their critical voice related to the EU, and are likely develop a more critical stance in the absence of membership prospects or any social dimension such as free movement of workers and benefits from structural funds.

This book fills a gap in the literature in two main ways. First, Turkey's EU membership question has not yet been analysed from a critical political economy perspective using the tools of historical materialism. The European studies literature has been mostly developed by pro-European scholars, whereas critical perspectives (e.g. critical political economy or feminism) are largely marginalised for being Eurosceptic (Manners and Whitman, 2016). There have been studies in critical political economy literature analysing the socio-economic content behind European integration (e.g. Bieler and Morton, 2001; Bieling et al., 2016; Bonefeld, 2015; Nousios et al., 2012; Ryner and Cafruny, 2017; van Apeldoorn et al., 2009) and enlargement (e.g. Bieler, 2000; Bohle, 2006; Holman, 1996; Shields, 2012). However, this book is the first to study Turkey's membership bid using the analytical tools of critical political economy. A few historical materialist inspired studies have employed a critical and historical perspective on Turkey's integration with Europe. Gehring acknowledges the role of the EU in consolidation of neoliberal restructuring in Turkey highlighting the need to develop a critical lens on EU integration to explicate deeper contradictions as a result of reforms embedded in 'Copenhagen's double-bias of democratic criteria and an agenda of accelerated neoliberalisation' (Gehring, 2021: 104–105). Yet his analysis does not uncover the coordinates of class struggle in the last two decades through an empirical focus on the position of Turkey's social forces. Axel Gehring's book presents a more comprehensive analysis; however, it is published in German (Gehring, 2019). Tekeli and İlkin's (1993a, 1993b, 2000) three-volume study presents a historical analysis of Turkey–EU relations from the 1950s through a focus on the positions of different fractions of capital, political elites and political parties. Manisalı (2002, 2005, 2009) developed a critical perspective to Turkey–EU relations with an emphasis on the Turkish market's dependence on the EU, the imperial character of relations and its uneven development. However, these existing studies did not present relations as an instance of class struggle and completely ignored the position of Turkish labour. More importantly, their analyses reflect methodological nationalism by presenting the actors' positions without considering the structure of global capitalism. Moreover, these works were published in Turkish. There are critical studies adapting a historical materialist perspective of the trajectory of Turkey's integration with globalisation and neoliberalism (e.g. Aydın, 2005; Önder, 2016; Yalman, 2009) and some recent studies from a critical political economy perspective of Turkey's state–society relations under authoritarian neoliberalism (e.g. Altınörs and Akçay, 2022; Babacan et al., 2021; Bedirhanoğlu, 2020; Gürcan and Mete, 2017; Önder, 2016; Şahin and Erol, 2021; Tansel, 2018; Yalman et al., 2018). However, in discussing transition, these studies take global structure, not the EU, as an instance of regionalisation. Yalman and Göksel (2017) highlight the need to develop a historical materialist perspective regarding Turkey–EU relations, filling a vacuum by presenting a critical narrative with a historical perspective. Yet their analyses do not rely on an empirical analysis of positions of social forces and they highlight the EU's role in Turkey's neoliberal transition without presenting alternatives. In a nutshell, there is no book from an overall historical materialist perspective in Turkish or in English.

The second gap that this book fills is through its empirical research. The literature on Turkey–EU relations has largely been limited to analysing political decisions – in other words, the politics of enlargement. Some studies have empirically analysed the position of capital and political parties vis-à-vis membership (e.g. Çarkoğlu and Rubin, 2003; Öniş, 2007). However, they have not presented this as an instance of class struggle. In particular, they have ignored the opposition of labour and other social groups disadvantaged by globalisation. Alternatives to EU membership in Turkey's society have been neglected or only considered in relation to alternative foreign policy alignments of Turkey, like strengthening relations with Turkic states (e.g. Yeşilada, 2013) or alternatives to full membership like privileged partnership (e.g. Karakaş, 2013) and calls for a new and more flexible start of Turkey-EU relations discussed as 'concentric circles' or a 'spaghetti bowl' (e.g. Müftüler-Baç, 2017). More importantly, opposition is often identified with conservative and nationalist groups around identity politics (e.g. Yılmaz, 2011). The literature has turned a blind eye to debating alternatives among disadvantaged groups as a result of negative repercussions of neoliberal restructuring and globalisation carried through the EU membership perspective. However, there is more space for opposition in Turkey due to the uneven development of Turkey's integration. Since completing the Customs Union in 1996, Turkey has not only opened its market to competitive European firms but also liberalised its economy without any compensatory protective mechanisms of membership for disadvantaged groups, such as structural funds and/or free movement of workers, to alleviate social tensions.

This book addresses its research questions through an empirical study conducted in three rounds of interviews. The first round was conducted with sixty-nine interviewees in May 2010 and December 2011 when I was a PhD candidate at the University of Nottingham. At that time, there was a pro-European political atmosphere in Turkey. Some interviews were repeated in January/February 2017 at a historical juncture characterised by deglobalisation and a crisis of liberalism and populism. The third round of interviews took place in June/July 2022 and 2023. In total, 109 interviews were conducted. The interviews included five categories of questions to unravel the rationale behind the supportive and/or critical stance of social forces: globalisation, the effects of participation in the Internal Market and eurozone, social policy, foreign policy and democratisation. The collected data was supported by cross-checking with primary resources. The interview participants included five categories of actors: representatives of capital, labour and political parties, state officials, and representatives of social forces in the social factory of capitalism around struggles of ecology, patriarchy, human rights and migration. Regarding the first category, I consider the textile and automotive sectors as internationally oriented, given their privileged position within Turkey's export-promotion strategy, whereas I consider small and medium-sized enterprises (SMEs) and the agricultural sector as nationally oriented. Turkey's agriculture sector, which is not included in the Customs Union except for processed agricultural products, remains sheltered and produces for the domestic market. The interviews are presented as anonymous as it is the position of institutions rather than individual opinions that are taken as the bases for analysis.

Regarding the attitudes of these five categories, I assume that internationally oriented capital will support EU membership as the means to stimulate exports and consolidate an open market economy. Conversely, nationally oriented capital will oppose membership because it will be negatively affected by the opening of markets to competition and elimination of state subsidies. Regarding labour's position, there is more space in Turkey to expect an alternative to EU membership as Turkey participated in the Customs Union prior to membership without any of the compensatory social measures associated with full membership. Drawing on Bieler (2000: 48; 2005: 461), I hypothesise that trade unions that organise workers in international/ transnational production sectors will support membership, whereas trade unions organising workers employed in nationally oriented sectors will be more critical. For the last three categories I integrate political and civil society into the analysis to question whether social forces can transcend their economic-corporate phase and consolidate or contest hegemony in political and civil society. Regarding the third category, political parties, I assume that right-wing political parties will support membership in line with their support of globalisation, whereas political parties whose social base rests on workers, SMEs, peasants and public employees will develop a more critical stance. The fourth category, officials from state institutions, are more likely to favour membership if their institutions are linked to the global economy. Conversely, state institutions that implement policies for groups disadvantaged by globalisation, such as planning offices and ministries of labour, are likely to be sidelined. Lastly, I consider struggles over ecology and patriarchy as examples of resistance to the discipline of capital across the entire reproductive system and expect their representatives to contest globalisation.

Chapter 1, 'Historical materialism: encountering the post-Marxist critique', introduces the conceptual framework, specifically the social relations of production, class, intra-class struggle, passive revolution, hegemony and uneven and combined development. It operationalises the research design and lays out the coordinates of intra-class struggle. It then engages with the post-Marxist critique. Historical materialist scholarship is asserted to be in crisis, especially following the neoliberal turn in the 1980s and the collapse of the socialist project. The poststructural and post-Marxist critique is an important one, with some feminists 'divorcing' from Marxism (e.g. Hartmann, 1979) and post-Marxists criticising historical materialism for economic essentialism and class reductionism. For instance, Laclau and Mouffe in *Hegemony and Socialist Strategy* (1985) criticise Marxism for class and economic reductionism. They introduce radical and plural democracy to encompass struggles of exploitation and domination. Similarly, Hardt and Negri (2000 and 2004) claim in *Empire* that the 'postmodernisation of the global economy' has engendered a new political subjectivity, substituting industrial labour with the multitude. In response, historical materialist scholars criticise post-Marxism and claim that the social relations of production remain central to historical materialist analyses. I address various important questions raised by this debate: Does historical materialism overlook plural forms of social antagonisms, thereby confining agency to production and class? How do Marxist scholars respond to these critiques? What is the legacy of the post-Marxist critique after the economic crisis and the rise of populism? The post-Marxist critique of historical materialism is important given the current historical context of deindustrialisation, digitalisation, rising individualism and prevailing identity politics. It also establishes a conceptual basis to integrate struggles over political recognition, such as feminist and ecological struggles, in the following empirical chapters. After laying out the disagreements, I argue that post-Marxism operates within capitalism's dualisms – the separation between economics and politics – a condition that 'de-socialises the material'. In contrast, historical materialism goes beyond the ideational-material dualism to present the struggle within the sphere of social reproduction as an internal relationship in a dialectical manner as a totality – in agreement with van der Pijl (1998: 36 and 47) that it is the 'discipline of capital over the entire reproductive system' that has to be resisted. Bieler and Morton (2018: 150) locate it as 'class struggle in the social factory of capitalism'. Accordingly, in the following empirical chapters I discuss alternatives to EU membership as class struggle within capitalist discipline.

Chapter 2, 'Integration of a peripheral country into the capitalist world system: Turkey's political economy', situates Turkey–EU relations within the uneven development of global capitalism and highlights particular coordinates of class struggle historically. This prepares the ground for discussing the current struggle among social forces in the following three empirical chapters. The chapter primarily draws on concepts and categories from the historical materialist literature, with particular emphasis on Gramsci and Gramscian historical materialism and the literature on the political economy of Turkey. The analysis is structured into three distinct historical periods based on the coordinates of capitalist accumulation: the Fordist period of the 1960s and 1970s; the neoliberal turn in the 1980s; and the post-2008 authoritarian neoliberal period. Turkey–EU relations are analysed at the end of each section to address the following questions. How can we read Turkey's transition to capitalism under structural conditions of uneven exchange? How has neoliberal restructuring during the 1980s impacted

Turkey–EU relations? How have the Great Recession, the COVID-19 pandemic, rising populism and authoritarianism transformed the new coordinates of core–periphery relations and conditioned the future of Turkey–EU relations? I argue that during Keynesian embedded liberalism, there was no clear consensus on membership. Instead, relations reflected a tug of war between those social forces favouring industrialisation through protectionism, and those supporting liberalisation through the Customs Union. Following the neoliberal turn, Turkey applied for membership in 1987 and joined the Customs Union in 1995 in the absence of a labour perspective. I then read Turkey's current AKP regime as an example of *trasformismo* as a condition of the 'formation of an ever more extensive ruling class' that has consolidated neoliberal restructuring (Gramsci, 1971: 58). In the 2010s, the Gezi Park protests, 15 July 2016 coup attempt and the change to a presidential regime, coupled with the contradictions of dependent financialisation and the state's increasingly coercive mechanisms, engendered an authoritarian neoliberal regime. During this period, Turkey–EU relations are discussed outside the membership perspective while developing in a transactional manner by promoting cooperation in particular strategic sectors, such as migration, health and/or person-to-person contact.

Chapter 3, 'Globalisation and class struggle between Turkish capital and labour during the 2000s reform process', examines the class struggle between capital and labour in the 2000s to address the following questions. Was there a pro-European hegemonic project in the 2000s and, if so, which social forces supported it? Was the pro-membership project hegemonic with capital groups able to lead society by presenting the project on a universal terrain in civil society? Was the labour movement able to come up with an alternative to the neoliberal pro-membership perspective? If not, how can we account for their failure? I argue that internationally oriented capital promoted EU membership to stimulate competitiveness whereas nationally oriented capital either adapted to globalisation by promoting national champions or gave their consent as they were already integrated into the global economy, mostly via outsourcing. The pro-membership project thus became hegemonic with capital groups able to present membership on a universal terrain using arguments that went beyond their vested interests. In response, labour developed two class strategies for contesting pro-membership. Internationally oriented labour accepted globalisation as 'irresistible' and therefore advocated an international struggle. Thus, they defend membership under the motto, 'Another globalisation and Europe is possible'. Nationally oriented labour was concerned that the liberalisation required by membership would cause deindustrialisation. Nevertheless, they supported membership so long as they benefitted from EU structural funds.

Chapter 4, 'Globalisation and struggle in political and civil society', extends the class struggle in the 2000s to three further categories: political parties, state institutions and the social factory of capitalism. It questions to what extent the ruling class could transcend their economic vested interests – the economic-corporate phase – in articulating their project on a universal terrain for the hegemonic moment in political and civil society. I also question whether counter-hegemonic social forces could transcend their economic-corporate phase and contest pro-membership in political and civil society. Could struggles around ecology, feminism, human rights and migration form a united struggle? I argue that the pro-membership project was hegemonic as ideas associated with membership were defended on universal terms in political and civil society. I suggest that, rather than one project for and one project against EU membership, there were two rival class strategies contesting pro-membership in Turkey in the 2000s: neo-mercantilism and Ha–vet (No–Yes), neither of which provided an overall alternative. The former opposed the capitalist nature of European integration and stood for Social Europe under the motto 'Another Europe is possible'. The latter advocated 'membership on equal terms and conditions', supporting membership so long as Turkey benefitted from the EU's social policy, structural funds and the free movement of workers.

Chapter 5, 'Deglobalisation? Reconsidering the struggle under authoritarian neoliberalism', revisits the struggle in the 2010s within the conjuncture of global capitalism and probable future coordinates of core–periphery relations characterised by deglobalisation, populism, the crisis of neoliberalism and the COVID-19 pandemic. Scholars often describe Turkey's political landscape under AKP rule after 2013 as an authoritarian turn or democratic backsliding. Discussions emerge about a 'New Turkey' with a new capitalist structure and political and institutional set-up (e.g. Buğra and Savaşkan, 2014; Özbudun, 2014). Turkey experienced dismantling of the separation of powers as well as other institutions of the modern nation-state, privatisation and personification of power as well as polarisation of society into two camps, increasing coercion and suppression of dissent. In this period, Erdoğan called on Turkey to follow the Chinese model in its growth strategy (*Hürriyet Daily*, 2021). Chapter 5 considers the new coordinates of dependence between core and periphery in the 2010s and how EU–Turkey relations will be redefined in this context. The pull factors of EU membership (e.g. membership would consolidate democracy and stimulate growth) are increasingly questioned in tandem with rising populist politics as well as the uneven development of economic integration and socio-economic disparities between Europe's core and periphery. In such a context, what arguments can social forces offer to continue sustaining the pro-membership project? How are Turkish industry's competitive sectors in manufacturing, such as textiles and the automotive industry, influenced by changes in the global supply chain stimulated by the COVID-19 pandemic and geostrategic rivalry? I then consider the stance of labour as well as representatives in political and civil society. How does Turkish labour perceive the struggle? Has labour's 'yes, but' stance changed? Is there a 'Lexit' (a Left exit) debate regarding the Customs Union? How do social forces in the social factory of capitalism debate membership within the current context of authoritarian neoliberalism?

1

Historical materialism: encountering the post-Marxist critique

Historical materialism is asserted to have been in crisis at various junctures in history via critique of economic essentialism and class reductionism. Proponents often refer to social change while defending its crises such as dislocations in capitalism, rising individualism in capitalist societies, informalisation and digitalisation in economies. It was especially after the collapse of the Soviet Union and the socialist project that historical materialism was announced as anachronistic. Yet it was through the 1980s neoliberal restructuring and rise of identity politics, coupled with postmodernist and poststructural critique, that historical materialist scholarship was severely criticised. In return, historical materialist scholars argue for its renewal. This chapter engages with a debate between post-Marxism and historical materialism. The post-Marxist critique is an important one given the current historical context of deindustrialisation, digitalisation, rising individualism and prevailing identity politics. It problematises and intervenes in the relation between identity and class politics pre-eminent in contemporary social theory and political practice. In terms of political praxis, radical democracy is also asserted as an alternative to socialism. As Wood (1995: 271) contends, radical democracy has also been seen as a substitute for socialism among various fractions of the Left since the 1990s. This debate is equally decisive in uncovering contours to integrate struggles over political recognition – e.g. feminist and ecological struggles in the following empirical chapters.

This chapter first introduces the historical materialist conceptual framework that will be employed in the following chapters. It operationalises the research design and lays out the coordinates of intra-class struggle after the 2000s. The chapter then engages with the post-Marxist critique and lays out the historical materialist arguments. The following questions are discussed: What are the criticisms of post-Marxist scholarship to historical materialism? Does historical materialism overlook plural forms of social antagonisms, thereby confining agency to production and class? How do Marxist scholars respond to these critiques? After laying out the disagreements, I argue that post-Marxism operates within capitalism's dualisms of economics and politics, as well as state and civil society relations. It thus 'de-socialises the material' and fails to present a critique to domination under global capitalism. In contrast, historical materialism goes beyond this ideational-material dualism to present the struggle within the sphere of social reproduction as a social totality. It equally treats economics and politics as well as states and markets as an internal relationship in a dialectical manner. Accordingly, in the following empirical chapters I discuss alternatives to EU membership alongside environment struggles, human rights and the patriarchy as class struggle in the capitalist discipline.

The research design: operationalising historical materialism

This book specifically embarks on two historical materialist categories in explaining Turkey's integration with European structures: uneven and combined development and hegemony. Trotsky (1929/2007: 121) refers to uneven and combined development while arguing that socialism in one country or national socialism was 'economically and politically untenable'. For him, capitalism's historical evolution shows that it developed unevenly while generating dependencies among capitalist countries, a condition he referred to as the 'law of uneven development' (Trotsky, 1928/1957: 21). As Trotsky noted:

> it would have been more correct to say that the entire history of mankind is governed by the law of uneven development ... Capitalism finds various sections of mankind at different stages of development, each with its profound internal contradictions. The extreme diversity in the levels attained, and the extraordinary unevenness in the rate of development of the different sections of mankind during the various epochs, serve as the starting point of capitalism. Capitalism gains mastery only gradually over the inherited unevenness (Trotsky, 1928/1957: 19)

The international character of capitalism equally generates its combined nature. To refer to Trotsky (1930/2000: 5) again, 'The law of combined development reveals itself most indubitably, however, in the history and character of Russian industry. Arising late, Russian industry did not repeat the development of the advanced countries, but inserted itself into this development, adapting their latest achievement to its own backwardness.' As he explained: 'binding all countries together with its mode of production and its commerce, capitalism has converted the whole world into a single economic and political organism' (Trotsky, 1906/2007: 87). Trotsky also refers to dependence among advanced and backward countries:

> Every backward country integrated with capitalism has passed through various stages of decreasing or increasing dependence upon the other capitalist countries, but in general the tendency of capitalist development is toward a colossal growth of world ties, which is expressed in the growing volume of foreign trade, including, of course, capital export. (Trotsky, 1929/2007: 136–137)

Similarly, Anievas and Nişancıoğlu (2015: 46) argue that the combined development of capitalism constantly results in the existence of developmentally differentiated societies due to the 'multilinear, causally polycentric, and co-constitutive' nature of their interconnectedness. They define the combined nature of capitalism as follows:

> the ways in which the internal relations of any given society are determined by their interactive relations with other developmentally differentiated societies, while the very interactivity of these relations produces amalgamated sociopolitical institutions, socio-economic systems, ideologies and material practices melding the native and foreign, the 'advanced' and 'backward', within any given social formation. (Anievas and Nişancıoğlu, 2015: 48)

Rosenberg (e.g. 2013 and 2021) has further developed uneven and combined development in international relations theory. He contends that the analytical category of uneven and combined development contributes to overcoming the 'predominance of internalism' or 'methodological nationalism' in social sciences, which is 'the explanation of social phenomena by reference to the inner characteristics alone of a given society or type of society' (Rosenberg, 2013: 569). It contributes to grasping the 'international' through 'visualising parts and whole together, both simultaneously and in their interaction' (Rosenberg, 2021: 148). To quote Rosenberg (2021: 149):

> there has always existed an 'international' dimension of some kind; that the horizon of social causality and political agency has never been restricted exclusively to conditions *inside* a given society; and that any general social theories that do not include this inter-societal dimension *must* rest upon a false abstraction of the historical process. (emphasis in original)

Similarly, Anievas and Nişancıoğlu claim that the theory of uneven and combined development presents an internationalist historiography in explicating a particular social phenomenon. For instance, they argue that the origins of capitalism and the rise of the West have been pre-eminently studied through a simple Eurocentric narrative that positions Europe as 'the privileged or sole author of history' (Anievas and Nişancıoğlu, 2015: 94–95 and 276). This not only explains the origins of capitalism as a '*sui generis* development unique to Europe' but also depicts non-European societies as 'passive bystander[s], at the receiving end of Europe's colonial whip, or a comparative foil – an Other – against which the specificity and superiority of Europe is defined' (Anievas and Nişancıoğlu, 2015: 4). However, they claim that the origin of capitalism is not simply 'an intra-European phenomenon, but a decidedly international (or intersocietal) one: one in which non-European agency relentlessly impinged upon and (re)directed the trajectory and nature of European development' (Anievas and Nişancıoğlu, 2015: 4). Similarly, Nişancıoğlu (2014: 331 and 332) argues that uneven and combined development overcomes both the ontological singularity and unilinear conception of history embedded in assumptions of Eurocentric international relations theory. For instance, the Ottoman role in trade and military conflict with the Habsburgs was decisive in the rise of modern nation-state and the internationalisation of merchant activity in Europe (Nişancıoğlu, 2014: 346). Thus Nişancıoğlu (2014: 346) states: 'there were numerous other causal chains – vectors of uneven and combined development – both European and extra-European that must be incorporated into a full understanding of capitalism's origins'. Duzgun also argues that uneven and combined development enables our analysis to 'capture the interactive, temporal and cumulative constitutions of world historical development' (Duzgun, 2022: 300).

Rosenberg and Boyle (e.g. 2019) contend that the uneven and combined development is not confined to late industrialisation but is applicable to other historical specificities. Similarly, Bieler and Morton acknowledge that capitalism's uneven and combined development explains not only its expansion into non-capitalist geographies through state formation processes on the periphery but also the current coordinates of capitalist social relations within global capitalism, including China's integration into global capitalism and Greece's integration into the European core (Bieler and Morton, 2018: 98–99). Yet Callinicos, in the letters exchanged with Rosenberg on the 'transhistorical' general abstractions of uneven and combined development, highlights that analyses embarking on uneven and combined development have to be attentive to 'the structures and tendencies of definite modes of production' in explicating the 'international' and 'specific modalities of the inter-societal' (Callinicos and Rosenberg, 2010: 169–170). Similarly, Bieler (2013: 172) emphasises the need to uncover the specific coordinates of capitalist social relations of production of the specific historical period in discussing the uneven historical development of capitalism. Morton (2010b: 215) also argues that there is a need to be careful about 'the actual modalities of historical and empirical unevenness and the combination of different stages of development within capitalism as a mode of production'.

The second historical materialist category that this book embarks on is hegemony. For Gramsci, hegemony is a moment in which the ruling class takes 'moral and intellectual leadership' by transcending 'the corporate limits of the purely economic class, and can and must become the interests of other subordinate groups too' (Gramsci, 1971: 181). Here, hegemony is a form of class rule secured both by consent and the coercive mechanisms of the state (Overbeek, 2000: 173). It is not limited to state domination; rather, it encompasses material resources, institutions and ideas. This definition implies that the struggle over hegemony proceeds on two levels. At the economic-corporate level, the 'tradesman feels obliged to stand by another tradesman, a manufacturer by another manufacturer, etc', while the hegemonic moment is reached when 'the corporate limits of the purely economic class' is transcended by forming relations of force (Gramsci, 1971: 181–82). The hegemonic level is political as it 'marks the decisive passage from the structure to the sphere of complex superstructures' (Gramsci, 1971: 181–182). This occurs when a particular social group prevails and gains an upper hand in the conflict by 'bringing about not only a unison of economic and political aims, but also intellectual and moral unity, posing all the questions around which the struggle rages not on a corporate but on a "universal" plane' (Gramsci, 1971: 181–182). Bates neatly sums up the Gramscian concept of hegemony as a form of rule led by a particular class that has convinced 'others of the validity of its world view' (Bates, 1975: 352 and 355). In other words, hegemony emphasises that people are 'not ruled by force alone, but also by ideas' (Bates, 1975: 351). It stands as a form of intellectual and moral unity on a 'universal' plane (Gramsci, 1971: 181–182).

This definition has two particular merits. First, Gramsci observes that 'even bourgeois hegemony is not automatic but achieved through conscious political action and organisation' (Hobsbawm, 1977: 209). It advances the classical conception to encompass one that 'describes structures of bourgeois power in the West' (Anderson, 1976: 20). Second, Gramsci extends the struggle over hegemony to the working class and subaltern groups. Indeed, his reference to the 'need for the Left to break out of an "economic-corporate" outlook and construct a hegemonic politics of its own' was a decisive theoretical opening (Forgacs, 1989: 72). In *Some Theoretical and Practical Aspects of 'Economism'*, Gramsci (1971: 160) cogently observes that theoretical syndicalism prevents 'a subaltern group … from ever becoming dominant, or from developing beyond the economic-corporate stage and rising to the phase of ethical-political hegemony in civil society, and of domination in the State'. Consequently, he is considered a figure within historical materialism who emphasises 'the active, voluntarist side of Marxist theory, as opposed to the fatalistic reliance upon objective economic forces and scientific laws' (Femia, 2002: 117). His critique of spontaneity sits alongside his reference to the need for political contingency (Gramsci, 1971: 196). Following Thomas, it can be said that 'Gramsci's carceral research can be succinctly characterised as the search for an adequate theory of proletarian hegemony in the epoch of the "organic crisis" or the "passive revolution" of the bourgeois "integral State"' (Thomas, 2009: 136).

In the following chapters, the analysis of the struggle over hegemony in relation to Turkey's membership bid is based on the social relations of production. Marx describes production as a totality, a social body, social subject – in other words 'production in general' (Marx, 1857–1858/1973: 86). It is not simply the production of physical goods in factories but the social relations of production. As famously put by Marx (1857–1858/1973: 85) it is an abstraction and 'whenever we speak of production ... what is meant is always production at a definite stage of social development – production by social individuals'. To quote Marx: 'capital is not a thing, but a social relation between persons which is mediated through things' (Marx, 1867/1990: 932). Cox expresses this totality by stating that production is not limited to the 'supply of the physical requisites of life', but rather entails the creation of historical structures, institutions and relationships that determine modes of life and the accumulation of resources, which collectively constitute the 'material reproduction of society' (Cox, 1987: 396). Bieler and Morton (2018: 37) describe this ontological starting point of social relations of production as 'everyday patterns of behaviour involved in the production and consumption of physical goods as well as the discursive institutional and cultural tactics established to ensure the hegemony of existing social relations'. Hence, '*relations* of production' are central rather than '*forces* of production', pinpointing the material's dependence on social structures (van Apeldoorn, 2002: 17).

The book takes class struggle as the basis for its analysis. In *The Eighteenth Brumaire of Louis Bonaparte*, Marx (1852/1934: 106) describes class as referring to people who live under similar conditions 'that separate their mode of life, their interests, and their culture from those of the other classes, and put them in hostile opposition to the latter'. There are studies which examine European integration and enlargement as class struggle (e.g. Bieler, 2000; Cafruny and Ryner, 2003; Holman, 1996; Shields, 2003; van Apeldoorn, 2002). Yet 'due to the diversity of the way production is organised, there are rarely two homogenous classes opposing each other in capitalism' (Bieler, 2006: 32). Bieler argues that European enlargement outcomes should be studied as an open-ended struggle among different nationally, internationally and transnationally oriented social forces whose interests are determined by the structural factors of globalisation, and the transnationalisation of production and finance (Bieler, 2000: 1–4). In this sense, class struggle is not confined to national capital and labour but is examined in relation to various fractions of capital and labour (intra-class struggle). Similarly, Robinson remarks that accumulation in global capitalism entails not simply the geographical expansion of capital across national boundaries (internationalisation) but 'the fragmentation and decentralisation of complex production chains and the worldwide dispersal and functional integration of the different segments in these chains' (transnationalisation) (Robinson, 2004: 14–15). Therefore, the main struggle in the era of global capitalism is between national and transnational fractions of classes along the contradictory logics of national and global accumulation (Robinson, 2004: 37 and 49–53). Likewise, van Apeldoorn reads the current state of globalisation as a new phase in capitalism, determined by the transnationalisation of production, creating spatial fractionalisation while the related rival class strategies are increasingly important in analysing the social relations of production (van Apeldoorn, 2002: 27 and 32).

In discussing intra-class struggle, it is necessary to establish the main mechanism of integration of a particular country into the global capitalist structure. Internationalisation is related to countries integrating principally via trade, while transnationalisation occurs when the inflow and outflow of foreign direct investment (FDI) determines the main integration pattern (Bieler, 2006: 65). For Turkey's economy, the principal mechanism of integration with globalisation is trade. As Table 1.1 shows, the percentage of foreign trade in Turkey's gross domestic product (GDP) has increased steadily in recent decades, from 47 per cent in the 2000s to 60 per cent in 2020 and 79 per cent in 2022. The level of transnationalisation of production can be represented by data on inward and outward FDI (Bieler, 2006: 47–67). Table 1.2 shows that Turkey's FDI is still negligible in terms of capital accumulation.

Yet FDI flows tripled between 2006 and 2010 during Turkey's reform process. They plateaued during the 2010s before declining after 2019. It is imperative to uncover Turkey's FDI as a percentage of GDP as well. As Table 1.3 below shows FDI stocks as of GDP was 7 per cent in 1995, increasing to 8 per cent in 2000 and 15 per cent in 2005. Despite this steady increase, trade constitutes the main mechanism of Turkey's integration. Hence, Turkey's integration path exemplifies internationalism in the 2000s and is discussed in relation to internationally and nationally oriented sectors in Chapter 3. It is assumed that the internationally oriented social forces of capital and labour were more likely to favour an open economy and support regional integration because they benefitted from a borderless world in the 2000s. Conversely, the nationally oriented forces of capital and labour were likely to be more critical of integration because they depended on national protectionism and state subsidies (Bieler, 2000: 48; 2005: 465; 2006: 38). However, a word of caution is necessary here. Ultimately, the position of these social forces can only be uncovered through empirical study. Chapter 5 revisits this struggle over hegemony in the 2010s. It questions whether pro-membership is still hegemonic and whether there are any

Table 1.1 Ratio of foreign trade to GDP

	Imports of goods and services (% of GDP)	Exports of goods and services (% of GDP)	Total foreign trade (% of GDP)
1981–1990	17.2	13.7	30.9
1991–1995	19	16	36
1996–2000	24	21	45
2001–2005	23	23	46
2006–2010	26	22	48
2011	28	22	50
2012	28	24	52
2013	28	23	51
2014	28	25	53
2015	26	24	50
2016	25	23	48
2017	29	26	54
2018	31	31	62
2019	29	32	61
2020	32	28	60
2021	35	35	70
2022	42	37	79

Source: World Bank (2023) *National Accounts Exports and Imports of Goods and Services to GDP (1981–2022)*, https://data.worldbank.org/indicator/NE.EXP.GNFS.ZS?locations=TR
https://data.worldbank.org/indicator/NE.IMP.GNFS.ZS?locations=TR

alternatives. Table 1.3 shows that FDI inward and outward stocks as of GDP increased in the 2010s when compared with the 2000s. Yet it was 27 per cent in 2010 and 28 per cent in 2017. The average of FDI stocks as of GDP was 23 per cent in the 2010s. Although it peaked to 38 per cent in 2020, it is possible to observe fluctuations related to speculative capital, as will be discussed in Chapter 2. Hence, although there is more transnationalisation, international trade still constitutes the main mechanism of integration of Turkey with the global economy. Accordingly, in Chapter 5, the struggle in the 2010s is also discussed in relation to the international fraction of capital and labour. As Table 1.1. shows, the ratio of foreign trade to GDP averaged 52 per cent in the 2010s, increasing to 70 per cent in 2021 and 79 per cent in 2022.

An additional category in the research is the position of alternative subjectivities. The crux of the issue here is whether the struggle over hegemony is confined to the relations of production. If not, how can alternative

Table 1.2 FDI in Turkey

	Inward (millions of US dollars)	Outward (millions of US dollars)	FDI inward stock (millions of US dollars)	FDI outward stock (millions of US dollars)
1991–1995 (annual average)	756	53	13,437	1,279
1996–2000	846	448	17,302	2,382
2001–2005	3,790	592	36,487	6,388
2006–2010	15,950	1,720	133,137	16,736
2011	16,143	2,331	140,305	24,034
2012	13,745	4,107	181,066	30,471
2013	13,461	3,534	145,467	32,782
2014	12,969	6,682	168,645	40,088
2015	18,976	4,809	145,471	44,656
2016	13,651	2,954	132,882	38,020
2017	10,965	2,626	180,697	41,403
2018	12,840	3,605	134,524	49,935
2019	9,290	2,967	164,906	47,754
2020	7,880	3,240	211,573	52,487
2021	11,840	4,966	223,413	57,453
2022	12,881	4,715	236,294	62,168

Source: UN Trade and Development
UNCTAD (2023b) *FDI Inward Stock, by Region and Economy 1990–2022*, https://unctad.org/topic/investment/world-investment-report
UNCTAD (2023c) *FDI Outward Stock, by Region and Economy 1990–2022*, https://unctad.org/topic/investment/world-investment-report
UNCTAD (2023d) *World Investment Report 2023*, https://unctad.org/publication/world-investment-report-2023#anchor_download

subjectivities, such as struggles around gender, the environment or human rights, be incorporated in the research design? The following section revisits the debate between historical materialism and post-Marxism for two reasons. First, it aspires to answer how struggles around new social movements can be incorporated in the research design. Second, historical materialism has been accused of essentialism and reductionism in explaining transformations in capitalism in recent decades in parallel with the rise of identity politics and declining class politics. In response, scholars have argued for a renewal of historical materialism. The following section engages with post-Marxist critique to demonstrate how historical materialism is relevant to locating Turkey–EU relations within the historical specificities of global capitalism, and how to integrate social movements into the research design.

Table 1.3 FDI stocks as percentage of GDP

	FDI inward stock (millions of dollars)	FDI outward stock (millions of dollars)	FDI inward and outward stock (millions of dollars)	GDP (millions of dollars)	FDI stock as of GDP (%)
1990	11,150	1,150	12,300	207,570	5.9%
1995	14,933	1,418	16,351	233,253	7%
2000	18,812	3,668	22,480	274,295	8%
2005	71,429	8,315	79,744	506,315	15%
2006	95,472	8,866	104,338	557,076	18%
2007	155,676	12,210	167,886	681,321	24%
2008	81,328	17,846	99,174	770,449	12%
2009	144,700	22,250	166,950	649,289	25%
2010	188,329	22,509	210,838	776,967	27%
2011	137,995	27,681	165,676	838,786	19%
2012	192,219	30,968	223,187	880,556	25%
2013	152,565	33,329	185,894	957,799	19%
2014	183,869	39,569	223,438	938,934	23%
2015	158,730	35,673	194,403	864,314	22%
2016	149,599	38,662	188,261	869,683	21%
2017	197,001	45,847	242,848	858,989	28%
2018	145,302	44,875	190,177	778,382	24%
2019	160,648	48,875	209,523	759,935	27%
2020	229,961	49,924	279,885	720,289	38%
2021	139,970	51,752	191,722	819,034	23%
2022	164,909	56,681	221,590	–	–

Source: UN Trade and Development
UNCTAD (2023a) *Gross Domestic Product: Total and Per Capita*, https://unctadstat.unctad.org/datacentre/dataviewer/US.GDPTotal
UNCTAD (2023b) *FDI Inward Stock, by Region and Economy 1990–2022*, https://unctad.org/topic/investment/world-investment-report
UNCTAD (2023c) *FDI Outward Stock, by Region and Economy 1990–2022*, https://unctad.org/topic/investment/world-investment-report
UNCTAD (2023d) *World Investment Report 2023*, https://unctad.org/publication/world-investment-report-2023#anchor_download

The cultural turn and the post-Marxist critique to historical materialism

Certain historical developments have led some scholars to assert a crisis of Marxism (Callinicos et al., 2021: 1). The first example in the 1970s followed the decline of 1968 radical movements while the second in the 1980s followed the neoliberal turn and the collapse of the communist regimes (Callinicos et al., 2021: 1). Historical materialism was critiqued by postmodernist and poststructuralist scholars. The former emerged from the cultural turn of the 1980s. Eagleton (1996: vii) describes postmodernism as:

> a style of thought which is suspicious of classical notions of truth, reason, identity and objectivity, of the idea of universal progress or emancipation, of single frameworks, grand narratives or ultimate grounds of explanation. Against these Enlightenment norms, it sees the world as contingent, ungrounded, diverse, unstable, indeterminate, a set of disunified cultures or interpretations which breed a degree of scepticism about the objectivity of truth, history and norms, the givenness of natures and the coherence of identities.

Historical materialism is situated within the modernist paradigm. As such it is not exempt from postmodernist critique. According to Therborn (2008: 66), for example, 'Marxism is … the major manifestation of the dialectics of modernity, in a sociological as well as theoretical sense.' Marxism both flourished as a social force within the Enlightenment and the rise of the modern capitalist system and was also preoccupied with uncovering the contradictory nature of modernity (Therborn, 2008: 66). That is, 'Marxism was the theory of this dialectic of modernity as well as its practice' (Therborn, 2008: 66). In *Postmodernism, or, the Cultural Logic of Late Capitalism*, Jameson (1991: 35) discusses how postmodernism became the cultural expression of late capitalism, which also constituted the 'purest form of capital' through its expansion into uncommodified areas. The debate between Marxism and postmodernism falls outside the scope of this chapter. Suffice to mention that there is a large body of literature on critiques of modernity (e.g. Horkheimer and Adorno, 1973) and the Marxist responses (e.g. Anderson, 1998; Eagleton, 1996; Harvey, 1989; Jameson, 1991).

Poststructural critique is levelled by various scholars subscribing to diverse theoretical traditions that share a linguistic or cultural turn. As Howarth observes, it is tricky to decide 'who should count as a poststructuralist' (Howarth, 2013: 6). Howarth, indeed, depicts poststructural research as 'a loose style of theorising' with differing tendencies (Howarth, 2013: 13). He describes poststructural research as a social ontology which takes a certain critical position to structuralism and essentialism while being influenced from the linguistic turn (Howarth, 2013: 7–9). There are crucial differences and contestations with poststructuralist scholars more 'unified in their opposition to essentialism, scientism and certain forms of naturalism' (Howarth, 2013: 13). Howarth categorises the poststructural research agenda in three generations. The second generation of poststructural thinkers in the 1970s and 1980s developed a dialogue with Western Marxists such as Gramsci, Althusser and Poulantzas (Howarth, 2013: 15). It is this second generation of thinkers pioneered by Laclau and Mouffe's (1985) *Hegemony and Socialist Strategy* that falls into the scope of this chapter.

Laclau and Mouffe describe their project as post-Marxist. Yet the critique has gone beyond them to encompass several critical theorists aspiring to go beyond Marx (Tormey and Townshend, 2006: 2). Yet drawing the boundaries of post-Marxism is not an easy task. Callinicos et al. (2021: 1) define post-Marxism as an endeavour to question categories 'inherited from Marxism in a theoretical and political framework that simultaneously is itself influenced by Marxism but seeks to go decisively beyond it'. As such, Tormey and Townshend claim that the work of critical theorists, 'who have at one time or other asserted that there is a "crisis" of Marxism, that "Marxist" orthodoxy has collapsed, in turn necessitating a thinking through of Marx's work and legacy for reconstituting critique and as a political response to advanced capitalism', can be considered post-Marxist (Tormey and Townshend, 2006: 4). Despite taking varying theoretical positions, these theorists all problematise core Marxist concepts, such as the Marxist account of revolutionary subjectivity and history, Marxist positivism and the problem of democracy while arguing that there is no simple 'return' to Marx for an emancipatory project (Tormey and Townshend, 2006: 5–6). Based on this discussion, I next focus on the post-Marxist critique in relation to two specific works, namely Laclau and Mouffe's *Hegemony and Socialist Strategy* (1985) and Hardt and Negri's *Empire* (2000). Both of these works take Marxist categories as their starting point, yet aspire to go beyond them. Both of them assert that there is a need to reconsider political subjectivity because capitalist relations have been transformed. Both works aspire to enlarge the political space for democracy.

In *Hegemony and Socialist Strategy*, Laclau and Mouffe argue that historical materialism subscribes to two forms of essentialism: class as the sole unifying element of hegemonic formations, and the economic base as the determinant of antagonisms and the political sphere (Laclau and Mouffe, 1985: 69). They break with the base/superstructure model, the centrality of the working class as the revolutionary subjectivity and the production structure as the determinant of antagonisms in society (Laclau and Mouffe, 1985: 48–57). Instead, they interpreted them as constituting 'limits to hegemony' while also producing a form of 'political authoritarianism' (Laclau and Mouffe, 1985: 54 and 56–57). They argue for a plurality and diversity of social antagonisms in society, a position echoed by Howarth (2000), Howarth et al. (2000) and Torfing (1999), who criticise assigning a privileged position to social class in the hegemonic struggle due to their position in relations of production. This shift, they claim, is a necessary response to structural changes in capitalism, such as the decline of the classical working class in post-industrial countries, atypical forms of political struggle – especially on the periphery, the penetration of capitalist forms into social life and the proliferation of new forms of political struggle and new social movements, including feminist, ethnic and ecological protest movements (Laclau and Mouffe, 1985: 1). Accordingly, they articulate a strategical praxis of 'radical democracy' through which they believe the Left has to come to terms with democracy and pluralism (Laclau and Mouffe, 1985). This project of 'radical and plural democracy' integrates the struggles for 'redistribution' and 'recognition' within the Left (Laclau and Mouffe, 1985: xv and xviii). It is not a case of 'back to class struggle' but rather the advocacy of 'a chain of equivalence' through which workers' struggles can operate alongside new social movements of identity and ecologically based struggles (Laclau and Mouffe, 1985: xviii).

Based on this critique, Laclau and Mouffe aspire to 'radicalise' the Gramscian notion of hegemony. They dismiss the base/superstructure model, claiming that the relation between the hegemonised task and class is contingent rather than necessary, and that 'a relation of contradiction can exist between two objects of discourse' independent of the relations of production (Laclau and Mouffe, 1985: 86 and 110). In parallel with poststructuralism, they conceive of society as an 'impossible object of analysis'. The terrain of the social can never be closed, they claim, so there can be no absolute or determinant fixing of the identities of social subjects in articulatory practices or political subjectivity (Laclau and Mouffe, 1985: 112–113). Thus, structural undecidability conditions hegemony (Laclau and Mouffe, 1985: xii). In the hegemonic relation, 'a certain particularity assumes the representation of a universality' by linking different identities and political forces around a common project (Laclau and Mouffe, 1985: x–xiii). Hegemony is no longer conceived of as the unification of political forces around interests; rather, 'the concept of hegemony supposes a theoretical field dominated by the category of articulation' (Laclau and Mouffe, 1985: 93). Hegemonic projects aspire to stabilise meanings or hegemonic formations by articulating 'nodal points' or 'master-signifiers' which partially fix the identities of particular signifiers (Howarth, 2000: 110). Hence, they wish to radicalise democratic struggles so that political identities are not subsumed under class but rather in the plural form as 'multiple hegemonic articulations' (Laclau and Mouffe, 1985: 137).

Similarly, in *Empire* (2000), Hardt and Negri claimed that productive processes have been transformed by 'postmodernisation of the global economy' as well as the passage from modernity to postmodernity, which necessitates rethinking political subjectivity and the nature of work and wealth (Hardt and Negri, 2000: 258). They argue that Lenin's imperialism has been replaced by an empire, in line with transformations in the global economy. The empire has replaced nation-states and the metropolis-colony nexus (Hardt and Negri, 2000: xii). It is 'a decentred and deterritorialising apparatus of rule that progressively incorporates the entire global realm within its open, expanding frontiers' (Hardt and Negri, 2000: xii). In *Empire*, they claim that industrial labour in mass factories is reduced and being replaced with 'immaterial labour' under the new informational economy dominated by services (Hardt and Negri, 2000: 28 and 29). Immaterial labour is 'labour that produces an immaterial good, such as services, a cultural product, knowledge, or communication' (Hardt and Negri, 2000: 28 and 290). All struggles unite against one common enemy, namely the international disciplinary order (Hardt and Negri, 2000: 261). They further claim that the imperialist period is over as well as the division of labour and pre-eminent Marxist theoretical assumption that the main struggle is between the capital of the First World and the labour of the Third World (Hardt and Negri, 2000: 264). Instead, the international proletariat is united and struggles accumulate around the empire (Hardt and Negri, 2000: 263). They acknowledge the monopoly tendency of labour by arguing that current capitalist dynamics produce 'an ever more extreme separation of a small minority that controls enormous wealth from multitudes that live in poverty at the limit of powerlessness' (Hardt and Negri, 2000: 43). The multitude, Hardt and Negri (2004: 107) claim, 'gives the concept of the proletariat its fullest definition as all those who labour and produce under the rule of capital'. Hardt and Negri highlight two dislocations behind this transition. First, shifts in the global economy have altered the hegemonic status of the industrial working class (Hardt and Negri, 2004: xv). Second, it is no longer simply industrial production but social reproduction – including relationships, communications and forms of life – that have to be inserted into the analysis (Hardt and Negri, 2004: xv). In this era, agency for social change is the multitude which is an open and inclusive concept encompassing diverse figures of social production (Hardt and Negri, 2004: xv). They claim that the 'multitude is composed of innumerable internal differences that can never be reduced to a unity or a single identity – different cultures, races, ethnicities, genders, and sexual orientations; different forms of labour; different ways of living; different views of the world; and different desires' (Hardt and Negri, 2004: xiv). These struggles transcend economic struggles to encompass ecological struggles or struggles over the mode of life (Hardt and Negri, 2000: 269).

These assumptions were experienced in global politics in the 2010s under the post-truth and populist era. Radical democracy achieved electoral victory through Syriza in Greece and Podemos in Spain. Yet they failed to generate a plausible alternative and soon were defeated by populist politics and the New Right. Moreover, Khan and Wenman (2017: 513) highlight that poststructuralism is accused of setting the ground for Brexit and the election victory of Donald Trump through its talk on anti-foundationalism and anti-essentialism which all create a basis for populist politicians to 'manipulate "the truth" to suit their own cynical objectives'. Yet Khan and Wenman do not agree with this critique. They instead argue that the current post-truth era is not a result of poststructuralists disseminating ideas about the 'groundlessness of all truth claims', but rather 'modern politics has always been "post-truth" which has become intensified due to the digitalisation of the public sphere (Khan and Wenman, 2017: 514). Hardt and Negri revisit their project and their argument on multitude for the politics of praxis in their 2019 essay. Here, the crux of the issue is to find a plausible answer to the question 'how can a multiplicity act politically, with the sustained power to bring about real social transformations?' (Hardt and Negri, 2019). Hardt and Negri call for a return to the concept of class, which they name as 'class prime', to get organised and be politically effective (Hardt and Negri, 2019). They argue that globalisation has transformed class into a multitude while the need for political activism requires the multitude to be transformed into a class prime (Hardt and Negri, 2019). They summarise the historical evolution of political subjectivity as 'class-multitude-class prime' (C-M-C) (Hardt and Negri, 2019). The class prime is 'an internally articulated multiplicity oriented equally in struggle against capital, patriarchy, white supremacy and other axes of domination (Hardt and Negri, 2019).

A critical reply to post-Marxism and the relevance of historical materialism

In response to these critiques of economic essentialism and class reductionism, a group of scholars have reclaimed Marxism's intellectual revitalisation in the last decade. Especially following the 2007–08 Great Recession, scholars benefitted from Marxist analytical tools to explain the crisis of capitalism and the collapse of political liberalism. While mainstream economists returned to Marx to explain the capitalist crisis, historical materialist scholars explained why Marx remains relevant to understanding the current historical specificity of global capitalism (Munck, 2016: 197). For instance, Dumenil and Levy argue that, in *Capital Volume III*, Marx provides the tools to uncover capitalism's historical tendencies such as distribution, accumulation, employment and production (Dumenil and Levy, 2008: 105). According to Munck (2016: 196) Marx provides the necessary tools to grasp '"general laws" of capitalist accumulation, its relationship to employment, inter-capitalist competition and the impact of the capitalist cycle'. This sub-section considers the questions posed by poststructural and post-Marxist research and explains historical materialist responses to these critiques.

First, at the heart of the debate between historical materialism and post-Marxism is the relation between materialism and idealism. Post-Marxist scholarship accuses historical materialism of economic essentialism. They claim to transcend the duality between idealism and materialism through discourse theory. They highlight the 'material character of every discursive structure' (e.g. Geras, 1987; Laclau and Mouffe, 1985: 108–109; Torfing, 1999: 45 and 94). Against the critique of economic essentialism, historical materialist scholars contend that the central category of analysis is social relations of production as a social totality. As Wood (1986: 59) asks, 'is it not the first premise of historical materialism that material production is a *social* phenomenon?'. For instance, Gramsci criticises the 'fatalism of philosophy of praxis' and/or 'vulgar materialism', reading it as a consequence of the failure to develop an 'immanent thought to [the] philosophy of praxis' (Gramsci, 1977: 34). In this sense, Gramsci ultimately argues that economism has to be combated in both the theory of historiography and the theory and practice of politics (Gramsci, 1971: 165). Bieler and Morton (2018: 6) contend that a pre-eminent tendency within the literature on global politics is separating the material *content* and/or ideational *form* in analysing 'the international' (emphasis in original). Rather, they argue that historical materialism overcomes this dualism through its dialectical conception of the material content and ideational form in explicating the international sphere (Bieler and Morton, 2018: 8). In their analysis of the current conjuncture of global crisis, war and global capitalism, they suggest rethinking the 'international' as an 'internal relation' conceiving of capital as a social relation within the dynamics of class struggle, relations of production and state–civil–society relations (Bieler and Morton, 2018: 9). Rather than conceiving of politics (or the state) and economics (or the market) as externally related, the philosophy of internal relations uncovers the relationship between global capitalism and accumulation with geopolitical rivalry and global war (Bieler and Morton, 2018: 22).

In return, historical materialist scholars criticised post-Marxism for prioritising the ideational and neglecting the material. Wood criticises post-Marxism for its 'autonomisation of ideology and politics from any social base' (Wood, 1986: 2). That is, it reorients the socialist project to 'social collectivities – "popular alliances" – whose identity, principles of cohesion, objectives, and capacity for collective action are not rooted in any specific social relations or interests but are constituted by politics and ideology themselves' (Wood, 1986: 5). As such, poststructuralism separates and prioritises the ideational over the material, an error which prevents it from unravelling the social actors behind power mechanisms and questioning the underlying power structure behind a particular discourse (Bieler and Morton, 2008: 112–113). From such a vantage point, the post-Marxist conception of the struggle over hegemony ends up 'abstracting forms of collective agency from the prevailing social order and isolating and separating issues from social conditions and material interests' (Morton, 2006: 48–49). Hence, post-Marxism is accused of operating within capitalism's structured separation of economics and politics – a condition that 'de-socialises the material' (Wood, 1981: 70). As Wood (1981: 67) convincingly argues, the separation of economics and politics has always been immanent to capitalism, and constitutes its 'most effective defense mechanism'. Indeed, Wood (1990: 60) argues that one of the functions of post-Marxism is 'to conceptualise away from capitalism'. For her, what is alarming is not that post-Marxism 'violate[s] some doctrinaire Marxist prejudice concerning the privileged status of class', but rather that it fails to critically engage with capitalism, seeking 'to sweep the whole question under the rug' (Wood, 1990: 79). Similarly, Aronowitz (1986–87: 11–12) criticises Laclau and Mouffe for leaving little room for political economy while Žižek (2000: 97) posits that the absence of class analyses in postmodernist critical thought (such as Laclau and Mouffe's) signifies a 'theoretical retreat from the problem of domination within capitalism'. In this sense, while postmodernism politicises language and gender, drawing attention to issues that were previously viewed as apolitical or private, it fails to repoliticise capitalism. Its reading of the political is predicated on a 'depoliticisation of the economy' (Žižek, 2000: 98). For Žižek, it is the form of contemporary capitalism that renders political subjectivities dispersed, shifted and contingent; and postmodern analyses will never be sufficiently political so long as it continues to neglect the economic sphere (Žižek, 2000: 108). Yet Žižek contends without a radical repoliticisation of the economy, 'all the talk about active citizenship, about public discussion leading to responsible collective decisions, and so on, will remain limited to the "cultural" issues of religious, sexual, ethnic and other way-of-life differences' (Žižek, 1999, 353).

The second area of disagreement concerns the relation between state and society. Laclau and Mouffe deconstruct the Marxist conception of state as an instrument of the ruling class in capitalist accumulation (Laclau and Mouffe, 1985: 139). However, they offer no hints about how to approach the state's role in the hegemonic struggle. On the one hand, this is consistent with their critical stance towards the classical conception of power. In line with poststructuralism, they argue that 'power is not something one can seize, because power is constitutive of the ensemble of social relations' (Laclau and Mouffe, 2002: 146–147). Accordingly, they define the field of articulatory practices within the 'open, non-sutured character of the social' as the core of hegemonic relations. It is the existence of a variety of hegemonic nodal points – that are antagonistic – which renders relations hegemonic (Laclau and Mouffe, 1985: 138–139). To put it bluntly, 'hegemony is, quite simply, a political type of relation, a form, if one so wishes, of politics, but not a determinable location within a topography of the social' (Laclau and Mouffe, 1985: 139). In this conception, the struggle over hegemony is no longer related to the seizure of state power. So they remain silent in *Hegemony and Socialist Strategy* on the role or status of the state within the struggle over hegemony. In my view, this position has the political consequence of overlooking the state's role in the struggle over hegemony while failing to contest the instruments of the capitalist state.

Moreover, Laclau and Mouffe overlook neoliberal civil society, which helps the ruling class to articulate its vested interests on a universal terrain. Given that the state is undertheorised and neoliberal civil society is uncontested – and coupled with their separation of politics and economics – Laclau and Mouffe's discourse theory operates within the neoliberal order's separation of the state and civil society. This separation has been widely criticised. Buttigieg (2005: 35–37) contends that it risks misconstruing 'power relations within, among and across states', strategically disabling leftist struggle. Similarly, Wood (1990: 60) claims that the conceptual opposition of the state and civil society means that '"civil society" [is] in danger of becoming an alibi for capitalism'. Though this definition of civil society opens new avenues for emancipatory projects of Leftist politics, it retreats from the problem of capitalism (Wood, 1990: 63). As Wood cogently observes, such a stance overlooks the 'oppressions of civil society' (Wood, 1990: 63). More importantly, such a definition of civil society generates 'new forms of freedoms and equality', but equally 'constitute[s] a new form of social power, in which many coercive functions that once belonged to the state [are] relocated in the "private" sphere, in private property, class exploitation, and market imperatives' (Wood, 1990: 73). Indeed, Wood claims that the 'irony' of these 'new pluralisms' is that they end up 'making invisible the power relations which constitute capitalism', despite aspiring to articulate 'an antagonism to all power relations in all their diverse forms' (Wood, 1990: 78). Similarly, Bieler and Morton (2004: 307–308) criticise the direct treatment of global civil society as a platform generating resistance, given that such a reading conceives of the state's relationship with the market as one of exteriority and fails to recognise that civil society frequently operates as an agent of globalisation. Rather, historical materialist conceptual tools pave the way to treat the state as a social relationship. The challenge for Bieler and Morton (2018: 123) is 'to conceptualise the state as a condensation of class forces in a way that emphasises its internal relations with social property relations, with the wider interstate system and with global capitalism'. The historical materialist ontology of internal relations can account for this embedded relation between global capitalism and geopolitics (Bieler and Morton, 2018: 123).

Third, the international is untheorised in post-Marxism. In *Hegemony and Socialist Strategy*, Laclau and Mouffe differentiate between advanced industrial societies, in which politics is dominated by democratic struggles, and the Third World, where struggles fall into two antagonistic camps. Apart from this differentiation, the analyses are not equipped with an understanding of the international sphere in post-Marxism and discourse theory. For historical materialist scholarship, the international sphere is salient not only in relation to the uneven and combined development of capitalism but also concerning its role within the struggle over hegemony in a national context. Marx considered the world market while explaining the capitalist system. For instance, he refers to the role of the colonial system in the expansion of capitalism, which was essential to transforming dependent countries from a feudal to a capitalist mode of production (Marx, 1867/1990: 915–916). The colonial system equally increased trade and enabled the concentration of capital. To quote Marx: 'The colonies provided a market for the budding manufactures, and a vast increase in accumulation which was guaranteed by the mother country's monopoly of the market' (Marx, 1867/1990: 918). Similarly for Trotsky (1929/2007: 119), 'Internationalism is no abstract principle but a theoretical and political reflection of the character of world economy, of the world development of productive forces and the world scale of the class struggle.' To quote Trotsky: 'Marxism takes its point of departure from world economy not as a sum of national parts but as a mighty and independent reality that has been created by the international division of labor and the world market' (Trotsky, 1929/2007: 131). In his analysis of hegemony, Gramsci contends that 'international relations … follow (logically) fundamental social relations' and the 'geographical position of a national State follows (logically) structural changes, although it also reacts back upon them to a certain extent' (Gramsci, 1971: 176). He further posits that 'the line of development is towards internationalism, but the point of departure is "national"' (Gramsci, 1971: 240). Moreover, Gramsci argues that 'capitalism is a world historical phenomenon, and its uneven development means that individual nations cannot be at the same level of economic development at the same time' (Gramsci, 1977: 69). Thus, Morton contends, Gramsci presents a theoretical framework that 'displays an awareness of the uneven development of social power relations and class struggle that provides a stimulus to taking the "national" social form as a point of arrival intertwined with the mediations and active reactions of "the international" dimension' (Morton, 2007b: 621).

Fourth, an additional category of debate is historicism. Laclau and Mouffe argue that Gramsci fails to develop a 'radical historicist' analysis. They attribute this to the essentialism they believe Gramsci develops around the political centrality of the working class (Laclau and Mouffe, 1985: 70).

Conversely, historical materialist scholarship criticises post-Marxism for its ahistoricism. For instance, Morton criticises Laclau and Mouffe in their treatment of history for 'austere historicism', which 'reduces past forms of thought to their precise historical context and tends to relegate Gramsci to history' (Morton, 2007a: 27). He argues that Laclau and Mouffe assert a break with the past that prevents 'the texts of historical materialism (such as the *Prison Notebooks*) from generating new meanings in different contexts' (Morton, 2007a: 26). Hence, Laclau and Mouffe close off the possibility of analysing capitalist development historically. They overemphasise rupture from industrial societies without considering the continuities and redefinitions and reconstitutions of the hegemony of the ruling class. According to Morton, they define antagonism independently of historical processes so that history 'becomes a succession of articulatory practices discursively produced and formed' (Morton, 2006: 49). This is criticised by Wood (1986: 75) as randomisation of history. She contends that Laclau and Mouffe present an ahistorical view of the world that leaves us with nothing but contingency. To quote Wood (1986: 75), 'in the absence of a simple, mechanical, and crude determinism, there apparently remains nothing but absolute contingency – or rather, that there is no history, no determinate historical conditions, relations, processes'. The kernel of historical materialism, Wood highlights, is historicity and 'the specificity of capitalism, as a moment with historical origins as well as an end, with a systemic logic specific to it' (Wood, 1995: 5). It aspires to explain specificity of capitalism or any mode of production without any transhistorical natural law but through focusing on 'historically specific social relations, contradictions and struggles' (Wood, 1995: 6).

Scholars question to what extent Gramscian conceptual tools can be applied to different geographies and/or different historical conjunctures (e.g. Bellamy, 1990; Germain and Kenny, 1998). Morton discusses historicism and how Gramscian ideas can be situated in and beyond their context (Morton, 2007a: 15–38). He is critical of both ahistorical and mechanical treatment of Gramsci's theory. Morton accuses the former of 'restrictive or austere historicism' which reduces Gramscian ideas to the context in which Gramsci lived (Morton, 2007a: 25). The latter applies past forms of thought without reconsidering historical and geographical specificities and social conditions. Here, to quote Hall (1987: 16), Gramsci is a thinker who provides the tools to 'ask the right kinds of questions' rather than someone to follow like 'an Old Testament prophet' who '"has the answers" or "holds the key" to our present troubles' (Hall, 1987: 16). Similarly, Buci-Glucksmann (1980: ix) proposes to consider the limits of Gramsci, highlighting that 'it is no use falling into an ideological Gramsci-ism'. Rather, there is a need to 'locate Gramsci in history, his history, his own time, in order to de-ideologize our analysis and measure the real importance of his concepts today' (Buci-Glucksmann

1980: 11). Indeed, in his criticism of 'vulgar materialism', Gramsci refers to 'absolute historicism' (Gramsci, 1971: 419–472):

> It has been forgotten that in the case of a very common expression (historical materialism) one should put the accent on the first term –'historical' – and not on the second, which is of metaphysical origin. The philosophy of praxis is absolute 'historicism', the absolute secularisation and earthliness of thought, an absolute humanism of history. It is along this line that one must trace the thread of the new conception of the world (Gramsci, 1971: 465).

According to Morton, absolute historicism presents a dialectical understanding of history as 'an approach to philosophy and concrete political activity that conceives the historical process as a synthesis of past and present' (Morton, 2007a: 24).

The final area of debate concerns agency and structure. Post-Marxist and poststructural scholars criticise historical materialism for its essentialist and structuralist conception of society. The structure has a negative connotation in poststructuralism because it is believed to hinder freedom and emancipation. They argue that society is not a fully intelligible and structural totality; rather, it encompasses an 'excess of meaning'. Hence 'society as a unitary and intelligible object … is an impossibility' (Torfing, 1999: 113). Torfing summarises this stance by claiming that Laclau and Mouffe fail to theorise the 'subject before its subjectivation' (Torfing, 1999: 56). In this, they follow the poststructuralist position that emphasises the formation of political subjectivities while avoiding the formulation of a new theory of subject. This stems from the attempt to understand various new social movements within gendered, racial, urban and environmental politics following the abandonment of the idea of a 'universal class' (Torfing, 1999: 56). Laclau and Mouffe are cautious not to propose a form of unity from these particularisms as a new subjectivity, believing it a stance against radicalism (Laclau and Mouffe, 1985: 167). Rather, they articulate a 'proliferation of particularisms' based around the logic of autonomy through which each struggle 'retains its differential specificity' (Laclau and Mouffe, 1985: 164 and 182). According to Wenman (2013: 189) one of the reasons why *Hegemony and Socialist Strategy* has been very influential is related to their emphasis on collective struggle, strategic questions and political alliance building for emancipation. Here, Wenman (2013: 189) contends, Laclau and Mouffe follow Gramscian and Machiavellian legacy without conceiving of poststructuralism as an 'unqualified celebration of the politics of diversity'. Yet still, the definition of 'social totality', Laclau and Mouffe offer, remains ambiguous and does not go beyond a vague claim that 'radical' struggles over 'the seizure of power in the classical sense' (by which they mean struggles in which political space can be divided in two) tend not to be developed in advanced industrial societies (Laclau and Mouffe, 1985: 131–132).

This stance is criticised for confusing authority with authoritarianism (Sim, 2000: 31). Wood (1995: 1) argues that if post-Marxist hostility to social totality extends to capitalism as a social totality, this scholarship will treat the market as a 'universal and inevitable law of nature'. Such an ontological stance, Wood contends, not only closes all critical engagement with the totalising power of capitalism, but also reiterates the liberal grand narrative of the 'end of history' (Wood, 1995: 1). It therefore stands, Eagleton claims, 'in the end part of the problem rather than of the solution' because the probable future scenario (he warned presciently back in the 1990s) is rising fascism (Eagleton, 1996: 133–134). Similarly, for Wood (1986: 63), although the post-Marxist project may have the best democratic intentions, there are clear dangers in dislocations like subordination of the socialist struggle to pluralist democratic struggles and replacing class with subject positions. That is, the autonomisation of political movements from social relations and interests may have dangerous consequences of either becoming instruments of the dominant interest (capital groups), or being degraded into despotic arbitrariness (Wood, 1986: 188). Indeed, for Wood, unless class politics can become a unifying force, it is highly likely that the new social movements will 'generate periodic and momentary displays of popular support but destined to leave the capitalist order intact' without being able to present an emancipatory project (Wood, 1986: 199). Rather, the new social movements aim to have electoral victory as an end in itself (Wood, 1986: 197).

This book does not agree with post-Marxism that there is class essentialism within historical materialism or that the current dynamics of globalisation require us to conceive of class struggle as multitude in *Empire*. Contrarily, the research embarks on historical materialism and takes the social relations of production as its basis in discussing the struggle over hegemony in the following empirical chapters. Historical materialism does not exclude contradictions around patriarchy, human rights and the environment. Embarking on Bieler and Morton's ontology of an internal relationship, contradictions over patriarchy, the environment and human rights in the following empirical chapters are analysed as an instance of class struggle. Bieler and Morton (2018: 133–134) posit that a radical dialectic of political identities requires conceiving of class struggle beyond the workplace to encompass reproductive labour in the nexus of the extended social factory. They argue that race, gender, ecology and sexuality are 'internally constitutive of class, rather than external to it' (Bieler and Morton, 2018: 132). Hence, the focus is on capitalist social relations as a whole in the sphere of the social factory 'which encompasses productive and unproductive wage labour as well as non-wage labour in the production, appropriation and distribution of surplus value' (Bieler and Morton, 2018: 142). Wood discusses this in relation to extra-economic goods. She highlights that struggle for emancipation is not only based on the 'economic' terrain but has extended to extra-economic goods encompassing struggles around 'gender emancipation, racial equality, peace, ecological health and democratic citizenship' (Wood, 1995: 264). According to van der Pijl, it is the 'discipline of capital over the entire reproductive system' and its 'exploitation of the social and natural substratum' that has to be resisted (van der Pijl, 1998: 36 and 47). That is, capitalist discipline 'subjects new spheres to the logic of exploitation and profit', including 'the destruction of the biosphere, and all the terrains on which the corrupting influences of money and profit are souring the joys and quality of life, from sports and leisure to art, education and health – even a funeral' (van der Pijl, 1998: 48). Federici (2012: 93) discusses this in relation to the need to incorporate reproduction to Marxist theory. She discusses the question of reproduction in relation to feminism and describes it as 'the complex of activities and relations by which our life and labour are daily reconstituted' (Federici, 2012: 5). To quote Federici (2012: 2), 'the reproduction of human beings is the foundation of every economic and political system, and the immense amount of paid and unpaid domestic work done by women in the home is what keeps the world moving'. Here, Federici (2012: 7) refers to Mario Tronti's *Operai e Capitale* (1966), the concept of the social factory, in which capitalist hegemony is so advanced that 'every social relation is subsumed under capital and the distinction between society and factory collapses, so that society becomes a factory and social relations *directly become relations of production*' (emphasis in original). Similarly, Bhattacharya contends that social reproduction theory asks 'if workers' labour produces all the wealth in society, who then produces the worker?'. Accordingly, social reproduction theory treats labour necessary for the production of commodities and labour required to produce people within the systemic totality of capitalism (Bhattacharya, 2017: 1–2). Put alternatively, class struggle is not confined to production of commodities alone, but extends to homes, scholars and hospitals as a social totality in addition to workplaces (Bhattacharya, 2017: 3).

Conclusion

This chapter introduced the conceptual framework that is employed in the following chapters while reading Turkey's trajectory of integration with the European structures. The analyses especially draw on two historical materialist categories: hegemony and uneven and combined development. While the former paved the way to discussing the struggle over EU membership among different fractions of capital and labour within the global capitalist structure, the latter contributes to situating Turkey's membership trajectory in uneven and combined development of capitalism internationally. The chapter then laid out the main contours of both intra- and inter-class struggle. Class struggle in the 2000s is discussed in Chapter 3 as an instance of internationalism and as a struggle between nationally and internationally oriented sectors. It is assumed that internationally oriented fractions of capital and labour will support membership in line with their support to open economies, while nationally oriented labour and capital will develop a critical stance due to their concern to compete with the European market in the 2000s. Class coordinates for the 2010s are then reconsidered. Data on FDI stocks revealed that transnationalism was increasing in the 2010s, yet international trade still constitutes the main mechanism of integration of Turkey's economy with the global economy. However, it is ultimately empirical research that determines the main contours of class struggle.

The chapter next concentrated on the critiques of historical materialism and their responses. Poststructural and post-Marxist critiques have become pre-eminent, especially since the 1980s neoliberal turn and the collapse of the socialist project. Here, two works are particularly examined: Laclau and Mouffe's *Hegemony and Socialist Strategy* (1985) and Hardt and Negri's *Empire* (2000). They were selected as these scholars depart from Marxism, but aspire to go beyond it through revising its main contours. They argue that capitalism is structurally transformed and there is a need to reconstitute the critique to advanced capitalism while reconsidering political praxis following the collapse of the socialist project. They are both critical of historical materialist premises regarding political subjectivity, history and structure. While Laclau and Mouffe criticise historical materialism for class reductionism and economic essentialism, Hardt and Negri argue that postmodernisation of the global economy transformed the nature of work while substituting the nation-state with the empire. They both problematise political subjectivity. While Laclau and Mouffe propose radical contingency to integrate new social movements and struggles of political recognition in a radical and plural imaginary, Hardt and Negri contend that industrial workers are substituted by immaterial labour in service economies. The current dynamics of the class under global and postmodern capitalism requires a new political imaginary, the multitude which unites against the international disciplinary order of the empire. While Laclau and Mouffe explicate their reasoning as integrating the struggles of political recognition, Hardt and Negri refer to social reproduction as the space for political struggle. Ultimately, they both advocate enlarging the space for democracy as political praxis.

The disagreements between post-Marxism and historical materialism are debated in relation to five categories: the relation between material and ideational, state and civil society, international sphere, historicism and agency-structure. I argue that post-Marxist scholarship separated economics from politics and treats the relation between state and civil society as an exteriority. It thus 'de-socializes the material', operates within capitalism's dualisms and fails to provide a critique of domination under global capitalism. Post-Marxism untheorised the international dimension. Its treatment of history is equally problematic in analysing capitalist development historically. Historical materialist conceptual tools pave the way to treating the relation between the economic and the political as well as the state and civil society as an internal relation in a dialectical manner while presenting the struggle within the sphere of social reproduction as a social totality. The relation between class and identity politics is analysed as an internal relation in the following empirical chapters in a dialectical way.

2

Integration of a peripheral country into the capitalist world system: Turkey's political economy

This chapter provides a political economy reading of Turkey's social formation by situating it within the structural dynamics of the global political economy. Each section ends by considering the main coordinates of Turkey's integration with European structures. In line with Gramscian historical materialism, the chapter discusses class struggle at the national level within the conditions of the international (Gramsci, 1971: 176). The chapter also provides the historical background of state–market relations in Turkey, specifically the historical coordinates of the class struggle, to prepare the ground for the empirical analyses in the following three chapters. It does so by structuring the analyses on three levels: the social relations of production, the form of the state, and the world order. Following Cox (1987: 11–12), production is not confined to the production of goods within the manufacturing sector; rather, it refers to the social relations of production as a social totality. There are different forms of state depending on the pre-eminent accumulation strategy and configuration of social forces upon which historical blocs are formed (Cox, 1987: 105) while world orders are engendered by the social relations of production and particular forms of state (Cox, 1987: 109). My analysis starts after the Second World War, when the EEC was formed and Turkey applied for an association partnership. The analysis is presented in three historical periods based on the coordinates of capitalist accumulation and uneven exchange between the EU and Turkey: the Fordist period of the 1960s and 1970s; the neoliberal turn in the 1980s; and the post-2008 authoritarian neoliberal period.

The chapter investigates how we can read Turkey's integration into European structures under structural conditions of uneven exchange, and asks how neoliberal restructuring during the 1980s has impacted Turkey–EU relations. It then questions how the rise and fall of the AKP governments are read using the tools provided by critical political economy literature. How have the Great Recession, the COVID-19 pandemic and the rise of authoritarian neoliberalism transformed new coordinates of core–periphery relations and conditioned the future of Turkey–EU relations? The chapter argues that there was a tug of war between Keynesian embedded liberalism, the main development understanding underlying Turkey's import-substitution industrialisation (ISI) strategy and liberalisation engendered by the Customs Union. There was little consensus regarding membership, with particular groups adapting the following motto about the EEC: 'They are the partners and we are the market.' Moreover, Turkey prolonged timetables to liberalise its trade regime as envisaged by the Additional Protocol. It was after the 1980s neoliberal turn and the containment of its labour movement that Turkey applied for full membership and joined the Customs Union after liberalising its trade regime and adapting structural adjustment policies.

The chapter then argues that AKP hegemony in the 2000s can be read as *trasformismo* representing continuity with the previous right-wing political parties in consolidating neoliberalism with a moderate form of Islam. The party successfully led society providing moral and intellectual leadership through a populist discourse based on presenting the main struggle in society as one against the so-called 'strong state' and the Kemalist elite. Thus, the chapter argues, the AKP not only extended the ruling class but also disarticulated dissent through populism within a historical conjuncture of deteriorating socio-economic conditions of the social forces that are disadvantaged from globalisation and neoliberal restructuring. The 2010s is then discussed as financialisation which engenders cycles of crises due to contradictions embedded in the growth model of emerging markets on the periphery with the AKP government resorting to coercive state policies following the Gezi Park protests, 15 July 2016 coup attempt and the COVID-19 pandemic. This period is studied as a crisis of neoliberal hegemony and authoritarian neoliberalism. In this period of global crises, Turkey–EU relations are discussed not within the context of membership but the cooperation of prioritised issues such as migration, visa liberalisation and person-to-person cooperation, among others. The analysis starts by examining Turkey's post-war reconstruction under Pax Americana. The discussion then proceeds with the neoliberal transition before identifying the main political economic coordinates in the last decade under authoritarian neoliberalism.

Hegemony under Pax Americana

Fordism and import-substitution industrialisation in Turkey

The Ottoman Empire started to integrate with capitalism in the late nineteenth century under the liberal world order. An old Turkish saying of the period, 'If you want to hang yourself, use an English rope' (quoted in Boratav,

2007: 1) suggests that the Ottoman Empire was subjected to capitalist relations via trade and exchange before its social class structure became capitalist. The Ottoman economy was indeed pre-capitalist, relying on agricultural production (Zürcher, 2005: 16). However, its relations with core capitalist countries were uneven due to capitulations and its dependence on foreign capital to finance modernisation in the declining empire. Though it was not colonised, it was dependent and forced to make concessions, which Keyder (1987: 37–38) defines as 'debt imperialism'. Before World War I, the welfare-nationalist consensus collapsed as rival imperialisms among major industrial powers replaced this liberal laissez-faire order (Cox, 1987: 151–210). According to Cox (1987: 161), the 'welfare-nationalist' state planned economies under state capitalism and corporatism. While core capitalist countries stimulated industrialisation by protectionism and expanding markets through their colonies (Cox, 1987: 154), developing countries on the periphery, transformed into fascist/corporative states, aspired to 'catch up' with capitalist regimes through 'passive revolution' (Cox, 1987: 163). Hence, Gramsci reads the bourgeois revolution in Italy as a passive revolution (Gramsci, 1971: 114), contending that 'what was involved was not a social group which "led" other groups, but a State which … "led" the group which should have been "leading" and was able to put at the latter's disposal an army and a politico-diplomatic strength' (Gramsci, 1971: 105). Gramsci refers to the '"Piedmont"-type function' of the state, which 'replaces the local social groups in leading a struggle of renewal' while describing it as '"domination" without that of "leadership": dictatorship without hegemony' (Gramsci, 1971: 105–106).

Morton uses passive revolution to examine modern state formation on the periphery within the 'causal conditioning of the "international" and uneven and combined development of capitalism' (Morton, 2007a: 41). He argues that passive revolution uncovers 'class strategies of transitions to capitalism by tracing mechanisms tied to the state, which have assisted in the emergence of capitalism to become the primary organ of primitive accumulation and social development' (Morton, 2007b: 601). According to van der Pijl (1998: 79), the condition of passive revolution explicates the state/society complex on the periphery, where social class formation is slow and the strong state 'confiscates' society through its power over the bureaucracy. As van der Pijl noted (1998: 80): 'One might say that by aiming to catch up with the leading social system of production in the world economy, every contender state has by definition been "capitalist" already before it "turned capitalist"'. Importantly, Gramsci studies the Italian state formation process within the uneven and combined development of capitalism. He writes:

when the impetus of progress is not tightly linked to a vast local economic development which is artificially limited and repressed, but is instead the reflection of international developments which transmit their ideological currents to the periphery ... then the group which is the bearer of the new ideas is not the economic group but the intellectual stratum, and the conception of the State advocated by them changes aspect; it is conceived of as something in itself, as a rational absolute (Gramsci, 1971: 116–17).

Indeed, a reformist bureaucracy organised under the Committee of Union and Progress emerged in Turkey in the late nineteenth century. Following World War I, consolidating the 'national economy' was prioritised coupled with a critique of the liberal trade regime, which left nationalist industries underdeveloped (Toprak, 1995: 2–17). The republic pursued 'etatism' through a protectionist trade regime and state initiative to cultivate indigenous industry and a national bourgeoisie (Keyder, 1987: 106–107). Erol reads the republic's capitalist transition as a passive revolution, as an outcome of the Ottoman Empire's class configuration and the path to expanding capitalist accumulation in Turkey within the uneven and combined development of capitalism structurally (Erol, 2020: 132).

The liberal regime was reconstructed after the Second World War. Cox (1987) names this period, founded upon Fordism (mass production and mass consumption) under US hegemony, Pax Americana. Production was internationalised, whereby global trade connected national economies by 'geographical extension of economic activity across borders' (Robinson, 2004: 10 and 14). Ruggie describes the compromise during this period as 'embedded liberalism', in which the state implemented Keynesian welfare state policies and intervened in the market to guarantee full employment and create demand (Ruggie, 1982: 393 and 399). However, while core capitalist countries adopted the neoliberal state, neo-mercantilist developmentalist states prevailed on the periphery (Cox, 1987: 235). Cox identifies the historical bloc that founded the latter form as a coalition of the petty bourgeoisie, which was 'very largely bureaucratic and consisting of government and big corporation employees', organised workers' groups and small business people (Cox, 1987: 235). Yet these developmentalist states were not delinked from the world capitalist economy because they depended on capitalist accumulation related to technology transfer and foreign capital (Cox, 1987: 232). Through state corporatism, the developmentalist states also generated a compromise between industrial capital and organised labour (Cox, 1981: 145–146), with planning offices, ministries of industry and labour playing a more active institutional role in government (Cox, 1987: 234).

Meanwhile, Turkey integrated with the Western alliance by joining various Western institutional structures, namely NATO, the Council of Europe, the World Bank (WB) and the Organisation for Economic Cooperation and

Development (OECD), and receiving Truman and Marshall grants. Due to its geostrategic position close to the Soviet threat, Turkey was seen as strategically important for the Western Alliance and its containment policy. Turkey was also incorporated into Pax Americana by adapting liberal economic policies during the 1950s and establishing a multiparty political regime following the victory of the Democrat Party (DP) in the 1950 elections. The DP appealed to the public through populism and an anti-elitist discourse through its election slogan 'Enough is enough, let the nation speak'. The party promoted economic liberalism against previous protectionism and state interventionism while aspiring to protect religious freedoms and local traditions against the Republican People's Party's (CHP) political impositions during the single-party period (Keyder, 1987: 117). According to Aydın (2005: 28–29), the DP's agrarian policies made industrialisation secondary in line with the international division of labour within the Western alliance, which designated Turkey as a supplier of food and raw materials in return for foreign capital inflows. For Sakallıoğlu, the DP period was based on larger farmers and small-town merchants, who demanded a liberal regime to guarantee external borrowing (Sakallıoğlu, 1992: 713). Yalman, however, describes the 1950s as 'planless industrialisation' rather than a rupture from the planned economy period (Yalman, 2009: 190 and 198), arguing that the DP did not abandon industrialisation while the balance of social forces remained unchanged (Yalman, 2009: 190 and 211). By 1954, in its second term in office, the DP government faced economic stagnation, which was created by external balance deficits that could not be offset by agricultural exports. Furthermore, the DP's strong anti-communist stance was irritating Turkey's liberal intelligentsia.

Following the 1960 military coup, the government implemented the ISI strategy in tandem with the embedded liberalism and Fordist accumulation based on demand management in the world order. Economic management involved three successive five-year plans, from 1963 to 1978, while the public sector successfully protected national industries through quotas, high tariffs and an overvalued exchange rate. Institutionally, the State Planning Organisation (DPT) played a decisive supervisory role in the economy. Through this programme, industrialisation's share in gross national product overtook that of agriculture after 1973 (Ahmad, 1993: 134). Yalman (2009: 217) reads this period as a new hegemonic project under developmentalism. The social basis of the historical bloc under developmentalism comprised the industrial bourgeoisie and industrial workers, supported by the Kemalist bureaucratic cadres and the peasantry (Boratav, 2003: 130–141). Boratav (2003: 130–141) argues that this period was populist in that the ISI was expected to benefit all societal segments: workers would benefit from higher real wages and better working conditions under state corporatism; industrial capital would be protected from competition in the international markets; peasants would be guaranteed minimum prices and agricultural subsidies. Indeed, the state form was 'developmentalist', in line with peripheral countries' state corporatism under Pax Americana based on a compromise between the petty bourgeoisie and small organised worker groups (Cox, 1981: 145–146). Thus, Turkey's developmentalist state protected domestic industry while controlling foreign exchange and foreign trade to benefit domestic industry and the petty bourgeoisie. It also institutionalised corporatism by naming itself as a 'social state' in the 1961 Constitution, which also granted rights to strike and collective bargaining for the working class (Önder, 1999: 45). The ISI was thus based on a mutual accommodation in labour–capital relations, considering that the industrial bourgeoisie and labour aristocracies set real wages through industrial bargaining (Keyder, 1996: 151). There were considerable achievements for the labour movement as unionisation increased and trade unions politicised. Real wages were critical to stimulating demand since the pre-eminent Fordist accumulation strategy relied on generating domestic demand to foster production for the industrial bourgeoisie (Boratav, 2003: 124). Thus, the developmentalist state devised policies to regulate distribution relations to maintain high real wages and agricultural income.

Turkey–EEC relations: a tug of war between development and liberalisation

During this period of Fordist accumulation and the neo-mercantilist developmentalist state, relations between the EEC and Turkey can be described as a tug of war between social forces favouring liberalisation through the Customs Union and those social forces favouring ISI-based industrialisation and protectionism, with some fractions within organised labour criticising Europe under the motto 'We are the market and they are the partners'. Following Greece's application in 1959, Turkey applied to the EEC for associate membership, signing the Ankara Agreement on 12 September 1963 to establish an association partnership. The Ankara Agreement was aimed at Turkey joining the Customs Union, including consideration of full EU membership during the process. The partnership had three stages. The first preparatory stage required unilateral concessions by the EEC to reduce customs and protectionist barriers against Turkish products and provide financial assistance to Turkey. The second transitional stage, launched on 1 January 1973 after the Additional Protocol was signed, required Turkey to gradually align with the EEC's common external tariff and liberalise certain products listed in two groups, over twelve and twenty-two years. The third stage involved finalising the Customs Union through both sides liberalising their trade regimes for manufactured products and processed agricultural goods.

However, I argue that there was little consensus during this period among Turkey's social forces regarding EEC membership or eliminating protectionism. The social forces underpinning the ISI strategy were domestic bourgeoisie and organised labour, who expected protectionism and the cultivation of domestic industry. Those social forces were sceptical of liberalisation. Tekeli and İlkin (1993b) analysed the position of these social forces. Given the lack of empirical analyses of the period, their study can help reveal the position of these social forces. The commercial-industrial bourgeoisie and the liberal Justice Party supported signing the Additional Protocol without delay to boost productivity and make Turkey a strong partner within the Western alliance (Tekeli and İlkin, 1993b: 56–59 and 94–104). Yet the centre-left CHP, a fraction of the DPT and SMEs, organised under domestically oriented chambers of industry in Anatolia, were unwilling to open the economy to competition from Europe, and demanded protectionism and delays in the liberalisation programme under the Additional Protocol. Meanwhile, organised labour and the Workers' Party of Turkey (TİP) resisted the EEC under the motto 'they are the partners and we are the market', criticising the EEC as an imperialist bloc aiming to exploit Turkey while liberalisation was believed to hinder industrialisation and economic development (Tekeli and İlkin, 1993b: 94–104 and 113–115). Indeed, these tensions between liberalisation and industrialisation became clear after the Council of Ministers increased import tariffs to 50 per cent the day before signing the Additional Protocol (Tekeli and İlkin, 1993b: 92). Turkey also requested a five-year exemption due to economic crisis and repeatedly delayed liberalising trade with Europe in the 1970s. The DPT and the CHP also proposed revising the Additional Protocol to support the development of Turkish industry and agriculture (Tekeli and İlkin, 1993b: 216–222).

Globalisation, the neoliberal turn and structural adjustment

The neoliberal turn after the 1980s

The historical bloc founded on Fordism started to disintegrate in the late 1970s in tandem with the economic crisis. Due to its debts, the US ended the Bretton Woods system by abandoning the fixed exchange rate regime. The 1973 oil crisis caused inflation and soaring costs of raw materials in the world economy (Cox, 1987: 277–278). Meanwhile, the neoliberal accumulation strategy engendered new coordinates for the social relations of production and form of state. The relations of production are transnationalised by disintegrating different phases of production across different geographies while integrating them on a transnational scale (Cox, 1981: 146). According to Robinson (2004: 14–15), transnationalisation denotes organising production on a global scale by 'the fragmentation and decentralisation of complex production chains and the worldwide dispersal and functional integration of the different segments in these chains'. This envisages a new division of labour in the global economy between core and peripheral countries, with the former conducting capital-intensive phases of production through technological innovation and a highly skilled workforce, while the latter conducting labour-intensive production through standardised technology and cheap labour (Cox, 1987: 319). Thatcherism and Reaganism substituted the economic strategy of tolerating inflation in return for employment with monetarism, whereby controlling inflation is the primary objective for economic growth while consolidating a predictable economic environment (Cox, 1987: 279).

Under this neoliberal strategy, the neo-mercantilist developmentalist state is redefined. The state is no longer a buffer between national industry and the external economic environment. Rather, the state is internationalised (Cox, 1981: 146) to promote international industrial competitiveness by securing the interests of export-oriented sectors and providing subsidies (Cox, 1987: 253–254 and 290). On the periphery, the internationalisation of the state prioritises those state institutions aligned with structural adjust- ment policies, particularly the finance ministry and prime ministers' offices with other ministries (e.g. industry, labour and planning offices) having a secondary position (Cox, 1981: 146). Under the Thatcher-Reagan model, the state abandons social policy goals, redistributionist tools and demand management (Cox, 1987: 286). Tripartism is discarded with the state institu- tions endorsing government–business alliances. The labour movements weaken and further fragment around new divisions, specifically established/non- established and national/international labour, while labour is put into a defensive position (Cox, 1981: 148). Established workers in larger enterprises are unionised, skilled and working under stable and secure conditions, whereas non-established workers, mostly composed of immigrants, minorities and women, are outside trade union solidarities (Cox, 1981: 148). An additional fraction is between internationally oriented labour, who are employed in export-oriented enterprises in the global economy and are not concerned about internationalised production, and nationally oriented labour, which needs protection from global trade to survive (Cox, 1981: 148). Hence, internationally oriented labour has the potential to ally with inter- national capital, not due to the absence of class antagonism but rather because international capital can, through enterprise corporatism, meet their concerns and isolate them from the issues facing labour generally (Cox,

1981: 148). Another split is promoted between public and private sector workers, with the former discredited as inefficient and damaging the public interest (Cox, 1987: 284). More importantly, another group comprised illegal workers, part-time female workers and migrant workers who are excluded from trade union solidarity (Cox, 1987: 284).

By the late 1970s, Turkey's ISI model was increasingly questioned due to world recession, foreign exchange bottlenecks, balance of payment deficits and political instability. Turkey's foreign currency shortage and the US economic embargo after Turkey's intervention in Cyprus in 1974 exacerbated the financial bottleneck. The ISI model was criticised for increasing Turkey's dependence on international borrowing, while the DPT was accused due to its protectionist policies and market interventions, rendering Turkish economy inefficient, expensive and cumbersome (Öniş, 1987: 28; Öniş and Webb, 1998: 325). Remarkably, just before the military coup on 12 September 1980, Turkey replaced the ISI model with a major adjustment programme – the 24 January 1980 Stabilisation Programme. This aimed to promote exports through tax rebates and credit subsidies, and liberalise trade by eliminating tariffs and other restrictions. The programme aspired to 'reduce the rate of inflation … improve the balance-of-payments situation through rapid export-growth and, thereby, re-establish Turkey's international creditworthiness' (Baysan and Blitzer, 1990: 10). The state withered away from production by 'rationalising' state economic enterprises, left income distribution to market mechanisms and adapted tight monetary controls to decrease inflation. It liberalised the exchange rate regime and introduced flexible exchange rates, with the Turkish lira depreciated by 4.2 per cent annually from 1981 to 1987 (Baysan and Blitzer, 1990: 11). Meanwhile, Turkey's labour movement mobilised to protect real wages, with the Confederation of Progressive Trade Unions of Turkey (DİSK) openly supporting the TİP and advocating socialism. Meanwhile, street fighting intensified between the Grey Wolves – a militant youth movement affiliated with the Nationalist Movement Party (MHP) – and the Revolutionary Youth Federation of Turkey. After taking control, the military junta ruled the country until the November 1983 general elections.

The role of the Turkish military cannot be read as external to society and its class struggle, contrary to the strong state tradition, which considers the state to be independent of society and capitalist social relations. As Yalman (2009: 311) argues, the 1980 transition should be interpreted as a passive revolution on three grounds. First, the bourgeoisie failed to take a moral and intellectual leadership position in the transition to the new hegemony. In particular, the export-oriented bourgeoisie was not in a position to lead society into the neoliberal restructuring (Yalman, 2009: 265 and 274–278). Moreover, the military junta announced its commitment to the

24 January Stabilisation Programme, thereby guaranteeing to both international financial institutions and the domestic bourgeoisie that it would implement the programme (Yalman, 2009: 300). Second, the military junta was instrumental in providing political stability while containing the labour movement and controlling the democratic process. As already mentioned, the new neoliberal accumulation strategy around transnationalisation of production envisages a role of labour-intensive production for the periphery based on cheap labour, thereby making real wages a cost limiting industry's international competitiveness. Actually, the number of workers on strike rose from 6,414 in January 1980 to 57,000 after the introduction of the structural adjustment programme, while the workers started working three days after the military coup (Koç, 1998: 186–87). To put it bluntly, the military regime then contributed to reducing wages without societal resistance by banning unions and strikes, prosecuting unionists and smashing left-wing organic intellectuals (Boratav, 2003: 150). Third, the International Monetary Fund (IMF) and the WB endorsed neoliberal restructuring through financial support to strengthen NATO's southern flank following the end of détente, the Soviet invasion of Afghanistan and the 1979 Iranian Revolution (Öniş and Kirkpatrick, 1991: 11).

Notably, Callinicos criticises stretching the concept of passive revolution in understanding neoliberal transitions from 'a particular path *to* capitalist domination' during the modern state formation process, towards strategies of '*maintaining* capitalist domination' and/or 'restorations of capitalism' (emphases in original, Callinicos, 2010: 491–492 and 503). Morton, however, argues that passive revolution not only enables scrutiny of a condition of revolution without mass participation, but also helps us to understand:

> how a revolutionary form of political transformation is pressed into a conservative project of restoration while lacking a radical national-popular 'Jacobin' moment … Definitionally, then, a passive revolution can be a technique of statecraft which an emergent bourgeois class may deploy by drawing in subaltern social classes while establishing a new state on the basis of the institution of capitalism, as in the Risorgimento, or the expansion of capitalism as a mode of production, as in the case of 'Americanism and Fordism'. (Morton, 2010a: 317–318)

Similarly, Gramsci (1971: 108) questions whether passive revolution can 'be related to the concept of "war of position" in contrast to "war of manoeuvre?"', and whether passive revolution can be interpreted as a ruling class strategy for restoring capitalist social relations in the war of position rather than a condition limited to the bourgeois revolution.

In line with the neoliberal turn, the neoliberal form of state was established in Turkey's social formation. State economic enterprises were privatised while the state role in production withered. Tripartism was abandoned, with the military junta curtailing social rights guaranteed by the 1961 Constitution. Boratav (2003: 149) describes this period as 'capital's counter-attack against labour'. The regime presented real wages as a production cost reducing the competitiveness of Turkish products in global markets and campaigning against 'overpaid workers' (Önder, 1999: 54) by systematically keeping nominal wages below the annual inflation rate (Boratav, 1990: 209). The neoliberal form of state contained the labour movement by 'outlawing' DİSK for a decade while promoting new trade unions, limiting bargaining to real wages rather than a critique of general economic policies and banning action in certain economic sectors which were declared 'strategic' (Yalman, 2009: 316–317). Welfare state policies were replaced by charities (Yalman, 2009: 324). As Boratav concludes, 'lower wages may lose their significance in a social atmosphere where the wage as such starts to become a secondary element determining the welfare of the family' (Boratav, 1990: 224). For instance, municipalities distributed partial property rights to shanty towns and allocated building licences and land permission. The strategy of generating social mechanisms not only helped to prevent a social explosion but also reduced the need for trade union solidarity in serving the labour movement's interests (Boratav, 2005: 152–153). Yalman reads this new hegemony as 'putting an end to class-based politics' (Yalman, 2009: 308) through policies aiming to eliminate the 'saliency of class as the basis for collective identification and action' by a strategy of depoliticising society (Yalman, 2009: 309). In the neoliberal accumulation model, the disadvantaged social forces include wage earners, fixed income groups, low-ranked bureaucrats and agricultural workers (Boratav, 1990: 224). In the new dynamics of the relations of distribution, the tax burden disadvantaged those wage-earners with regular salaries (Boratav, 2003: 154) while structural adjustment encouraged industrialists towards rentier activities to take advantage of quick returns within the speculative economy (Boratav, 2005: 61; Önder, 1999: 68). The surplus thereby accrued to the rentier fraction, financial bourgeoisie, industrial and agricultural exporters (Boratav, 2003: 167–169).

Financial liberalisation and the rise of the AKP government as an example of trasformismo

Turkey's adjustment to neoliberalism can be considered in two phases: trade liberalisation and export promotion from 1980 to 1988 and financial market liberalisation and deregulation from 1988 to 2003 (Yeldan, 2006: 196). In 1989, Turkey abandoned controls on foreign capital transactions while opening its domestic asset markets to international competition and making the Turkish lira convertible (Cizre and Yeldan, 2005: 389). Financial liberalisation engendered deindustrialisation with the rentier fraction of capital benefitting from high, rapid returns from speculative capital (Aydın, 2005: 113–115). As Aydın (2005: 134) notes, to explicate the accumulation around financialisation 'the state had borrowed externally at a cheaper rate in order to pay its internal debts with phenomenally high interest rates'. During the 1990s, the economy was subjected to a cycle of crises and adjustment triggered by currency appreciations due to short-term speculative foreign capital inflows that reduced exports and increased the current account deficit, which in turn increased exchange rate risks and encouraged a rapid exit of foreign lenders (Akyüz ve Boratav, 2003: 1555). This rentier type of accumulation, coupled with short-term capital inflows and contraction in the productive sector, saw inflation and interest rates soar and was followed by the 1994 financial crisis (Akyüz and Boratav, 2003: 1552). The 1994 crisis was followed by three years of 7 per cent economic growth as exports and capital inflows recovered. In 1999, however, there was another financial crisis, with eight banks taken over by the Saving Deposit Insurance Fund, worsening public debts and deficits (Akyüz and Boratav, 2003: 1552). The economic contraction, and Turkey's fragile banking system, forced another stand-by agreement with the IMF in 1999. Due to low public revenues, the state turned to internal and external borrowing, with almost half of the budget allocated to interest payments before the 2001 crisis (Aydın, 2005: 106–107). Real rates in Turkey were 80 per cent in 2001, 60 per cent in 2002 and 75 per cent in 2003 (Yeldan, 2006: 202), while the domestic debt grew from 36.4 quadrillion Turkish lira in 2000 to 170 quadrillion Turkish lira by the end of 2002 (Aydın, 2005: 123).

In May 2001, Turkey announced a reform programme, Transition to a Stronger Turkish Economy, with Kemal Derviş, WB vice-president for the Middle East and North Africa region, announced as the economic minister to head a team of technocrats to implement it. The expectation was that such a team would avoid political interference, with Kemal Derviş providing the financial markets with security thanks to his links with transnational capital and foreign creditors. The programme put the blame for the crisis on the fragile banking sector, 'excessive' public sector employment, 'irrational' public spending, 'redundant' agricultural subsidies, financial deficits in social security institutions and 'inefficient' public economic enterprises (Central Bank, 2001: 1 and 4). It aimed to guarantee macroeconomic stability through a tight fiscal policy by controlling inflation, reforming the banking system, restricting public spending, implementing privatisation and replacing agricultural subsidies with direct income support mechanisms (Central Bank, 2001: 1 and 4). Put bluntly, it aimed to provide macroeconomic stability through structural adjustment to reassure foreign capital about investing in Turkey as an 'emerging market' (Aydın, 2005: 132).

General elections in 2002 took place during the ongoing economic crisis. Signalling society's deep resentment, none of the political parties forming the previous coalition government, namely the Democratic Left Party (DSP), MHP and Motherland Party (ANAP), won parliamentary seats because they failed to pass the 10 per cent election threshold. Instead, the newly founded AKP secured almost two-thirds of the seats with 34 per cent of the vote. It then consolidated its hegemony with 46 per cent of the vote in the 2007 elections and 49 per cent in 2011. Although it emerged from the conservative Millî Görüş[1] (National View) movement, the AKP came to terms with globalisation in the 2000s, defining itself as a 'conservative democratic' party after altering its previous statist/developmentalist, nationalist and anti-European position (Uzgel, 2009: 18). The international context in the 2000s was also conducive, with the New Right presenting Turkey under the AKP regime as a model for other Middle East 'Muslim democrats' with its moderate form of Islam (Uzgel, 2009: 21–22). The AKP's 'new' foreign policy orientation pioneered by the former foreign minister Ahmet Davutoğlu was equally well received. He called for a more active role for Turkey as a regional power within supranational organisations through soft power mechanisms, with Turkey acting as a bridge between West and East (Davutoğlu, 2008: 77–79; Davutoğlu, 2010).

I argue here that the AKP's hegemony can be read as *trasformismo*. Gramsci (1971: 58) originally used this term to describe the 'formation of an ever more extensive ruling class' whereby the party programmes of both right and left converge to such an extent that 'there cease[s] to be any substantive difference between them' (Gramsci, 1971: 58 footnote 8). However, he also used the term in describing the ruling class's strategy of leading 'even those [who] came from antagonistic groups and seemed irreconcilably hostile' (Gramsci, 1971: 59). Concurrent with Cox (1983: 166–167), *trasformismo* is the 'strategy of assimilating and domesticating potentially dangerous ideas by adjusting them to the policies of the dominant coalition and can thereby obstruct the formation of class-based organised opposition to established social and political power'. Hence, contrary to Tuğal (2009), who reads the AKP hegemony as a passive revolution, I argue that it represents *trasformismo* for two reasons. First, the AKP adapted the macroeconomic policies of the Transition to a Stronger Turkish Economy programme, thereby reconsolidating neoliberalism, despite presenting itself as a rupture from previous 'corrupted' right-wing political parties. More specifically, the AKP extended the ruling class by appealing to Turkey's SMEs as its social base and integrating SMEs into the neoliberal hegemony. Internationally oriented capital supported the government on the expectation that the AKP regime would implement the Transition to a Stronger Turkish Economy programme strongly with an AKP majority in the parliament.

Meanwhile, national oriented SMEs endorsed the AKP regime to render SMEs competitive in international markets (Interview 55). As the interviewee from the AKP noted, the party aimed to strengthen SMEs, which it considered Turkey's truly 'competitive' and productive industrial segments (Interview 55). Moreover, the AKP was expected to consolidate democracy by increasing the welfare of the middle-income groups (Interview 55).

Second, the AKP successfully disarticulated dissent by incorporating disadvantaged groups from globalisation into capitalist discipline through an identity-based populist discourse. Attracted by the AKP's populist discourse, which characterised the main struggle in society as being 'the people versus the elites', those social forces disadvantaged by globalisation, which might have supported a progressive alternative political project, instead supported the populist dissent against the so-called 'strong state establishment'. The interviewee from the AKP paradoxically defined the party as a 'social democratic political party' by referencing 'development' and 'justice' in its name (Interview 55). The AKP's discourse was well received by low-income groups, though the party not only had no political agenda to improve labour conditions but was also aligned with social mechanisms based on charities in line with the individualistic welfare mechanisms of the hyperliberal form of state. In its 2001 election manifesto, the party referred to disabled, retired, unemployed, poor and diseased people in discussing its social policy with a shallow reference to labour (AKP, 2001: 40). It promised to guarantee 'social justice' by providing assistance with health expenses for dependent people, distributing coal and schoolbooks for poor people and increasing salaries for disabled people (AKP, 2007: 90–96). However, it did not aim to transform the relations of distribution in Turkish society to the benefit of lower and middle income groups. For instance, the AKP has promoted the competitiveness of the Turkish economy in global markets through a low wage labour policy while turning a blind eye to the informal economy (Bakırezer and Demirer, 2009: 175). Moreover, the bulk of taxes is collected by indirect taxation, which disproportionately burdens middle- and low-income groups (Bakırezer and Demirer, 2009: 167).

Turkish membership application and reform process in the 2000s

Despite being part of the Additional Protocol, trade was not liberalised during the ISI period. On the contrary, Turkey froze liberalisation in 1978 and did not reduce trade barriers against EEC products until the 1980s. In 1988, for instance, although the Additional Protocol envisaged full removal of tariffs by 1985 for products in the twelve-year list, Turkey only reduced 20 per cent of them and 10 per cent of tariffs on the twenty-year list (Tekeli and İlkin, 2000: 185–186). Moreover, until the late 1980s, it resorted to protectionism through non-tariff barriers such as duties and equities. Turkey only started liberalising its trade with the EEC after 1989, following its application for full EEC membership on 14 April 1987. The ANAP government and Prime Minister Turgut Özal argued that membership would complete Turkey's modernisation, help Turkey to reach the level of European civilisation, consolidate democracy and end Turkey's international isolation following the Cyprus intervention and international conflicts with Greece (Özal, 1991). Tekeli and İlkin (2000: 100–101) argue that the ANAP government expected that membership would consolidate export-led growth strategy while providing financial assistance for its neoliberal programme. Right-wing political parties endorsed the membership perspective while certain left-wing intellectuals, social democratic political parties and Kurdish groups also reconsidered their former critical stance because they believed that membership could help reform the anti-democratic practices institutionalised by the military regime (Tekeli and İlkin, 2000: 103–104). In contrast, religious-conservative parties were openly critical based on the motto cited earlier that 'They are the partners and we are the market' (Tekeli and İlkin, 2000: 100–104). Meanwhile, the labour movement remained weak following the military coup, given that DİSK was banned from politics from 1980 to 1992 while the Confederation of Turkish Trade Unions (Türk-İş) adapted the position of the government (Tekeli and İlkin, 2000: 105–106).

The European Commission declared Turkey eligible for membership while admitting that the European Community (EC) was not ready for another enlargement as it was preoccupied with completing the Single Market by 1992. The European Commission also asked Turkey to consolidate its democracy and market economy, provide a stable macroeconomic structure, reduce inflation and unemployment, guarantee adequate social protections for workers and deepen the Customs Union (European Commission, 1989). After 1988, Turkey prepared a 'precipitated tariff reduction list' and started to implement tariff reductions for European products (Interview 47).

Regarding the position of social forces concerning how joining the Customs Union would affect the economy, Turkey's internationally oriented capital fraction believed it could contribute to Turkey's products being more competitive on international markets (Interview 3, 14, 16; TÜSİAD, 2008: 19; MESS, 1994: 17). They expected the Customs Union to bolster Turkey's production capacity and bring technology transfer (Interviews 3 and 16). The Turkish Industry and Business Association (TÜSİAD) expected membership to bring macro-economic stability through the Maastricht criteria while helping Turkey to comply with international trade rules (TÜSİAD, 1996: 55–56). In line with export promotion and state subsidies for leading export sectors, the concerns of Turkey's textile industry were prioritised in negotiations, with the Undersecretariat of Foreign Trade providing an organic link between bureaucracy and textile exporters (Interview 47). Similarly, the automotive industry supported the Customs Union on the condition that imports of secondhand vehicles should require special permission (Interview 47). In line with the hypothesis, internationally oriented textile sector labour also supported the Customs Union because it would eliminate quotas, so long as Turkey could gain EC membership (Interview 6). Indeed, both the Textile Workers' Union (Tekstil-İş) and the Textile, Knitting, Clothing, and Leather Industry Workers' Union of Turkey (Teksif) supported the Customs Union (Interviews 6 and 13). The Tekstil-İş representative, for example, claimed that the Customs Union would enable the standardisation of textile production while increasing product quality (Interview 6).

In contrast, and as expected from the hypothesis, nationally oriented capital raised concerns with the Customs Union regarding liberalisation. Turkish SMEs were expected to struggle to compete with European competitors (MÜSİAD, 1996: 109). Their representatives argued that imports of raw materials would harm domestic SMEs while rising imports would damage the trade balance, thereby generating a foreign exchange bottleneck in Turkey's economy (İSO, 1995: 16 and 30; MESS, 1994: 28; MÜSİAD, 1995: 53). Meanwhile, the terms and conditions of international trade would put extra pressure on SMEs (MÜSİAD, 1996: 108). Moreover, as Turkey would also have to comply with the EU's foreign economic regime, Turkey's privileged economic relations with other economic blocs, such as the Economic Cooperation Organisation, Islamic Conference Economic Council and Black Sea Economic Cooperation, would be impaired (MÜSİAD, 1995: 53). Indeed, the Independent Industrialists and Businessmen Association (MÜSİAD) proposed that the Middle Eastern developing countries and the Turkic republics should form a new economic regional bloc: the Cotton Union (MÜSİAD, 1996: 4). Certain labour groups also disagreed with the 'membership first' policy of the Türk-İş and the claim of the Confederation of Turkish Real Trade Unions (Hak-İş) that 'they are the partners and we are the market'. Türk-İş expected that the Customs Union would exaggerate Turkey's economic problems by increasing unemployment and reducing the independence of Turkey's foreign trade regime (Türk-İş, 2002b: 235–241). Similarly, Hak-İş was against the Customs Union, reasoning that it would damage Turkey's industry and make it dependent on the EU, yet without Turkey's participation in EU decision making (Hak-İş, 1992: 180–181; 1995: 82–83; 1999: 49).

Despite these dissident voices, the EU–Turkey Association Council completed the Customs Union on 6 March 1995. At the 1997 Luxembourg European Council, however, the EU decided to launch a new accession wave in 1998 to include ten Central and East European applicants and Cyprus, but not Turkey (European Council, 1997). The Luxembourg Summit conclusions were disappointing for Turkey as it was excluded from the Big Bang Enlargement, even though a decade had passed since its full membership application in 1987. Turkey then froze political relations with the EU until the 1999 Helsinki European Council, at which Turkey was finally declared a candidate 'destined to join the Union on the basis of the same criteria as applied to other candidate States' while also benefiting from a preaccession strategy (European Council, 1999). The screening process started with the EU issuing its first Accession Partnership for Turkey on 8 March 2001, which set short- and medium-term priorities for Turkey's alignment with the EU acquis. Turkey published its 'National Programme for the Adaption of the EU acquis' on 19 March 2001. Another milestone in Turkey–EU relations was the EU's decision on 3 October 2005 to open accession negotiations. However, these stalled in 2007, with only one chapter, Science and Research, provisionally closed. The EU suspended eight other negotiation chapters until Turkey agreed to implement the Additional Protocol for all members, including the Greek Cypriot Administration of Southern Cyprus. As part of its enlargement strategy, the EU has issued progress reports that assess the candidate country's progress towards membership and Turkey has published its National Programme. Particularly, in its first two terms in office, the AKP continued to carry the reform process, with Turkey–EU relations mostly discussed in terms of enlargement. However, as mentioned earlier, the reform process slowed after 2007 as relations gradually deteriorated under the historical conjuncture of the Great Recession and rising populism.

The global crisis and the rise of authoritarian neoliberalism

The global crisis and the new coordinates of core–periphery dependence

The 2007–08 Great Recession started with the collapse of US mortgage-backed securities, a bursting speculative financial bubble, leading to bankruptcies and bailout programmes globally. Overbeek (2012: 31) reads this as a crisis of overaccumulation, whereas van der Pijl (2019: 241) explains it as an accumulation crisis of money-dealing capital. It is based on the contradictions of financialisation as an accumulation strategy. Lapavitsas (2009: 143 and 146) argues that financialisation in the current conjuncture of global capitalism is not simply the dominance of banks over industrial and commercial capital. Rather, he identifies financialisation with the financial sector's growing autonomy as financial institutions gain new sources of profitability through financial expropriation and investment banking while labour groups resort to private finance to fulfil their basic needs of housing, consumption, education, health and old-age provision (Lapavitsas, 2009: 146). Lapavitsas (2013: 10) argues that financialisation has three characteristics: non-financial enterprises involved in financial transactions; banks operating in open financial markets and making transactions for profits; and individuals and households relying on the financial system to access goods like housing, education, health and transport. Hence, the novelty of the Great Recession is that financialised accumulation now includes wage earners rather than just the elites – for instance, the bourgeoisie and upper classes (Becker and Jäger, 2010: 6). Becker and Jäger (2010: 6) describe the crisis as popular financialisation, with large segments becoming indebted thanks to mortgage and consumer credits.

Scholars have identified various contradictions within financial globalisation. First, globalisation provides capital mobility, which enables employers to corner labour by threatening labour movements to 'accept lower wages, or else we move abroad' (Rodrik, 2017: 19). This has generated underbidding, putting national labour movements in competition to attract foreign capital (e.g. Bieler et al., 2008a; Bieler and Lindberg, 2011). Second, capital has become more difficult to tax thanks to its mobility, forcing governments to fund themselves through taxing consumption (indirect taxation) or income (Rodrik, 2017: 19). Hence, Piketty (2014: 347) argues that declining corporate taxes constitute a decisive cause of rising inequalities under the financial globalisation. To refer to Piketty (2014: 347):

> the recent rise of tax competition in a world of free-flowing capital has led many governments to exempt capital income from the progressive income tax … The result is an endless race to the bottom, leading, for example, to cuts in corporate tax rates and to the exemption of interest, dividends, and other financial revenues from the taxes to which labor incomes are subject.

Third, globalisation and capital mobility have led to a concentration of wealth and rising inequalities. In the *Seventeen Contradictions and the End of Capitalism*, Harvey (2015: 91) pinpoints the concentration of wealth as a crucial contradiction:

> between the incredible increase in the productive forces (broadly understood as technological capacities and powers) and capital's incapacity to utilise that productivity for the common welfare because of its commitment to the prevailing class relations and their associated mechanisms of class reproduction, class domination and class rule. Left to itself, the argument goes, capital is bound to produce an increasingly vulnerable oligarchic and plutocratic class structure under which the mass of the world's population is left to hustle a living or starve to death.

The Great Recession and the COVID-19 pandemic further accelerated inequalities. According to Piketty, the top decile's share of US national income fell from 45–50 per cent in the 1910s and 1920s, to 30–35 per cent by the end of the 1940s, and remained unchanged until the 1980s, when it soared to 45–50 per cent by the 2000s (Piketty, 2014: 23). According to Ruchir Sharma, the COVID-19 pandemic caused a further concentration of wealth, with the ultra-rich's share in GDP rising from 11 per cent to 17 per cent in France, 20 per cent to 30 per cent in Sweden and doubling in China (Sharma, 2021). Billionaires in Mexico and Russia now control 75 and 60 per cent of national wealth, respectively (Sharma, 2021). Similarly, the world's richest 2 per cent owns more than 50 per cent of global assets while almost 90 per cent of the world's proletariat work under precarious conditions or are unprotected, with many people marginalised and dispossessed (Gill, 2016: 35). Gill (2016: 34) describes the contradictions of market civilisation as 'me-oriented, consumerist, exploitative of human beings and nature … and ecologically myopic'. For Saval (2016), there is a similarity between Karl Polanyi's time, when labour, land and money were turned into 'fictitious commodities' and the current conjuncture under global capitalism, characterised by globalisation and financialisation, in which 'it seems like almost every social good is capable of being monetised: health, happiness, education, housing, communication, even citizenship have all become commodities sold and purchased on the market'. Indeed, in the *Great Transformation* (1944), Polanyi demonstrates how the unregulated markets of the laissez-faire period disembedded the economy from society, generating a double movement in which society reacted back with the rise of the First World War.

Scholars within Gramscian historical materialism analyse the main coordinates of the geopolitics of global capitalism following the 2008 Great Recession as a crisis of neoliberal hegemony – and/or authoritarian neoliberalism. The neoliberal project is not hegemonic because significant societal segments have not consented to neoliberal governance (van Apeldoorn et al., 2012: 479). Hence, van Apeldoorn argues that the rule of the neoliberal power bloc in Europe (pioneered by financial capital and industrial transnational corporations) is not hegemonic as the European Trade Union Confederation (ETUC) is increasing its critical stance and there have been cycles of protests against austerity on the European periphery, especially in Greece and Spain (van Apeldoorn, 2013: 199). Yet the absence of a viable counter-hegemonic project renders neoliberalism resilient (van Apeldoorn and Overbeek, 2012: 3). As the ruling classes cannot offer material rewards for the larger population, they resort to a 'politics of fear' accompanied by 'the contamination of the public sphere by distortion and misrepresentation of fact by the governing classes and media', which fuels fear by terrorism and xenophobia while demonising selected foreign leaders (van der Pijl, 2019: 257).

Institutionalist studies read this politics as populist (e.g. Müller, 2016) whereas critical political economy refers to 'authoritarian neoliberalism' (e.g. Bruff, 2014; Jessop, 2019; Tansel, 2017 and 2018). Bruff (2014: 113) defines authoritarian neoliberalism as 'the reconfiguring of the state into a less democratic entity through constitutional and legal changes that seek to insulate it from social and political conflict'. He contends that this does not signify a rupture with the previous neoliberal period, although it is qualitatively different because of its punitive nature that replaces legal and constitutional mechanisms with penal and criminal policies (Bruff, 2014: 116). Albo and Fanelli (2014: 7) name it as 'disciplinary democracy' which 'deploys anti-democratic measures that marginalises, and even criminalises, dissent in defense of austerity and market freedoms'. In this era, power is concentrated in the executive at the expense of parliaments with economic management centred around special economic agencies directly reporting to the executive (Albo and Fanelli, 2014: 14). Albo and Fanelli characterise this era with two features: total privatisation (e.g. water, healthcare, infrastructure, transport, education, pensions) and disciplining dissent through policing political protest (Albo and Fanelli, 2014: 14–19 and 26). The rise of right-wing populist politics has led to the expansion of the state's role in surveillance and coercion and restrictions on civil and political liberties (Albo and Fanelli, 2014: 20). The state resorts to coercive mechanisms by naming protests related to the economy and/or the environment as a threat to economic recovery or competitiveness, increasing fines and criminal charges for 'illegal' protests (Albo and Fanelli, 2014: 22). To quote Albo and Fanelli (2014: 22): 'The various surveillance, organizational and technical capacities developed in the "fight against terrorism" are now also used for domestic scrutiny and "pacification" of protests', from 'facial recognition systems, telephone, computer and electronics hacking, and metadata mining'. Within such a context, democracy is limited to '"free elections" and the formalism of "parliamentary procedures"' (Albo and Fanelli, 2014: 22). Albo and Fanelli (2014: 25) note that the 'substance of democracy as a process of struggle between social classes and groups over alternate socio-economic orders, and the development of citizenship capacities, has been eviscerated'.

In explicating the material basis of the rise of authoritarianism, Saad-Filho refers to dislocations caused by neoliberalism such as delocalisation of production to the East, elimination of skilled jobs, erosion of public sector employment, declining employment stability and deteriorating labour conditions (Saad-Filho, 2018). Political impotency, crisis of representation and declining influence of labour groups in the political sphere also contributed to the rise of authoritarianism (Saad-Filho, 2018). According to Rosenberg and Boyle, the uneven historical development of capitalism is the reason behind current populist politics. Manufacturing was transferred from the Global North to the Global South thanks to Chinese primitive industrialisation and its link to transnationalised production (Rosenberg and Boyle, 2019: 43). Rosenberg and Boyle (2019: 51) state: 'China found a path to rapid industrialisation by exploiting the social, technological and financial results of more advanced development elsewhere.' This 'China shock' has generated deindustrialisation and a decline in manufacturing employment accompanied with rising inequalities, polarisation of the labour market and a widening gap between low-skilled and high-skilled jobs, preparing the ground for Brexit and election victory for the former US President Donald Trump (Rosenberg and Boyle, 2019: 46).

In the literature, populist conjuncture is compared with the fascist regimes of the inter-war period, with Löwy (2019) and Toscano (2023) naming it as post-fascism. For Löwy, it is problematic to describe it as populism. Populism as a term is broadly defined as 'people against the elite' and as such it confuses the issue while 'making them more acceptable, if not sympathetic (who is not for the people against the elite?) carefully avoiding problematic terms: racism, xenophobia, fascism, far right' (Löwy, 2019). As such, it is also plausible to refer to Gramsci as he was writing during the inter-war period within the context of the Great Depression and rising fascism. According to Buci-Glucksmann, Gramsci differentiates two forms of bourgeois domination/leadership between the liberal state and the 'totalitarian and police character of the fascist state' (Buci-Glucksmann, 1980: 293). To quote Buci-Glucksmann (1980: 293), 'these tendencies all converge in a single point, the maintenance of capitalist exploitation "under the new conditions that make liberal economic policy impossible (at least in its full content and extension)"'. Buci-Glucksmann (1980: 305) refers to Gramsci's note on 'Self-Criticism and the Hypocrisy of Self-Criticism' and his reference to 'implicit' and 'tacit' parliamentarism through which the parliamentary regime is suppressed while 'its foundations in capitalist profit are left intact'. To quote Gramsci (1971: 255) '"Implicit" and "tacit parliamentarism" is far more dangerous than the explicit variety, since it has all its defects without its positive values ... The entire subject needs re-examining, especially with respect to the "implicit" party system and parliamentarism, i.e. that which functions like "black markets" and "illegal lotteries".' The concept of Caesarism encompasses different dimensions of the fascist period with reference to the expansion of the state, capitalist crisis and organic crisis of the hegemonic apparatus (Buci-Glucksmann, 1980: 313). Yet Saad-Filho argues that there is a considerable difference with the inter-war period as authoritarian leaders rise through strategies of 'political tricks, expensive publicity, modern technologies, planned agitation, and brute force' rather than street clashes between their militias and communists (Saad-Filho, 2018).

Regarding the form of the state, although mainstream literature interprets the current conjuncture as the return of 'state capitalism' or 'rebound of the state', critical studies reconsider state functions in terms of the new dynamics of capitalist accumulation. Importantly, they consider states and markets as being internally rather than externally related or opposite phenomena (e.g. Bieler and Morton, 2018; van Apeldoorn and Graaff, 2022). As van Apeldoorn and Graaff (2022: 307) put it:

> Our key conceptual point remains that we cannot understand these shifts in terms of any mythical return of the state or a misleading dichotomy between 'state-led' and a hypothetical 'stateless' economy, but only as a reconfiguration of the various roles states play (and always have played) within and vis-à-vis (global) capital accumulation and capitalist markets.

The state continues to restore and reinforce the power of capital through austerity policies, erosion of wages, privatisation and commodification of welfare and health (van Apeldoorn et al., 2012: 472 and 478). Liberal states also continue to perform their roles of market creation (e.g. commodification and/or privatisation), market correction (ameliorating market failures), market direction and external representation for domestic capital (van Apeldoorn et al., 2012: 474). Nevertheless, the neoliberal state's role was transformed after the Great Recession (van Apeldoorn et al., 2012: 472; van Apeldoorn and Graaff, 2022: 307). In particular, in the core capitalist countries, the state has taken a more active role in saving the financial sector from collapse through bailouts and stimulus programmes, whereas on the periphery the state has sustained accumulation through capital controls, demand stimulus and/or structural investments (van Apeldoorn et al., 2012: 472). Similarly, the state has played a more prominent role in market directing, such as developing policies to reshore production following disruptions to the world supply chain during the COVID-19 pandemic (van Apeldoorn and Graaff, 2022: 322). Here, van Apeldoorn and Graaff (2022: 322) refer to US President Biden's policy of supporting US manufacturing 'to win the twenty-first century' or Europe's decision to enforce 'strategic autonomy' in its industrial policy. Similarly, in the Global South, the Chinese state increased its market-directing role by 'promoting the global expansion of the Chinese transnationalising state capital' (van Apeldoorn and Graaff, 2022: 322).

It is also important to reconsider core–periphery dynamics in this period. Despite the talk about the rise of the East with reference to BRICS and emerging markets, and the rise of statist capitalisms challenging the West with a rebound of developmentalism, van Apeldoorn et al. (2012: 483) argue that the state on the periphery has not protected industrial capital as it did during the Keynesian era of the catch-up or developmentalist model. Rather, these countries have integrated into the global economy to gain a prominent place within the neoliberal rules of the game (van Apeldoorn et al., 2012: 483). Hence, in agreement with Bieler and Morton (2018: 167), development in the Global South has to be understood within the uneven and combined development of global capitalism. For instance, Chinese development has relied on a 'low wage growth strategy' based on 'cheap labour, necessary for assembling the various parts into final products for export to North American and European markets' (Bieler and Morton, 2018: 167). Despite the talk about the rise of the East, 'there can be no question of developmental "catch-up", not for China or any other country in the Global South', given widening inequalities and polarisation between the Global North and the Global South (Bieler and Morton, 2018: 168 and 173).

Digitalisation is expected to further deepen inequalities and the development gap between core and periphery. For instance, Rodrik expects automation to prevent developing countries from converging economically with core capitalist countries (Rodrik, 2015: 23–24). Automation will trigger deindustrialisation in developing countries while generating unemployment and labour polarisation by increasing wage differences (Acemoğlu and Autor, 2010: 3; Dahlman et al., 2016: 28). Hence, digital transformation will actually widen the gap between skilled and unskilled workers as well as between developed and developing countries. Rodrik describes automation in developing countries as 'premature deindustrialisation', positing that deindustrialisation has started as they shift their economies towards the service sector without 'proper experience of industrialisation' (Rodrik, 2015: 4). Hence, Rodrik expects that automation will likely decrease economic growth while widening inequalities, thereby eroding the social base of liberal democratic regimes (Rodrik, 2015: 23). Moreover, datafication without transparency, data security and institutional guarantees over personal privacy will likely generate more surveillance of citizens and labour under 'surveillance capitalism' (Cole et al., 2021: 80). For instance, the WB warns that information without accountability will increase control over citizens (World Bank, 2016: 18).

The rise of authoritarian neoliberalism in Turkey

Studies in the mainstream literature contend that the AKP government between 2002 and 2007 played a positive role in democratisation and Europeanisation (e.g. İnsel, 2003; Öniş, 2009: 34). The party was expected to consolidate democracy by struggling against military tutelage and statist bureaucracy while helping to find a peaceful solution to the Kurdish problem (Öniş, 2013: 105) and enhance the middle classes, which would help Turkey to 'normalise' its democracy (İnsel, 2003). Later, however, the AKP regime has increasingly resorted to coercive mechanisms with the police force replacing the military, especially after the Gezi Park protests in 2013. After the failed coup attempt of 15 July 2016, the government declared a state of emergency, under which Turkey held the 2017 constitutional referendum that replaced the parliamentary regime with a presidential one. The new regime abolished the office of the Prime Minister, strengthened the executive, dismantled the separation of powers and eliminated judiciary independence while weakening the rule of law. The mainstream literature reads AKP rule after 2010 as illiberal democracy or democratic backsliding (e.g. Müftüler-Baç and Keyman, 2015; Özbudun, 2014 and 2015). However, these studies struggle to explain how democratisation in the 2000s ended up generating authoritarianism in the 2010s. Instead, they refer to concepts like post-Kemalism (Öniş, 2015), bounded communities (Öniş, 2015) and/or neighbourhood pressure (Çakır, 2008).

The critical political economy literature criticises mainstream research for reading AKP rule as composed of 'democratic' and 'authoritarian' phases. This stems from 'a binary conception of "politics" and "economics" (as well as "state" and civil society")' and turning a blind eye to the structural dynamics of the global political economy (Tansel, 2018: 198). Indeed, AKP rule represents continuity rather than rupture in terms of neoliberal restructuring (e.g. Bedirhanoğlu et al., 2020, Tansel, 2018; Türkeş, 2016; Uzgel, 2020; Yıldızoğlu, 2015). Yet the post-2011/2013 period is often read as authoritarian neoliberalism (e.g. Altınörs and Akçay, 2022; Tansel, 2018) or a new neoliberal state (Bedirhanoğlu et al., 2020). This authoritarian turn can hardly be explained without reference to the contradictions and crisis of global financialisation and the vulnerabilities of the growth pattern that emerging economies followed in the last two decades. During the Great Recession, the then prime minister, Erdoğan, claimed that 'the crisis will pass at a tangent to Turkey' (*Financial Times*, 2009). However, the economy was hit by the global contraction, especially after 2008. Indeed, countries in the Global South have become more vulnerable to shocks and crises because emerging markets have integrated into the global financial system by liberalising international capital flows and opening their markets to foreign investors and banks (Akyüz, 2017: 133). Scholars refer to three contradictions especially affecting emerging markets in the Global South. First, the growth pattern in the post-2001 crisis period has been 'jobless growth', which has generated declining real wages and persistent unemployment (Onaran, 2009: 246 and 252). Second, the growth pattern has been unsustainable as emerging countries' growth rates are dependent on 'continued and, in fact, increased inflows of capital' (Akyüz, 2012: 7). Third, the concentration of wealth and declining real wages of middle and lower income groups in core capitalist countries have generated 'underconsumption and a structural demand gap', which can hardly be compensated by bubble-driven spending (Akyüz, 2017: 51). This stems from declining wages in core capitalist countries parallel to the concentration of wealth and growing inequalities in global income distribution due to financialisation, globalisation and welfare state cuts (Akyüz, 2013: 2).

This structural crisis of dependent financialisation has compelled the AKP to resort to coercive politics in the last decade. Regarding social forces, the historical bloc underpinning the AKP government disintegrated as liberal intellectuals withdrew their support after the Gezi Park protests, large and medium-sized enterprises abandoned the bloc due to the AKP's unorthodox economic policies while the EU and the US became more critical of the AKP regime (Türkeş, 2016: 204–207). Following the 2015 elections, when the AKP was forced to establish a coalition with the nationalist MHP after it failed to maintain its parliamentary majority, it resorted to coercive mechanisms. Under the presidential system, the Kurdish peace process was shelved, parliament's role was reduced and the separation of powers was discarded (Türkeş, 2016: 207; Yıldızoğlu, 2015: 11). The failure of the Arab Spring, the ongoing Syrian war and rising authoritarianism under the presidential regime ended the narrative in the 2000s of the AKP as a model for the Middle Eastern countries with its moderate form of Islam (Yıldızoğlu, 2015: 58). Bedirhanoğlu et al. (2020: 3) read this period as the 'new neoliberal state', characterised by 'the privatisation and personification of state power, the rise of coercion, discretionary economic management, and the crippling of basic modern state institutions through processes such as deconstitutionalisation and Islamisation'. According to Altınörs and Akçay (2022: 17), the AKP allied with Turkey's nationalist-conservative forces after 2018, which consolidated the authoritarian fix. Executive power is further concentrated in the presidency while parliament is weakened with presidential decrees replacing legislative power (Altınörs and Akçay, 2022: 17). In compensating for its failure to sustain surplus value production, the AKP has expanded commodification to new spheres such as health, education, social security and infrastructure through promoting public–private partnerships and a commodified nature further benefitting the construction sector (Ercan and Oğuz, 2020: 107).

In the 2010s, the state–capital nexus and state–bourgeoisie relations have been transformed. The AKP has repoliticised economic management, taking back power from 'depoliticised' independent regulatory agencies to the executive (Ercan and Oğuz, 2020: 105). Indeed, an important characteristic of the 2010s is AKP's policy shift from acting as a 'neutral arbiter' or 'referee' vis-à-vis competing interest groups in society as advocated by liberalism to a policy 'undermining the autonomy of the independent regulatory agencies' (Bozkurt, 2021: 3). For instance, the Turkish Wealth Fund (Türkiye Varlık Fonu) was founded in August 2016 by transferring a number of public assets, including companies in strategic sectors, licences and real estate. The fund has shares with public companies such as Halkbank, Ziraat Bank, Botaş, Türksat, Borsa-İstanbul and Turkish Airlines, among others. It is directly administered by President Erdoğan, it benefits from tax exemptions and it is audit free (Ercan and Oğuz, 2020: 111). Similarly, following the 2016 coup attempt, the assets of companies linked to the Fethullah Gülen Terrorist Organisation were transferred to the Savings Deposit Insurance Fund (Tasarruf Mevduatı Sigorta Fonu) through emergency decrees under the state of emergency (Ercan and Oğuz, 2020: 111). The fund has been managed by the President since 2018 with almost 937 state-owned companies, endowing President Erdoğan with the final authority to decide (Kutun, 2020: 143). In the last couple of years, the pre-eminent controversy has been between the independence of the Central Bank, and President Erdoğan's pressure to keep interest rates low to encourage consumption through credits and shield his party's indebted political base from paying excessive credit rates, particularly for the housing sector (Kutun, 2020: 141). This controversy caused the governor of the Central Bank to be changed on six occasions between 2016 and 2024.

Similarly, public procurement law changed twenty-nine times between 2003 and 2013, curtailing its autonomy and mechanisms of transparent bidding (Buğra and Savaşkan, 2014: 126). The AKP regime benefits from public procurement, especially in social housing, infrastructural construction and municipal services as a mechanism for rent creation and distribution for the benefit of 'politically connected' private firms (Gürakar, 2016: 108 and 109). Esen and Gumuscu (2018: 349) argue that the AKP has established a 'loyal business class' since 2002 by rewarding and/or punishing capital groups. To quote Esen and Gumuscu (2018: 351), 'the AKP *politicised the state institutions* (debt collection, tax authorities, privatisation, public procurement), weakened judicial oversight, and *eroded the rule of law* to distribute public resources to its supporters, transfer capital from its opponents to its cronies, and to discipline dissidents in business circles' (emphasis in original). In particular, Esen and Gumuscu (2018: 354) highlight three mechanisms – namely public spending, privatisation of public goods and transfer of private capital to privileged business circles, especially related to construction, mining, health and energy sectors that generated a 'symbiotic relationship between the government and business actors'. In return, the loyal business class has supported the electoral basis of the party through donations and investments in pro-government media (Esen and Gumuscu, 2018: 361).

Regarding social forces, financialisation is not a class-neutral phenomenon; rather '[it] shifts the balance of power between classes and reconfigures relations within the capital-owning classes' (Yalman et al., 2019: 7). As Marois (2019: 132) highlights, 'financial restructuring has come at the expense of the people', especially organised labour and the popular classes. For instance, household debt and consumers credits contribute to the transfer of resources from non-capital-owning classes to the beneficiaries of financialisation (Yalman et al., 2019: 13). The independence of financial institutions, like the treasury, central bank and ministries of finance and economy, have resulted in policies that ignore the popular democratic demands and priorities of the labour movement (Yalman et al., 2019: 12). In addition, the labour movement remains disciplined by the AKP's neoliberal policies through 'flexibilisation, deunionisation, insecurity, precarity, privatisation, commodification, financialisation and restructuring' (Erol and Şahin, 2021: 3). The AKP's increased authoritarianism involves disciplining labour, lowering real wages and excluding collective labour groups' representatives from policy-making (Bozkurt-Güngen, 2018: 220 and 233).

In 2023, Turkey was named one of the ten worst countries for workers as employers resorted to systematic union-busting practices (ITUC, 2023). Trade union density declined from 12 per cent in 2000 to 6.3 per cent in 2012, although it increased to 9.9 per cent in 2019, compared to the OECD average of 20 per cent in 2000 and 15 per cent in 2019 (OECD, 2023). It is possible to highlight three particular reasons for this. First, the COVID-19 pandemic has worsened Turkey's working conditions with the state and capitalists perceiving it as an 'opportunity' to attract investments to Turkey through its cheap labour in a historical conjuncture when core capitalist countries reconsidered the global supply chain (Erol and Şahin, 2021: 2). Second, there is also a need to refer to refugees in discussing the deteriorating labour movement in Turkey. As Erol argues, refugee and migrant workers lowered wages, increased the reserve army and stimulated aggregate demand while reducing costs for SMEs (E. Erol, 2021: 149). After Syria fell into civil war, Turkey adopted an open-door policy for Syrian migrants, with official numbers reaching four million Syrian refugees and asylum seekers and almost 300,000 refugees and asylum seekers from Afghanistan, Iraq and Iran, as of mid-2022 (UNHCR, 2023). However, the real numbers are unclear because unregistered refugees are not counted in these official statistics. Erol argues that despite the negative discourse, refugee workers have helped alleviate Turkey's worsening economic crisis under authoritarian neoliberalism (E. Erol, 2021: 148). In particular, SMEs have taken advantage of refugee workers by employing them in the informal economy for lower wages (E. Erol, 2021: 139).

Third, the AKP's systematic anti-labour policies and commodification have further negatively impacted the labour movement. For instance, Çelik describes the labour regime in the AKP period as 'authoritarian flexibilisation' (Çelik, 2015: 623). It is authoritarian in cutting collective labour relations while consolidating flexibility in individual labour relations (Çelik, 2015: 623).

It does so through promoting 'conservative charity-social policy derive' by informal mechanisms which contribute to ameliorating the socio-economic conditions of the lower social classes (Çelik, 2015: 622). These policies rest on aid and charities on an irregular basis mostly under the guidance of the party mechanisms through paternalist and clientelist characteristics rather than institutionalising social policy (Çelik, 2015: 622). Çelik contends that they are clientelist as 'they establish customer relations instead of social rights based on relations between a citizen and his or her government' and paternalistic because 'collective rights have been restricted, organisation has been restrained, and obedience has been prioritised' (Çelik, 2015: 623). It has consolidated flexibility in labour relations through various working arrangements such as outsourcing employment through sub-employers or subcontracted workers and/or allowing private agencies to 'rent' employees to another employer (Çelik, 2015: 624). This is coupled with dislocations in the labour market through the erosion of public sector employment, triggered by privatisation of the health and education sectors. Importantly, Gürcan and Mete study the combined development of capitalism in the neoliberal period in working-class capacities. Here, they observe that combined development is not only related to trade liberalisation, financialisation and privatisation, but also to labour flexibilisation (Gürcan and Mete, 2017: 148). They uncover uneven development especially among labour groups employed under precarious working conditions, particularly in Islamo-conservative practices of Anatolian enterprises which control labour through their clientelistic ties with the AKP and charity-driven paternalistic strategies (Gürcan and Mete, 2017: 148). Indeed, the AKP has institutionalised labour flexibilisation through practices such as promoting sub-contracting and rental labour as well as relegation of workers to 4-C and 4-B status organised in newly privatised enterprises (Gürcan and Mete, 2017: 149). While 4-B status leads to employment through renewable contracts, 4-C status transfers permanent employment in the public sector to non-unionised temporary employment with lower wages (Gürcan and Mete, 2017: 102). Privatisation of public enterprises and expansion of neoliberalism to public services such as health and education have all expanded labour flexibilisation under the AKP regime (Gürcan and Mete, 2017: 149).

Although the AKP government's policies have worsened socio-economic conditions for labour and the popular classes, they continue to support the party. As Erol (2019: 672) highlights, this can hardly be explained in terms of 'the so-called "false consciousness" of the working masses'. Rather, it is possible to refer to four factors. First, the AKP's social policy coincides with the neoliberal form of social policy, substituting the welfare state with welfare governance directed to ameliorate social insecurities due to market dislocations (Özden, 2014: 530). The AKP's populist jargon has generated

flexibility by rejecting full-time wage labour as the 'normal' form of employment while promoting flexibility to eliminate the 'rigidities' and 'privileges'
of formal labour employment (Özden, 2014: 513–514). Second, the AKP's
social policy and innovative assistance programmes have addressed the basic
needs of poor segments, thereby 'depoliticising the longstanding social
problems of the country, turning poverty and inequality into an administrative
problem' while preventing the articulation of any viable project for transforming social relations (Özden, 2014: 485–486). This neoliberal populism is
associated with 'a conservative understanding of society that features
membership in a homogenous and amorphous community and nation'
(Özden, 2014: 488). The AKP's social assistance programmes have worked
as 'a complex web of social assistance involving local municipalities, faith-
based charitable organisations and public poverty reduction programmes'
(Özden, 2014: 519). Neoliberal populism went beyond wages to encompass
strategies in the sphere of social reproduction, 'whereby the destructive
consequences of neoliberal policies were alleviated through social assistance
programmes, addressing specific areas such as health, education and so
forth' (Bozkurt, 2013: 377–378). Third, neoliberal populism and identity
politics were effective behind the support of labour and the popular classes
for the AKP regime. As highlighted by Özden (2014: 529), these policies
coincide with the charismatic image of Erdoğan 'as the "father of the poor"
who grew up amongst them and is still one of them'. Fourth, financialisation
has generated financial inclusion to compensate labour for their deteriorating
socio-economic conditions (M. Erol, 2021: 25). As Uzgel notes, 'after all,
neoliberalism is not only about the markets and the states, but also about
how to administer a society that lives with declining wages, higher consumerism and a huge increase in consumer debt' (Uzgel, 2020: 66).

In recent years, Turkey's economy once again became crisis prone. The
Turkish lira collapsed in January 2018, losing half of its value against the
US dollar in two years. Turkey's current account deficit remains 'unchecked
as the government sought consumption/construction-led, debt-driven economic
expansion which has added very little to productive capacity and export
potential' (Akyüz, 2018). The government has tried to finance deficits by
selling national assets and external borrowing (Akyüz, 2018). Under orthodox
policies, cuts in capital inflows and currency depreciations force governments
in emerging markets to take precautions by raising interest rates and deploying
reserves (Akyüz, 2020). Turkey, however, has not followed these orthodox
recipes. Instead, it has borrowed from international markets at great expense
due to the declining lira and the loss of reserves (Akyüz, 2020). In July
2023, the economy faced uncertainty regarding the lira's future, losses in
reserves, rising inflation and growing current account deficits, all within a
volatile political environment, generating the possibility that the currency

turmoil could turn into a debt crisis (Akyüz, 2020). According to Bedirhanoğlu (2020: 35), the current regime has two options: to follow conventional neoliberal policies which would weaken Erdoğan's regime as neoliberal recipes would damage the AKP's own constituency of the poor; to adopt a non-conventional approach that could cause material breakdown and/or a shift in axis of Turkey's international alliances.

Reconsidering Turkey–EU relations: an uncertain partnership

After 2010, enlargement was taken off the agenda, both in Turkey and the EU. The pull factors of EU enlargement weakened following the 2007–08 eurozone crisis and the far right's rise in European politics. Arguments that enlargement would consolidate democracy and increase wealth in newly acceding countries have been increasingly questioned, especially after Brexit and the Greek referendum to exit the eurozone. The backsliding from democracy and the rule of law under populist regimes in Poland and Hungary severely put the EU's capability for promoting democracy into question.

Turkey–EU relations have deteriorated following the 2013 Gezi Park protests, and the AKP government has increasingly excluded opposition groups from politics. The EU criticised the excessive force used against Gezi Park protesters while the European Parliament issued a special resolution on 13 June 2013, calling on the AKP government to stop the 'disproportionate and excessive' use of force, investigate the police violence and guarantee all citizens the right to freedom of expression, peaceful assembly and peaceful protest (European Parliament, 2013). Following the 15 July 2016 coup attempt and subsequent state of emergency, the EU has openly criticised the democratic backsliding in Turkey. The AKP government condemned the EU's 'misreading' of the coup attempt, claiming that the EU's 'cold and critical attitude' had engendered a confidence crisis for Turkey (Ministry of Foreign Affairs, 2022). In return, the EU claimed that it had condemned the coup attempt 'immediately and strongly' and stood for democracy in Turkey. However, the 'disproportionate scale and scope of measures taken in its aftermath raise serious concerns' in the EU (Council of the EU, 2018: 12). In 2017, due to concerns over backsliding from democracy and human rights, the Council of Europe restarted monitoring Turkey (*Guardian*, 2017). In its 2018 report, the European Commission identified backsliding regarding judicial independence, public administration reforms and freedom of association, assembly and expression (European Commission, 2018). In addition, tensions in the Eastern Mediterranean escalated between Turkey and Greece, further damaging relations. Condemning Turkey's drilling activities in the Eastern Mediterranean as 'illegal', the EU halted the Association Council and EU–Turkey high-level dialogue meetings while reducing preaccession assistance to Turkey (Council of the EU, 2019).

Currently, only one chapter has been closed in the accession negotiations with sixteen chapters blocked after Turkey refused to extend the Customs Union to Cyprus. As Bal (2022a: 147) noted, during the 2010s both Turkey and the EU adopted a pragmatic approach in the absence of a consensus on Turkey's social transformation through membership, while the EU's role in improving civil society in Turkey became 'selective, palliative and therefore unsustainable'. Indeed, Turkey–EU relations in the 2010s have become transactional, with specific topics being prioritised rather than considered within the context of enlargement or membership. Turkey–EU relations have focused on particular issues of bilateral cooperation such as migration management and visa liberalisation, and improving people-to-people contacts, Erasmus+ and/or Horizon Europe. The EU has promoted bilateral sectoral cooperation, especially on energy, education and transport (European Union, 2016: 35), while the European Council has highlighted the need to improve people-to people-contact and mobility (European Council, 2021: 6). The European Council of 25 March 2021 identified 'public health, climate and counter-terrorism as well as regional issues' as areas to further stimulate bilateral cooperation (European Council, 2021: 6). In its *Strategic Compass* (European Union, 2022), the EU discussed Turkey in terms of 'tailored bilateral partnerships' (European Union, 2022: 55). Given this historical conjuncture, Chapter 5 explains how Turkey's social forces interpret EU membership and whether membership perspective continues to be hegemonic in state and society.

Conclusion

This chapter situated Turkey's integration with the EU within the structural dynamics of global capitalism and social relations of production to provide a historical analysis of Turkey's political economy for the subsequent empirical analyses. Drawing on Gramscian historical materialism, it adopted a three-category analytical framework, namely social relations of production, form of state and world order. The chapter argued that Kemalist modernisation and etatist policies aspired to cultivate Turkey's national industry and bourgeoisie within a world order of rival imperialisms. Then, under Pax Americana, Turkey was incorporated into the Western bloc through the Ankara Agreement, which envisaged completing the Customs Union and implied a probability of EU membership. However, during the neo-mercantilist-developmentalist period, Turkey's social forces were reluctant to implement the liberalisation foreseen in the Additional Protocol, with labour groups openly resisting the

EEC, based on the motto 'They are the partners and we are the market'. The chapter thus identified these relations as a tug of war between social forces supporting protectionism and developmentalism, such as SMEs, social democratic political parties and certain labour groups, and those supporting liberalisation in order to join the Customs Union. Indeed, the tariff reductions envisaged by the Additional Protocol were constantly delayed in this period until the 1980s neoliberal turn.

On 24 January 1980, Turkey adopted an economic programme that substituted ISI and Keynesian demand management with an export-promotion strategy. It then applied for membership of the EU while reducing trade protections against European products. The 1980 neoliberal restructuring was again institutionalised as a passive revolution because the ruling classes were unable and unwilling to lead society in the hegemonic struggle by providing moral and intellectual leadership through taking consent from subordinate social forces around the export-promotion strategy. The military regime was key to suppressing the labour movement and reducing wages, which neoliberalism considered a 'production cost' for countries trying to become more competitive in global markets. It was in such a socio-economic transformation that Turkey applied for full membership and joined the Customs Union, which was presented to society as important to provide foreign assistance in neoliberal restructuring and make Turkey's enterprises competitive in international markets. The labour movement remained weak, with left-wing-oriented trade unions banned from politics until the 1990s.

I then read the 1990s financialisation as causing cycles of crises under coalition governments until the 2002 elections that brought the AKP to power. Turkey was presented as a model Middle Eastern country with its moderate form of Islam and an emerging market bearing the potential to consolidate democracy through enlarging the middle-classes and struggling against the so-called military and bureaucratic elite. However, the chapter concurred with the critical political economy literature in interpreting the AKP regime as continuity rather than rupture from the previous neoliberal right-wing governments. It reads the AKP regime as *trasformismo* in consolidating neoliberal restructuring by enlarging the ruling class through integrating Turkish SMEs around the neoliberal project while disarticulating dissent through neoliberal populist tools and aligning with neoliberal social policy. In the last decade, however, vulnerabilities of the growth pattern of dependent financialisation came to the fore with Turkey affected by the Great Recession due to a halt in FDI and underconsumption in core capitalist countries. Following the Gezi Park protests, the 15 July 2016 coup attempt and the consolidation of presidential regime by referendum enabled Turkey's authoritarian turn. In such a historical context, Turkey–EU relations no longer centre on membership. Rather, they involve transactional cooperation over particular issues such as migration, visa liberalisation and person-to-person cooperation. The following chapters discuss the position of social forces in the hegemonic struggle over EU membership both in the 2000s and 2010s. It is ultimately class positions in the open-ended struggle which determine the future coordinates of Turkey–EU relations.

Note

1 The Millî Görüş (National View) was founded by Necmettin Erbakan in 1969 and its conservative political agenda was followed by a number of subsequently founded political parties. The Millî Nizam Partisi (MNP – National Order Party) was established in 1970 and disbanded in 1971 due to allegations of aiming to found a state based on Islam. It was then succeeded by the Millî Selamet Partisi (MSP – National Salvation Party) which was banned following the 1980 military coup. As its successor, its supporters established the Refah Partisi (RP – Welfare Party) in 1983. The party increased its votes after the 1980s: it got 9.8 per cent and 17 per cent in 1989 and 1991 elections. The party received 21.4 per cent of votes in the 1995 elections, getting 158 seats in the parliament. Necmettin Erbakan formed a coalition government with the centre-right party, the Doğru Yol Partisi (DYP – True Path Party), led by Çiller, on 28 June 1996, and stayed in power until 2 July 1997. Erbakan had to resign following the 28 February 1997 silent coup. It was then succeded by Fazilet Partisi (FP – Virtue Party), which was disbanded following a decision of the Constitutional Court in June 2001. In the 2000s, the ideas of National View were represented by two political parties, the Saadet Partisi (SP – Felicity Party) and the reformist AKP. Uzgel argues that the 28 February process was a turning point for the transformation within National View. Following the 28 February 1997 silent coup, the capital groups, also named 'green capital', started to search for a new political party, that would come to terms with globalisation and develop more cautious policies with secular/statist establishments in Turkey (Uzgel, 2009: 18).

3

Globalisation and class struggle between Turkish capital and labour during the 2000s reform process

This chapter reads Turkey's European trajectory within the structural dynamics of globalisation and neoliberal restructuring. While participating in the Customs Union, Turkey eliminated its trade protection measures. During the 1990s and 2000s, financial liberalisation and monetary reforms were introduced under the surveillance of EU reforms with the EU and IMF often named as the 'double anchors' of Turkey's structural adjustment programmes. This chapter uncovers the position of the representatives of capital and labour during the 2000s, after Turkey was declared an EU membership candidate at the 1999 Helsinki European Council. In doing so, the chapter emphasises intra-class and inter-class struggle while investigating whether there was a pro-membership project in Turkey that pioneered membership in the 2000s. If so, which social forces supported it? Was the project hegemonic with social forces able to lead society by presenting the project on a universal terrain? The chapter then asks whether there was an alternative to this pro-membership perspective and, if not, how to account for its failure.

Two industrial sectors are selected while addressing these questions. The first is the internationally oriented textile and automotive industries, given their privileged position within Turkey's export-promotion strategy since the 1980s. Both have been subsidised by the neoliberal state as leading sectors to stimulate international competitiveness. The second is nationally oriented SMEs and agriculture. These are presupposed to have a critical stance to globalisation and EU membership because they include sheltered sectors that primarily produce for Turkey's domestic market. Hence, they would be negatively affected by eliminating state subsidies and opening up markets to international competition, particularly because they primarily produce intermediate goods, which would have to compete with cheaper goods produced in global markets. Agriculture would be particularly affected by participation in the Internal Market as it is not included in the Customs Union (with the exception of processed agricultural products) and remains protected within the structural constraints of WB policies.

To investigate the position of internationally oriented capital, I interviewed representatives of the TÜSİAD,[1] the Turkish Exporters Assembly (TİM)[2] and the Turkish Confederation of Employer Associations (TİSK).[3] Regarding industrial sectors, I interviewed members of the Turkish Textile Employers' Association and the Automotive Manufacturers Association (OSD) as platforms representing the interests of capital groups in the internationally oriented textile and automotive industries.[4] For nationally oriented capital, I interviewed members of the Union of Chambers and Commodity Exchanges of Turkey (TOBB), the MÜSİAD, İstanbul Chamber of Commerce (İSO) and OSTİM Organised Industrial Region in Ankara as institutions representing the interests of SMEs.[5] Finally, I interviewed members of the Union of Turkish Agricultural Chambers (TZOB) and the Agricultural Credit Cooperatives of Turkey as representatives of the agricultural sector.[6]

My analysis of civil society is guided by Gramsci's conception of it as a terrain where hegemony is both contested and consolidated as 'the trench-systems of modern warfare' in the war of position (Gramsci, 1971: 235 and 238). Accordingly, civil society representatives were interviewed to enquire whether the ruling class presents its economic vested interests as a universal vision by transcending its economic-corporate phase. These institutions were approached as platforms that enable the organic intellectuals of capital to articulate neoliberal discourse on a universal terrain. Essentially, the issue here concerns the hegemonic status of the pro-membership project in Turkey in the 2000s. Therefore, the Turkish Economic and Social Studies Foundation (TESEV) and the Economic Development Foundation (İKV) were analysed as institutional platforms, whose studies have decisively shaped and articulated ideas regarding Turkey's EU membership debate.[7]

It might be expected that Turkey's labour movement would develop a critical stance towards EU membership given that participation in the Internal Market would increase competition pressures on Turkish industry, leading to cuts in wages and social standards. Yet, following Bieler, it should be noted that globalisation has engendered cross-class alliances (Bieler, 2000: 155). Accordingly, it can be expected that trade unions in internationally oriented sectors, which are integrated with Europe's production structure via the Customs Union, are more likely to support Turkey's EU membership bid. I interviewed trade union representatives in the textile and automotive industries, which are already economically integrated with the Internal Market. In contrast, trade unions in nationally oriented sectors are more likely to be critical due to concerns over deindustrialisation and de-unionisation (these claims further draw on Bieler, 2000: 48; 2005: 461; 2006: 42). Nationally oriented labour, particularly in agriculture and the public sector, is not included in the Customs Union, so workers might expect to be disadvantaged by participation in the Internal Market via EU membership.

Public employees are also expected to be critical as the membership process entails further liberalisation, so public sectors like education and health would be subjected to privatisation and commodification. Additionally, they would also be negatively affected by weakening the welfare state. Yet these assumptions can only be cross-checked through uncovering their positions by the empirical data. The following section uncovers the position of capital and questions the hegemonic status of the pro-membership question. It then investigates whether labour can come up with an alternative.

Turkish capital and the pro-membership project

Internationally oriented capital, globalisation and membership

Internationally oriented capital viewed globalisation positively, because it enabled technology transfer, delocalisation of production and increased volume of trade (Interview 28). Interviewees from the textile and automotive industries argued that globalisation has forced industries to comply with the rules of international competition (Interviews 26 and 27). In return, closed economy policies were discarded because they led to high prices and lower quality products and services in Turkey's domestic market (Interviews 3 and 28). The interviewees had no concerns regarding the competitiveness of Turkish industry with Europe as the Customs Union has already opened the Turkish industry to international competition. Accordingly, they endorsed EU membership on three grounds. First, membership would stimulate competitiveness and increase exports (Interviews 3 and 27). For example, the automotive industry representative considered the Customs Union an 'educative process' to render Turkish industry a 'global actor' (Interview 26). Second, the European market is essential for Turkish industry as Turkey conducts more than 50 per cent of its foreign trade with EU countries (Interview 28). Third, the membership perspective and ongoing reform process were helping to consolidate a functioning market economy in Turkey (Interview 16). In particular, by bringing predictability and consolidating market stability, the membership perspective was crucial for stimulating FDI flows (Interviews 3 and 4). Finally, their sectors are already integrated with the European market via the Customs Union, and the interviewees did not expect additional economic benefits of participating in the Internal Market except that Turkey would become directly involved in EU decision making (Interviews 4, 14, 16 and 26).

Representatives of Turkey's internationally oriented capital endorsed arguments that transcend its vested economic interests by promoting membership on a universal terrain as a progressive process for society. TÜSİAD, for example, identified membership as a 'national project' (TÜSİAD, 2002: 1). It therefore articulated a strategy to present membership as an issue above party politics (Interview 3) that was required by an international treaty, hence no longer open to debate in Turkish society. Indeed, TÜSİAD asked experts to prepare reports on sensitive topics at critical junctures to gain support for the pro-membership project. This included reform proposals on constitutional change and position papers to open public debate on sensitive topics, such as the Kurdish question and human rights (e.g. TÜSİAD, 1997, 1999 and 2001). Another indication of its hegemonic status was that the pro-membership project was also defended on non-economic grounds, such as by supporting the European Social Model. The pro-membership project promoted a neoliberal conception of social policy, which presents competitiveness as a condition for employment and extends social rights on the basis of economic conditions (Interview 14). More importantly, it endorsed social dialogue as a viable model to protect the interests of the workplace collectively and increase cooperation to make businesses more competitive (Interview 14). Meanwhile, the EU was also expected to con-solidate democracy, rule of law and respect for human rights, which are considered preconditions for safeguarding market economies (Interviews 4, 16 and 28). The EU was also perceived as a 'peace project' (Interview 7), so membership would lead to improved dialogue in foreign policy (Interview 4). Finally, EU membership was presented as a necessity to enable modernisa-tion in Turkey to reach the standards of 'contemporary civilisation', a process that began with the founding of the republic and its Western orientation (Interview 14).

Nationally oriented capital adapting to globalisation and membership

Contrary to expectation, the interviews showed that representatives of nationally oriented capital supported EU membership. Indeed, interviewees from SMEs stressed that there was no alternative to globalisation, so the only viable survival strategy was to adapt to the market economy model by increasing competitiveness and exports (Interviews 10 and 31; MÜSİAD, 2005: 41–42; TOBB, 2011a: 454–455). They aspired to promote 'national champions' able to compete in the global market (TOBB, 2011b: 733). Furthermore, EU membership was the only viable strategy for Turkey to take due to globalisation (TOBB, 2011b: 687). They claimed that the membership process forced Turkey to comply with international rules and standards, and increased the quality and competitiveness of Turkish industry (Interviews 5 and 9; MÜSİAD, 2004a: 99). Membership would provide an 'anchor' for stability and security that would increase Turkey's credibility, attract FDI and guarantee democracy and the rule of law (Interviews 5 and 31). Economic integration with the EU was also 'irreversible' due to the volume of trade with the EU, tourism income and FDI (MÜSİAD, 2001: 38–39). Finally, EU membership would consolidate institutionalisation by encouraging a political culture governed by rules and meritocracy rather than patronage relations (Interview 31).

This stance can be explained on two grounds. First, many SMEs have already encountered the effects of globalisation and the liberalisation of foreign trade, especially due to the Customs Union, either through bankruptcy or through adapting to new conditions. Therefore, it is 'out of question' to be concerned about the competitiveness of Turkish industry if it joined the Internal Market (Interview 5). Second, Turkey's SMEs are already integrated into global production through outsourcing and contract manufacturing. As Robinson (2004: 19–20) puts it, the global economy operates through 'multilayered networks of outsourcing, subcontracting, collaboration, and so on, that increasingly link local and national agents to global networks' within which agents either 'globalise or perish'. For instance, while only a minority of TOBB members are export-oriented SMEs, most SMEs either produce intermediate goods for the European market or conduct contract manufacturing on behalf of EU-based companies (Interview 31). Similarly, SMEs operating through OSTİM (a designated industrial zone in Ankara) are sometimes presented as the 'backyard' of Europe's production structure as they engage in contract manufacturing (Interview 10). Indeed, the OSTİM model provides an example of SMEs developing cooperative mechanisms in response to a decline in subsidies under the neoliberal state (Interview 10). The interviewee from OSTİM highlighted that although the majority of the SMEs produced supplier products, their products were assembled and then exported by other SMEs (Interview 10). This suggests that Turkey's nationally oriented capital was already integrated with, and dependent upon, international markets, making them somewhat internationally oriented as well.

Criticism of the EU membership process from SME representatives instead focused on national sensitivities rather than economic competitiveness, such as the EU's approach to the Kurdish and Armenian problems (Interview 10; MÜSİAD, 2004a: 17). In addition, proposals regarding permanent derogations and restrictions on the free movement of Turkish workers in Europe were considered unacceptable (MÜSİAD, 2004b: 13–14). Interviewees considered EU policy on the Cyprus problem as biased to the disadvantage of Turkey and Turkish Cypriots (MÜSİAD, 2006: 159). However, it is difficult for SMEs to provide an alternative independently from the political authority (Interview 31). Indeed, SMEs within TOBB viewed the pro-EU membership perspective as 'state policy' (Interview 31).

In line with the main hypothesis, the interviewee from the TZOB (which organises five million farmers producing for the domestic market) criticised globalisation and EU membership, mainly due to competitiveness. They stressed that Turkey's agriculture and animal husbandry could not compete in global markets for several reasons: Turkish farmers are poor; the agricultural structure is inefficient and fragile; unionisation is limited; holdings are divided into small plots; and technology remains underdeveloped (Interview 20). Moreover, globalisation reduces agricultural employment and prices so that agricultural producers cannot generate sufficient income (Interview 20). They also claimed that Turkish farmers cannot compete with European farmers (except in fruits and vegetables), which would lead to the closure of small farms if Turkey joined the EU. In addition, the interviewee highlighted that EU support for Central and Eastern European members was around 75 per cent lower than for older members (Interview 20). Moreover, the EU referred to permanent derogations in agriculture and its new support mechanism (implemented in 2012) would considerably curb agricultural support (Interview 20). Thus, the TZOB representative concluded that, as a regional institution, the EU could not protect Turkish agriculture from globalisation (Interview 20). Finally, the EU and World Trade Organization (WTO) policies overlap as EU countries are decisive in shaping WTO regulations. In particular, both endorse 'direct income support' models that discourage domestic production (Interview 20).

Was membership hegemonic in the 2000s?

Hegemony is a moment of intellectual and moral leadership that is presented on a universal terrain entailing transcendence of economic vested interests. It is plausible to argue that Turkey's pro-membership project was hegemonic in the 2000s. On the one hand, internationally oriented capital transcended its economic vested interests by articulating universal arguments at the ideational level in defending membership. The EU was presented as an anchor for consolidating democracy and civilising politics against the mechanisms of the 'strong state'. The European Social Model and the EU's neoliberal turn were well received, and social dialogue and social partnership were seen as viable social policy mechanisms. Moreover, dialogue in foreign policy was defended and Europe was articulated as a peace project. On the other hand, the arguments associated with EU membership were presented as progressive by particular civil society institutions – that are interpreted as neoliberal civil society – that aspire to produce 'objective and scientific' knowledge. They have a role to articulate ideas in favour of membership on sensitive topics at critical junctures. They are also instrumental for the organic intellectuals of capital to endorse membership on a universal terrain.

Yet it is also plausible to uncover their organic links with capital and to read them as 'fortresses and earthworks' (Gramsci, 1971: 238) that consolidate the neoliberal membership project.

Both TESEV and İKV are analysed here as such platforms. They endorsed EU membership as a 'development and democratisation project' in the 'public interest' (Interviews 107 and 108). Indeed, they played a decisive role in shaping the membership debate by commissioning researchers and scholars to write reports and by opening sensitive topics to public debate at critical junctures. For instance, the İKV initiated a platform supporting the elimination of the death penalty after Abdullah Öcalan, the leader of the Kurdistan Workers' Party (PKK), was arrested. They also launched a signature campaign supported by various intellectuals at a critical juncture before the 1999 Helsinki European Council (Interview 107). Similarly, these institutions have influenced public opinion and decision makers at the European level. A booklet was jointly published in 2014 by the Centre for European Policy Studies (CEPS) in Brussels and the Economics and Foreign Policy Forum in İstanbul, at a strategic time just before the EU was to decide to open accession negotiations with Turkey. One of the authors was Kemal Derviş, who was well known in Turkey for the 2001 Transition to a Stronger Turkish Economy programme and Turkey's financialisation, as explained in Chapter 2. The report concludes that EU policy-makers should not act based on religious and/or geographical prejudices. Instead, they should rely on universal norms and 'fairness and objectivity' in assessing Turkey's membership compatibility based on the Copenhagen criteria (Derviş et al. 2004: 25). Rather than culturalist and essentialist discourses that would deny membership, the report argued that Turkish membership would contribute to 'the process of democratic consolidation and societal modernisation' in Turkey, and help Europe reshape its political identity based on multiculturalism 'governed by the universal norms of democracy and a modern socially caring market economy' (Derviş et al., 2004: 25).

Was there an alternative? Labour debating the European membership perspective within the struggle against globalisation

It is difficult to operationalise labour in Turkey's social setting as trade unionism is highly fragmented. As of August 2023, there are twenty-one confederations with the main division being between industrial workers and public employees. There are eight confederations organising industrial workers in similar sectors, of which three are analysed here, namely Türk-İş, DİSK and Hak-İş, which together represented almost 97 per cent of all unionised industrial workers as of July 2021 (Official Gazette, 2021a). The 1980 neoliberal turn prevented public employees from organising with industrial workers, which has been a very powerful tool to fracture the labour movement. As a result, public employees are organised separately. There are thirteen confederations for public employees with trade unions in similar sectors. Four confederations are analysed here, namely the Confederation of Unions of Public Employees of Turkey[8] (Türkiye Kamu-Sen), the Confederation of Public Employees Trade Unions[9] (Kesk), the Confederation of Public Servants Trade Unions[10] (Memur-Sen) and the Confederation of United Public Workers' Unions[11] (Birleşik Kamu-İş), which together represented 94 per cent of all unionised public employees as of July 2021 (Official Gazette, 2021b). Internationally oriented labour is examined through the textile and automotive industries as well as two confederations, namely DİSK[12] and Hak-İş[13]. There is no public sector in the textile industry and almost 70 per cent of textile production is exported (Interviews 6 and 13). In the automotive industry, the United Metalworkers' Union (Birleşik Metal-İş) is organised only in the private sector, which mostly operates in international markets or works as supplier enterprises for international firms (Interview 29). At the confederation level, DİSK primarily organises in the private sector and has begun to organise workers in international and multinational enterprises (Interview 15). Hak-İş also mainly organises workers in the private sector (accounting for approximately 80 per cent of the firms in which it organises) and operates mostly in big enterprises – including transnational firms and former state economic enterprises that have been privatised (Interviews 11 and 23).

Nationally oriented labour, which was expected to be critical of globalisation and EU membership, is analysed below in relation to the agricultural sector and public employment. Türk-İş[14] organises industrial workers in public economic enterprises that primarily produce industrial goods for the domestic market. In agriculture, interviews were conducted with trade unions from four different confederations, namely the Turkish Forestry, Soil, Water, Agriculture and Agricultural Workers Trade Union (Tarım-İş), Real Trade Union for Workers in Agriculture, Land and the Water Industry (Öz Tarım-İş), the Union of Public Employees in Agriculture and Forestry of Turkey (Türk Tarım-Orman-Sen) and the Agriculture and Forestry Union (Tarım Orman-İş). Public employees are organised under four confederations namely Türkiye Kamu-Sen, Kesk, Memur-Sen and Birleşik Kamu-İş.

Internationally oriented labour and membership: 'Another globalisation and Europe is possible'

Representatives from trade unions organising in internationally oriented sectors described globalisation as 'irresistible' (Interview 13). They saw globalisation as creating a new division between countries whose production is based on advanced technologies produced by a skilled workforce and countries whose production is labour intensive with an unskilled workforce (DİSK, 1996: 69). Turkey falls within the latter category while the state operates to 'intensify the exploitation of labour' to be competitive in international markets (DİSK, 1996: 69; DİSK, 2000a: 6). The interviewees highlighted that globalisation has decreased labour's bargaining power and encouraged de-unionisation, while flexible, part-time and atypical work forms have increased (Interviews 13 and 17). This creates opportunities for capital to attack demands for unionisation and collective bargaining by threatening to move to other countries or cut wages for the sake of competitiveness (Interviews 2, 17 and 29). Additionally, globalisation attacks internationalism by generating competition and antagonism between workers in developed and developing countries (Interview 29).

Globalisation necessitates rethinking trade unionism as it has transformed the structure of mass production from large industrial complexes to small workplaces in informal economies, often using atypical and/or part-time employment (DİSK, 1996: 69). Accordingly, the classical tools of the Fordist period (e.g. strikes and unionisation) have to be modified for the global era (Interview 15). As one interviewee noted, the free movement of capital has 'dynamited' social rights acquired at the national level (Interview 15). From this perspective, internationally oriented labour sees the internationalisation of labour as the only viable way to struggle against globalisation (DİSK, 1996: 70–72). DİSK, therefore, believes that 'another globalisation, in the interest of workers, is possible' (Interview 15). Indeed, DİSK refers to strategies of international solidarity to enable international collective bargaining by organising all workers employed in a multinational enterprise (Interviews 8 and 15). The interviewees gave specific examples of such international solidarity mechanisms such as 'social responsibility declarations' and/or framework agreements[15] (Interviews 8, 15 and 29).

Representatives from the internationally oriented labour textile and automotive industries were content with the economic effects of liberalisation. They noted that Turkey conducts more than 50 per cent of its trade with the EU (Interview 6) and viewed the Customs Union positively as it consolidates market principles, which make Turkey's textile sector competitive in global markets (Interview 17). Thus, concurrent with this study's expectation, internationally oriented labour believed that Turkey has already been integrated with the European production structure and they were no longer concerned with the repercussions of participating in the Internal Market (Interviews 13 and 17). However, the reasons for their support varied. For example, despite describing the EU as a capitalist integration model, DİSK supported membership, citing the belief that 'another Europe is possible'

(DİSK, 2000a: 8–9; Interview 8). This motto reflects the assumption that internationally oriented labour would defend membership to regain its bargaining power lost at the national level due to globalisation. The interviewees from DİSK did not raise any concerns regarding integration into the Internal Market – which indicates that the workers they organise are employed in workplaces that are already integrated with the European market via the Customs Union. Indeed, they stated that Turkey has already been economically affected by the Customs Union (Interview 15). Thus, they interpreted the membership debate in relation to political criteria and social policy (DİSK, 2000a: 33). For example, they expected the European Social Model to improve working conditions in Turkey (Interviews 6 and 17). As the Customs Union was completed without positive integration, an additional argument to support membership was that membership would improve social standards (Interview 29), allow free movement of workers in Europe and contribute to finding a democratic solution to the Kurdish problem (Interview 15). The EU was equally seen as a peaceful project to encourage a reduction in military spending for combating terror in Eastern Turkey and dealing with Greece (Interviews 6 and 15).

There were also differences in the positions of internationally oriented trade unions. For instance, DİSK promotes a strategy of questioning capitalism ideologically through class struggle (DİSK, 2000b). It argues that confining unionism to collective bargaining is a neoliberal strategy limiting class struggle to narrow economism. Instead, DİSK seeks a united struggle of 'societal resistance' to create unity among retired and unemployed people, white-collar workers, female labour, students, migrant workers, peasants and workers employed in informal economies (Interview 8; DİSK, 1996: 70–71; DİSK, 2000a). In contrast, the Hak-İş representative viewed globalisation in a positive light believing that it engenders economic growth by transforming inefficient state enterprises and opening the traditional power mechanisms between the state and so-called 'big capital' into question (Interview 11). Thus, unionism advocated by Hak-İş operates within neoliberalism. Cox describes this stance as 'social partnership in Western Europe and business unionism in North America' (Cox, 1987: 374). Hak-İş describes its approach to trade unionism as facilitating an 'industrial democracy' (Interview 2) – an aim compatible with the mechanisms of 'social dialogue' proposed by the European model. For Hak-İş, 'class' is a social phenomenon rather than a 'front' (Interviews 2 and 18). Accordingly, labour and capital are 'social partners' and trade unionism should be based on cooperation rather than conflict (Interview 17). Hak-İş sees competitiveness and quality as 'common' problems for workers and employers (Interview 11). In this sense, references by Hak-İş to internationalism are deficient as it fails to advocate class struggle at the national level. Instead, it operates as an agent of *trasformismo* by organising disadvantaged groups within a neoliberal form of unionism. Accordingly, Hak-İş maintained a policy of unconditional support for membership in all its economic, political and social dimensions, without any 'reservations' (Interviews 2, 11, 18) with the European Social Model considered as an 'ideal model' for industrial relations (Interview 2), and the EU seen as a democratisation project and an 'anchor' to 'civilise' politics through freedom of speech and a culture of dialogue (Interviews 2 and 18).

Nationally oriented labour: 'Membership on equal terms and conditions'

The interviewees from nationally oriented labour argued that globalisation has generated deindustrialisation and de-unionisation, thereby damaging Turkey's economic development. Export-orientation enables capital to search for cheaper intermediate goods in world markets, forcing the closure of domestic enterprises that cannot compete with global prices (Interview 12). The agricultural labour representatives were highly critical, highlighting that Turkey is no longer agriculturally self-sufficient due to globalisation (Interview 19). Globalisation creates markets for international capital by curbing domestic production through direct support mechanisms or providing subsidies on the basis of land rather than production (Interview 22). Globalisation impoverishes the agricultural sector, generating proletarianisation, internal migration and illegal work (Interview 12). Similarly, the public employee interviewees accused globalisation of promoting the neoliberal campaign against the 'inefficient public sector', arguing that it generates commodification and views 'profitability' rather than the 'public good' as the determining factor for providing public services (Interview 30). Privatisation, they noted, reduces public sector employment as the state withdraws from fundamental sectors like education and health (Interviews 24 and 30). Importantly, globalisation also weakens the welfare state (Interviews 19 and 21) and encourages de-unionisation as capital groups squeeze wages and cut working standards by invoking the need for 'competitiveness' (Interviews 12 and 25). It also weakens the bargaining power of labour (Interview 23). Finally, the public sector interviewees criticised widening income disparities and decreasing welfare for public employees due to globalisation (Interview 25).

Nevertheless, despite these criticisms of globalisation, nationally oriented labour supported EU membership during the 2000s with the reservation that membership should be on 'equal terms and conditions'. Indeed, trade unions in Turkey's nationally oriented sectors were divided on whether EU membership would provide protectionism against the forces of globalisation or trigger further liberalisation. On the one hand, EU membership would entail further liberalisation that had to be resisted. It was expected to result in de-unionisation, subcontraction of work, an increase in black market work and further drops in social standards and welfare provisions (Interview 109). The interviewees criticised the European Social Model and the conception of 'social partners' which placed labour under the tutelage of capital (Interview 109). The EU was also criticised as a capitalist and imperialist union that exploited developing countries through strategies of dismemberment (Interview 109). Therefore, workers in core and peripheral countries in the capitalist system could not cooperate due to imperialism. In short, it was a fatal mistake to support EU membership in the belief that it could improve social policy (Koç, 2006: 71 and 106). Indeed, European trade unions were perceived as 'partners' with capital, as they share the surplus from imperialist exploitation. Hence, the nation-state was seen as a site of resistance against imperialism (Koç, 1998: 254 and 2004: 10–11). In 2001, Türk-İş initiated a campaign to reject common projects financed through the ETUC by Euro-Mediterranean Partnership resources. Türk-İş also published a booklet asserting that the EU did not intend to accept Turkey as a member on 'equal terms and conditions' but was pursuing a colonial strategy to dismantle its unitary state structure (Koç, 2001: 12–14). Türk-İş presented a report to the president, Ahmet Necdet Sezer, highlighting that while Türk-İş would support full EU membership, they believed that EU policy was reviving the Treaty of Sèvres[16] and seeking to dismember Turkey (Türk-İş, 2002c). In the mid-2000s, however, Türk-İş significantly changed its stance, which was criticised for excessive nationalism and for isolating Türk-İş from the accession process (Interview 1). In 2005, for example, it launched its 'Brussels Initiative' and organised a conference in collaboration with the Central Organisation of Finnish Trade Unions (SAK). Although Türk-İş retained reservations about political issues like the Kurdish, Cyprus and Armenian problems, its new approach supported EU membership, premised on a belief that it would improve social conditions in Turkey. It called the new policy 'membership on equal terms and conditions' (Interview 1).

On the other hand, trade unions in nationally oriented sectors equally highlighted that they had already been subjected to liberalisation as a result of structural adjustment policies adapted in line with WTO and WB rules. In this view, regionalism could be an effective strategy to protect against the effects of globalisation (Interview 19). In particular, the EU's agricultural funds and social policies were seen as viable mechanisms for protecting agriculture (Interview 19). The EU's agricultural policy was also depicted as a 'model' for providing self-sufficiency and protecting domestic production, in contrast to WTO, IMF and WB policies (Interview 19). In addition, because Turkey lacked the necessary social base for democracy to develop internally, EU membership could consolidate democracy while contributing to finding a democratic solution to the Kurdish problem (Interview 30). EU membership would result in Turkey adapting international norms and rules regarding social policy, and eliminating restrictions on the freedoms and rights of trade unions (Interview 24). Nationally oriented labour representatives were also united in their criticisms of the EU regarding political issues. They believed that the EU discriminated against Turkey in relation to the Cyprus problem by demanding unilateral concessions against Turkey's national interest (Interview 19). The EU was also seen as supporting a separatist solution to the Kurdish problem (Interview 19). Thus, these interviewees rejected the idea that the EU is a democratisation project. Instead, they argued that its imperialism impeded the consolidation of democracy (Interview 22). Indeed, they believed that democratic regimes can only be stabilised by internal societal dynamics (Interview 109). Finally, they rejected the EU's position on privileged partnerships, permanent derogations on the free movement of workers and structural funds (Interview 19).

Why not a united front among labour?

To understand why Turkey's labour movement has failed to develop a counter-hegemonic project against the pro-membership perspective, it is necessary to discuss the many reasons for division within the working class. First, globalisation has generated an intra-class struggle between internationally and nationally oriented labour (Bieler, 2000: 155). My empirical research shows that workers within internationally oriented sectors were no longer concerned about unemployment and deindustrialisation from integration with the Internal Market. Additionally, as globalisation is increasingly accepted as a 'fact', a process that cannot be reversed, interviewees in this sector supported internationalism and the struggle over 'Social Europe'. Second, globalisation has caused another division between formal and informal labour (Bieler et al., 2008a: 6), putting the latter at the risk of 'underbidding' and the constant 'threat of relocation' (Bieler et al., 2008b: 272). The interviews uncovered that a considerable number of Turkish workers operate in the informal economy, which weakens the base for unionisation. Notably, the bulk of workers in both SMEs and the informal economy were not organised at all (Interview 11). This recalls Cox's description of working class polarisation within the hyperliberal state. This is characterised by a 'relatively secure and protected minority, encompassed as a rule by enterprise corporatist relations', 'and a fragmented and relatively unprotected majority of non-established workers' (Cox, 1987: 281). As one interviewee noted, the mechanisms of 'wild capitalism' mostly operate within the informal economies of domestically oriented enterprises in Turkey's private sector, which feature subcontracted work and atypical forms of employment (Interview 15). My empirical research uncovered that the classical tools of trade unionism target the small workplaces themselves rather than transnational capital, resulting in capital fleeing to other geographies in response to demands for unionisation (Interview 12). Thus, globalisation has reinforced the split among formal and informal labour within the transnational chain of production.

In addition to these structural impediments, the Turkish labour movement faces various obstacles at a national level that have prevented a united stance since the 1980s neoliberal turn. First, the Turkish labour union movement is considerably fractured with twenty-one confederations (eight in industry and thirteen among public employees), each organised in overlapping sectors. Though they have similar socio-economic interests, political and ideological orientations prevent these trade unions from forming a united front as they are mostly organised under different confederations with different political orientations. There is also a divide between private and public sector unionism in industry. Second, Turkey's labour movement is restrained by anti-union legislation. To be eligible for collective bargaining, trade unions have to organise 10 per cent of workers in the same economic sector while overcoming a 50 per cent +1 threshold in the same enterprise (Çelik, 2013: 45). Moreover, public employees are not allowed to strike and face legal restrictions on their involvement in politics. One interviewee argued that these obstacles reduce public sector trade unions to the status of 'associations' (Interview 21). Third, the AKP's hegemony has created its own labour aristocracy, which conceives of unionism as a 'social partnership'. These unions have grown rapidly. For instance, Memur-Sen increased its membership from 41,871 in 2002 to 392,171 in 2010 and 1,004,152 in 2021 (Official Gazette 2002; 2010; and 2021b). Both Hak-İş among industrial workers and Memur-Sen among public employees are content to define themselves as 'partners' to capital. They see trade unions as part of 'populist politics' and work to settle tensions in society due to neoliberalism (Interview 21). For instance, when the AKP was transforming secure employment in the public sector, trade unions protested against the imposition of flexible, temporary forms of employment. To combat this, the AKP government directed newly employed public sector workers on contract status (that is known as 4B status) to join Memur-Sen. This largely explains why its membership grew from 35,000 in 2005 to 400,000 in 2012 (Interview 19). In return, Memur-Sen was authorised to conduct collective bargaining, weakening opposition to new, insecure forms of employment and the imposition of flexible markets in the public sector (Interview 22). These syndicalist trade unions exemplify *trasformismo*, the strategy of the ruling class to co-opt potentially antagonistic groups to capitalist discipline. The AKP integrated potentially antagonist and disadvantaged groups from globalisation into the neoliberal project by drawing support from SMEs and low-income groups through populism. Hence, the AKP disarticulated dissent from globalisation and neoliberal restructuring by presenting itself as a 'rupture' from previous right-wing political parties while using populist discourse to suggest that the main struggle was between 'the public' versus 'the elites'. Confederations of Hak-İş and Memur-Sen internalised the definition of labour–capital relations as a social partnership. In articulating a market economy model, they are co-opted to the idea that the 'collective' problems of labour and capital can be addressed through mechanisms of social dialogue (Interviews 11 and 25). Thus, they subscribe to a neoliberal understanding of social policy that puts the survival of the 'workplace' at the centre while viewing industrial relations as an arena for cooperation rather than conflict.

Conclusion

This chapter probed the positions of representatives of capital and labour in the 2000s regarding Turkey's EU membership bid. It was expected that internationally oriented capital would support membership to eliminate trade protectionism whereas nationally oriented capital would oppose it due to rising competition and reduced protectionism in their sheltered sector. There is more space in Turkey to expect an alternative from the labour movement as the Turkish economy has already faced competition with European and global enterprises via the Customs Union. Moreover, these sectors were subjected to competition without any compensatory social measures associated with EU membership that could alleviate social tensions – such as regional funds, agricultural and structural funds, and the free movement of workers.

Based on empirical research conducted in the 2000s, I argued in this chapter that the pro-membership was indeed hegemonic during this period. Although it was contested by two rival class strategies, neither provided an overall alternative. Internationally oriented capital pioneered EU membership as an anchor to stimulate competitiveness and consolidate a functioning market economy model while providing economic development and macroeconomic stability. The EU was equally presented as an anchor to consolidate democracy and a peaceful project. As such, the pro-membership project was hegemonic in that capital groups transcended their vested interests to present the project on a universal terrain with the support of certain actors in civil society. Contrary to expectations, Turkey's SMEs and its agriculture sector consented to the pro-membership project. This was because nationally oriented capital either adapted to globalisation by promoting 'national champions' through export promotion – that was seen as the only viable strategy of survival in the global era – or integrated with the transnational production structure via outsourcing and/or contract manufacturing, in line with the delocalisation of production. The only organisation that developed a critical stance was TZOB, on the grounds that EU membership would force small farms to close, and increase impoverishment and unemployment. However, this fraction was marginalised.

Turkey's labour movement was split on the membership question and contested the pro-membership project through two rival-class strategies, namely Ha–vet (No–Yes) and 'membership on equal terms and conditions'. However, neither offered an overall alternative. Internationally oriented labour accepted globalisation as inevitable and as something that can only be combated at the international level. They supported EU membership under the motto 'Another globalisation and Europe that benefits workers is possible.' Because Turkey was already in the Customs Union, labour in internationally oriented sectors was unconcerned about the implications of participating in the Internal Market. That is, the struggle against economic integration had already been lost in the 1990s. Accordingly, membership was expected to improve social standards in line with the European Social Model while offering free movement for Turkish workers in Europe. Moreover, internationally oriented labour believed that societal dynamics promoting democratisation in Turkey were constrained by 'strong state' mechanisms. Therefore, they considered that the EU reform process was key to containing the strong state – represented by the military and Kemalist cadres – and stimulating democratisation. As argued by Bieler (2006: 103), this support for EU social regulation does not, however, necessarily indicate that internationally/transnationally oriented labour agrees with neoliberal restructuring. Similarly, in the case of Turkey, the rationale of the 'yes, but' stance of internationally oriented labour differs from that of the pro-membership project. Hence, I argue that internationally oriented labour's support for membership does not show that it has been incorporated into the pro-membership project. Rather, it should be analysed as an alternative rival class strategy. That being said, unions like Hak-İş have internalised neoliberal restructuring. Therefore, their reference to internationalism is deficient because they have failed to advocate a struggle at the national level.

Nationally oriented labour in Turkey criticised EU membership for causing de-unionisation and deindustrialisation, although it was divided on its socio-economic impact. On the one hand, European integration was seen as a capitalist and imperialist integration model whose policies mirrored those of the WTO and WB. Thus, participating in the Internal Market was expected to have negative economic implications while membership would cause deindustrialisation and cuts in social standards due to the pressures of 'competitiveness'. Moreover, the European Social Model rested on a 'social partnership' that not only put labour under the tutelage of capital but sustained imperialist exploitation on the periphery. In this view, European workers shared the surplus created by imperialist exploitation. However, these ideas became marginalised in the late 2000s and this fraction changed its position to view membership as positive for social rights while maintaining its criticisms over national sensitivities. Certain unions within nationally oriented labour interpreted membership progressively to improve social standards as the struggle regarding the Customs Union had already been lost. Moreover, they argued that Turkey's agricultural sector had already been exposed to competition in tandem with structural adjustment policies outside membership. The EU's regionalism could provide protection against globalisation as the EU's common agricultural policy contradicted the WB's structural adjustment policies. During the 2000s, one issue that united nationally oriented labour was national concerns in debating the EU membership bid. Here, the EU was seen as an imperialist bloc trying to dismember Turkey by imposing additional conditions regarding the Cyprus, Armenian and Kurdish problems. Moreover, they argued that democracy could only be stabilised through Turkey's internal dynamics rather than incentives from an international anchor. Thus, these groups have developed a policy of 'membership on equal terms and conditions', highlighting that their support was conditional on Turkey benefitting from structural funds and the free movement of workers. As such, none of these rival class strategies provided an overall alternative. Yet the struggle over hegemony extends to political and civil society. Social forces have to be able to transcend their economic vested interests – the economic-corporate phase – in articulating their project on a universal plane for the hegemonic moment. This debate is the main focus in the following chapter.

Notes

1 TÜSİAD was founded in 1971 as the first voluntary-based organisation representing the interests of internationally oriented capital. It has organic links with European business groups. For instance, TÜSİAD has been a member of Business Europe since 1987. TÜSİAD members (e.g. Jak Jamhi and Güler Sabancı) have also become affiliated with the European Roundtable for Industrialists.
2 TİM was founded in 1993 to represent the interests of exporters organized in sixty-one exporter unions and twenty-seven sectors as an independent but affiliated institution of the Under-Secretariat of Foreign Trade (Interview 28).
3 TİSK was founded in 1962 as an umbrella institution to represent the interests of industry employers. It is currently composed of twenty-one employer associations, whose members mostly operate in international markets (Interview 14). It is the

institutional platform that represents employers in corporatist structures such as the Economic and Social Council, the Turkish Employment Agency and the Tripartite Advisory Board (Interview 14).

4 The Turkish Textile Employers' Association was founded in 1961 to represent the interests of textile producers. As the interviewee noted, the majority of its members operate in international markets with 65–70 per cent of its exports to EU countries (Interview 27). The Automotive Manufacturers Association was founded in 1974 to represent the interests of automotive industry employers. Its members mostly operate in international markets, with approximately 70 per cent of their exports to the European market (Interview 26).

5 TOBB was founded in 1952 as the first compulsory membership employer association. It represents 1.2 million enterprises from various sectors, and the majority of its enterprises are SMEs (Interview 31). The İSO has 15,000 members, 97 per cent of which are manufacturing SMEs, representing 40 per cent of Turkish firms in manufacturing and 35 per cent of Turkish exports (Interview 9). MÜSİAD was founded in 1990 in response to a belief that the state prioritised large İstanbul-based enterprises represented by TÜSİAD (Interview 5). It comprises around 3,000 SMEs (Interview 5). The OSTİM industrial zone in Ankara comprises 5,000 SMEs, operating in manufacturing, commerce and logistics (Interview 10).

6 The Union of Turkish Agricultural Chambers (TZOB) is an official professional platform based on compulsory membership, which organises the interests of five million farmers (Interview 20). It is mainly composed of small-scale producers who produce for the national market, though there are also larger firms operating in international markets (Interview 20).

7 These institutions also have the social function of opening certain sensitive issues to public debate by asking 'experts' (who, from a Gramscian perspective can be seen as 'traditional intellectuals') to write opinion papers. Both TESEV and İKV are presented to society as cultivating 'independent and scientific' knowledge that is 'objective and technical' in a positivist sense. They are understood to represent an independent and alternative view of 'civil society', an argument substantiated by the fact that they are financially independent from the state. Nevertheless, they are largely composed of traditional intellectuals, who form part of a 'social utopia by which the intellectuals think of themselves as "independent", autonomous, endowed with a character of their own' (Gramsci, 1971: 7–8). However, it is possible to unravel organic links between these intellectuals and capital. İKV, for example, was founded by the İstanbul Chamber of Commerce and the İstanbul Chamber of Industry in 1965 as a platform to prepare reports and develop a 'specialised' perspective for the private sector regarding integration with the EEC. The administrative boards of these institutions are formed by entrepreneurs. For instance, Jak Kamhi – the İKV's president between 1987 and 1992 – was a TÜSİAD Executive Committee member and a businessman in ERT for twelve years.

8 Türkiye Kamu-Sen was founded in 1992. It is the second largest confederation by membership and is organised in eleven branches in the public sector. It

criticises trade unionism based on class struggle, arguing instead that unionism is a social mechanism. It emphasises strengthening central authority and the state, and bases its ideology on nationalism (Interviews 19 and 24). As of July 2021, it had 430,183 members constituting 25 per cent of all unionised public employees (Official Gazette, 2021b).

9 Kesk, founded in 1995, is the third largest public employee confederation by membership. It promotes class struggle and believes that struggles over democracy and the Kurdish problem are inseparable from class (Interview 30). As of July 2021, Kesk had 132,225 members constituting 7 per cent of all unionised public employees (Official Gazette, 2021b).

10 Memur-Sen, founded in 1995, has increased its membership from 35,000 in 2005 to 400,000 in 2010 to become the largest confederation by membership under AKP hegemony (Interview 19). Memur-Sen defines its approach to trade unionism as 'societal trade unionism'. It advocates collaborative capital–labour relations built around social partnership (Interview 25). As of July 2021, Memur-Sen had 1,004,152 members constituting 58 per cent of all unionised public employees (Official Gazette, 2021b).

11 Birleşik Kamu-İş was founded in 2008 by former Kesk members after internal disagreements within Kesk regarding the rights of students to be educated in their specific mother tongue, including Kurdish. Certain members split from Kesk, accusing it of orienting unionism to solve the Kurdish problem. They claimed that this undermined unionism's basic principles by placing class struggle in a secondary position, so they founded Birleşik Kamu-İş (Interview 22). As of July 2021, Birleşik Kamu-İş had 68,600 members constituting 3.9 per cent of all unionised public employees (Official Gazette, 2021b).

12 DİSK was founded in 1967 by former Türk-İş trade unionists after criticising Türk-İş for collaborating with the state and keeping an apolitical stance with reference to party politics (yellow trade unionism). Before the 1980s, DİSK was defined as a socialist union according to its founding statute. However, this article was removed in 1992 (Interview 15). It was banned from 1980 to 1992 following the military coup. DİSK describes trade unionism as a democratic and class-based mass unionism that should be independent of the state, capital and political authority (DİSK, 2008). As of July 2021, DİSK has 206,640 members representing 9.7 per cent of all unionised industrial workers (Official Gazette, 2021a).

13 Hak-İş was founded in 1976 as a conservative confederation with references to religion. Because it conceives of class politics as imitation from Western civilisation, it argues that trade unionism should embrace Turkey's cultural codes (Hak-İş, 1995: 23 and 207). It has considerably increased its membership in tandem with the rise of political Islam. As of July 2021, Hak-İş had 730,516 members representing 34 per cent of all unionised industrial workers (Official Gazette, 2021a).

14 Türk-İş, Turkey's first confederation, was founded in 1952 by the state during the state corporatist period of 1945 and 1961. Within the context of the Cold War, Türk-İş categorised trade unionism as 'evolutionary and revolutionary', siding with the former as a model (Türk-İş, 2002a: 5). For instance, since its

inception, Türk-İş has followed the principle of remaining 'above party politics' because it renders trade unions dependant on political parties (Türk-İş, 2002a: 127). As of July 2021, Türk-İş had 1,154,177 members constituting 54 per cent of all unionised industrial workers (Official Gazette, 2021a).

15 International mechanisms are defended in the struggle against globalisation. For instance, trade unions in Europe have collaborated with Turkish trade unions to issue 'social responsibility declarations' to protect working standards in an international enterprise's workplace in Turkey (Interview 8). Another interviewee referred to framework agreements designed to control wage policies and apply equivalent social standards globally. Framework agreements help to reduce the informal economy, child labour and work accidents while improving health and safety. For instance, Birleşik Metal-İş has cooperated with the European Metalworkers' Federation to sign framework agreements (Interview 29). However, this mechanism is merely a moral declaration as it lacks recourse to legal sanctions in cases of breaches by companies (Interview 15). Hence, framework agreements can only ethically damage companies that do not comply with them (Interview 29).

16 Türk-İş criticised the European Parliament and its application of the political criteria on six points, which it finds unacceptable. The first is the EU's claim that Turkey is an 'occupier' in the Republic of Cyprus and that this constitutes an 'infringement of international law'. Second, the European Parliament expects Turkey to recognize the Armenian Genocide. Third, the EU policies towards minorities trigger ethnic separatism. Fourth, the EU supports Greece over problems in the Aegean Sea. Fifth, the EU wishes to declare the Patriarchate ecumenical and reopen the Clergy School in Heybeliada (which in Turkey is seen as a war academy central to Greek expansionism). Finally, the EU supports IMF policies in Turkey (Türk-İş, 2002b).

4

Globalisation and struggle in political and civil society

This chapter examines how the debate over globalisation and EU membership is discussed in political and civil society. More specifically, it asks whether social forces defending the EU membership perspective could have transcended the economic-corporate phase during the 2000s and endorsed the EU membership perspective on a universal terrain. If not, could counter-hegemonic social forces have developed a rival class strategy contesting EU membership and defended it by transcending their economic-corporate phase in the social factory of capitalism? In short, could rival class forces contest pro-membership in political and civil society? The chapter first introduces how struggles in political and civil society are analysed. Second, it uncovers the position of social forces in state institutions and political parties, and struggles around identity politics in the social factory of capitalism. Third, it questions why disadvantaged groups could not form a united front with labour groups. It concludes by presenting the struggle over EU membership in the 2000s as a hegemonic pro-membership project contested by two rival class strategies, namely Ha–vet and neo-mercantilism, which were unable to form an overall alternative.

Operationalising political and civil society through historical materialist lenses

The first category of analysis within political and civil society is political parties, evaluated in terms of their social basis. Here, my primary concern is their role in the struggle over hegemony in reflecting and reacting to the interests of social forces. Right-wing political parties can be expected to promote EU membership in line with their support for globalisation. Conversely, political parties whose social base includes SMEs, workers, peasants and public employees can be expected to develop a more critical stance to globalisation and EU membership. Within the political science literature, the dominant institutionalist analyses of Turkish politics examine party politics in terms of the 'centre–periphery cleavage'. This depicts the main cleavage in politics as the 'centre' composed of the Kemalist and secular elites, versus the 'periphery', composed of less developed segments in Anatolia, including various ethnic and religious groups (e.g. Heper, 1985; Mardin, 1973). This reading resonates with the pre-eminent understanding of the strong state tradition in Turkey's political science literature (Heper, 1985). In this reading, Turkey's social formation is considered to differ from those of European countries because it lacked both a mature bourgeois class to initiate the capitalist revolution (Keyder, 1987: 2) and a strong aristocratic class to replace the nobility (Heper, 1985: 32). These factors engendered 'bureaucratic reformism' in Turkey's social formation rather than the bourgeois capitalist revolution (Keyder, 1987: 2). Hence, the pre-eminent axis of politics in Turkey is not social class but a strong centre versus a weak periphery and civil society (Mardin, 1973: 170). Arguing against this approach, I embark on class analysis through examining political parties in relation to their social bases.

In this chapter, I examine party politics in the 2000s. The AKP first came to power in the 2002 elections with 34 per cent of the votes and a majority of two-thirds of the parliamentary seats (*Guardian*, 2002). In contrast, almost all the parties in the previous parliament, whether in the previous coalition government or opposition – the Democratic Left Party, the Nationalist Movement Party, the Motherland Party and the True Path Party – were left with no parliamentary representation after failing to pass the 10 per cent national electoral threshold (*Guardian*, 2002). The only exception was the CHP, which got 19 per cent of votes (*Guardian*, 2002). Whereas institutionalist analyses have interpreted the rise of the AKP in the 2000s as progressive for Turkish democracy to open up space for society against the dominance of the centre (e.g. İnsel, 2003; Keyman, 1999), I have argued elsewhere from a critical political economy perspective that the AKP's rise represents continuity rather than rupture (Uzgören, 2018: 294). Accordingly, in this chapter, I consider the AKP as the new face of right-wing politics. To quote Gramsci:

> The problem arises of whether the great industrialists have a permanent political party of their own. It seems to me that the reply must be in the negative. The great industrialists utilise all the existing parties turn by turn, but they do not have their own party. This does not mean that they are in any way 'agnostic' or 'apolitical'. Their interest is in a determinate balance of forces, which they obtain precisely by using their resources to reinforce one party or another in turn from the varied political checkerboard. (Gramsci, 1971: 155)

Indeed, the rise of the AKP can be read as an example of *trasformismo*. Gramsci originally used *trasformismo* to refer to a process whereby the right- and left-wing parties' political programmes converge to such an extent that 'there cease[s] to be any substantive difference between them' (Gramsci, 1971: 58, footnote 8). To put it alternatively, it refers to the 'formation of an ever more extensive ruling class' (Gramsci, 1971: 58). According to Cox, *trasformismo* can be extended to the 'strategy of assimilating and domesticating potentially dangerous ideas by adjusting them to the policies of the dominant coalition' (Cox, 1983: 166–167). The AKP can be read as *trasformismo* because the party's rise extended Turkey's ruling class by incorporating SMEs into the neoliberal hegemony while simultaneously weakening dissent by containing disadvantaged groups from globalisation through populist mechanisms such as charity and poverty reduction programmes (Uzgören, 2018: 296). Although one of the interviewees from the AKP defined the party as 'conservative democrat' and its social base as 'SMEs, farmers and artisans' (Interview 55), it actually represents the centre-right with conservative Islamist references by coming to terms with globalisation and neoliberalism. Indeed, President Erdoğan recently suggested regulating the state as a 'stock company' (Erdoğan, 2015) while AKP cabinet members own companies, such as the Minister of Tourism, Murat Ersoy (owning the ETS Tourism company), Minister of Health, Fahrettin Koca (chair of the administrative board of the Medipol company) and Minister of Education, Ziya Selçuk (owner of the Maya chain of private schools) (Cumhuriyet, 2018).

In the 2000s, political opposition was composed of a group of centre-left social democratic parties, emancipatory leftist political parties and the MHP. The two centre-left political parties were the CHP and the DSP. The CHP has been the main parliamentary opposition party since the 2002 election. In its 2007 election manifesto, the CHP defined its social base as SMEs, artisans, retirees, farmers, workers and the military (CHP, 2007: 30–42). However, the CHP has two fractions: a leftist social democratic fraction that emphasises welfare state policies and sees social class as the main political divide; and a republican fraction that emphasises policies around republicanism, modernism and secularism and sees the main political cleavage as between 'urban educated sects and uneducated segments' (Interviews 58 and 64). The CHP has been a member of the Socialist International since 1976 and the Party of European Socialism since 1999. The second centre-left political party, the DSP, also appeals to public sector employees, workers, farmers, retirees and SMEs (Interview 54).

Both the social democratic parties and Kurdish political parties refer to themselves as the 'emancipatory left'. They seek to distinguish themselves from the 'centre-left' and aspire to unite class struggle with identity politics regarding the struggles of citizens of Kurdish and Alevi origin (Interview 44). The Peace and Democracy Party (BDP), the Freedom and Solidarity

Party (ÖDP) – neither of which have passed the 10 per cent electoral threshold – fall into this category. They see the consolidation of democracy and the Kurdish problem as interconnected, and have developed organic links with the Kurdish political movement. The BDP defined itself as social democrat, emphasising policies to empower economic infrastructure in eastern Anatolia, describing its social base as workers and the poor (Interview 60). The BDP equally appealed to the Kurdish population, drawing support from capital deployed in eastern Anatolia in relation to identity politics and Kurdish sensitivities (Interview 60).

Finally, the right-wing, nationalist MHP appeals to lower-income groups and SMEs (Interview 59). In its 2007 election manifesto, the MHP defined SMEs as the 'backbone of the economy' which were critical for generating national champions (MHP, 2007: 46–48). The MHP describes its ideology as *ülkücülük* (idealism), meaning the promotion of 'love for and the ideal of serving one's state' and a 'devotion to the well-being of the state' (Çınar and Arıkan, 2002: 26 and 34).

The second category of analysis within political and civil society concerns state institutions, which are again analysed here as embedded in and internal to society. Gramsci's analyses of the integral state and Cox's analysis of the internationalisation of the state provide hints about operationalising the state. The Gramscian conception of the integral state describes the embeddedness of the state within society in terms of a social relationship that sits at the core of the struggle over hegemony (Gramsci, 1971: 263). As Gramsci (1971: 247) puts it:

> the State must be conceived of as an 'educator', in as much as it tends precisely to create a new type or level of civilisation ... Because one is acting essentially on economic forces, reorganising and developing the apparatus of economic production, creating a new structure, the conclusion must not be drawn that superstructural factors should be left to themselves, to develop spontaneously, to a haphazard and sporadic germination. The State, in this field, too, is an instrument of 'rationalisation', of acceleration and of Taylorisation. It operates according to a plan, urges, incites, and 'punishes'.

The analysis of the state in this chapter draws equally on Cox's conception of the internationalisation of the state that considers state institutions in relation to a state–society complex – 'form of state' – determined by the pre-eminent accumulation strategy (Cox, 1981: 146). While the necessities of international production engender intra-state compromise in adjusting national policies, a transition in state structure takes place that strengthens those ministries and other institutions related to the economy (such as central banks, ministries of finance and prime ministers' offices) in transmitting the global consensus to the national level (Cox, 1981: 146; 1987: 253–254).

Accordingly, I argue that, in the current era of the neoliberal form of state, state institutions linked to the global economy will favour EU membership with the rationale that Europeanisation will help Turkey adjust international rules determined by the global consensus and transnationalisation of production. Conversely, those state institutions that develop policies for social forces disadvantaged by globalisation are more likely to be sidelined in national policy-making and develop a more critical stance due to their concerns over relations of distribution and welfare cuts. More specifically, I predict that the interviewees from the Central Bank, the Ministry of Commerce and Industry, the Ministry of Foreign Affairs and the Secretariat General for EU Affairs favour globalisation and EU membership, whereas interviewees from the DPT, the Ministry of Labour and Social Security, the Ministry of Agriculture and Rural Affairs and the Small and Medium Enterprises Development Organisation (KOSGEB) have a more critical stance to an open economy.

The third category of analysis within political and civil society concerns struggles against the discipline of capital. I approach these struggles as an instance of class struggle in relation to the commodification of social relations. As I argued in Chapter 1, I disagree with the post-Marxist critique that historical materialism is class reductionist and economic determinist. Instead, throughout the book, I draw on historical materialism to treat the class struggle as not limited to the manufacturing sector but conceived within the social factory of capitalism. Here, I draw on van der Pijl (1998) and Bieler and Morton (2018), who argue that class struggle goes beyond the workplace to encompass reproductive labour in the nexus of the extended social factory (Bieler and Morton, 2018: 133–134). As van der Pijl notes, 'the issue is no longer that "capitalism" is showing signs of collapse, and "socialism" is around the corner … what is failing today is not capital but the capacity of society and nature to support its discipline' (van der Pijl, 1998: 48). Thus, what needs to be resisted is the penetration of capitalist logic into the process of social reproduction and its exploitation of nature and social relationships (van der Pijl, 1998: 36). Accordingly, I analyse contradictions around the climate crisis, patriarchy and abuses of human rights as instances of class struggle within the extended social factory of capitalism. To do so, I questioned the interviewees about the economic and social aspects of globalisation and EU membership, their conceptions of emancipation and their views about the relations of force with other social forces across the political spectrum.

Regarding the women's rights/feminist movement, I conducted interviews with five different groups. The Association for the Support and Training of Women Candidates (Ka-der) was founded in 1997 to empower women in political decision-making positions and support female candidates in municipal and general elections. Ka-der aims to establish women in at least 30 per cent of decision-making positions (Interviews 33, 34 and 43). The Association for the Support of Contemporary Life (ÇYDD) was founded in 1989 to defend secularism and modernity. It seeks to help women acquire economic independence by providing female students with scholarships (Interview 35). The Women's Centre, Education, Production, Consultation and Solidarity Foundation (Kamer) was founded in 1997 to struggle against honour killings, domestic violence and poverty, especially in eastern and south-eastern Anatolia (Interview 66). The Capital City Women's Platform is representative of the conservative-religious fraction of Turkey's women's rights movement. It aspires to challenge women's conditions within conservative Muslim communities while also campaigning against the headscarf ban in the public sphere (Interview 45). Finally, the Socialist Feminist Collective was founded in 2008 to fight against 'patriarchal capitalism' by raising the consciousness of salaried and unsalaried female labour as well as to campaign for recognition of women's 'emotional labour' in the private sphere (Interview 61).

Regarding struggles around the environment and human rights, I conducted interviews with four institutions. The Human Rights Association (İHD) was founded in 1986 by human rights activists and relatives of victims of abuse. It aims to raise public awareness about human rights and to institutionalise the protection of human rights at the state level (Interview 37). The Helsinki Citizens' Assembly was founded in 1993 to work for the peaceful coexistence of different cultural groups and the construction of fortress Europe by spreading norms and values such as the rule of law, the respect of human rights and citizenship (Interview 62). In Turkey, it focuses on the Kurdish problem, the Cyprus issue and relations with Armenia (Interview 62). The Association for Human Rights and Solidarity for the Oppressed, Mazlumder, aims to contribute to finding a peaceful solution to the Kurdish problem and campaigned during the 2000s against the headscarf ban as a violation of human rights (Interview 38). Greenpeace Mediterranean is the regional office of Greenpeace International, which works for the environment, peace and increased dialogue domestically and internationally (Interview 63).

Position of political parties in the debate over membership

In Chapter 2, I read the AKP rule as *trasformismo* because it both extended the ruling class around the neoliberal hegemony and also weakened dissent by co-opting groups disadvantaged by globalisation through ad hoc individualistic instruments such as charities in place of formal social policy mechanisms. Although the interviewee from the AKP defined the party as 'conservative democrat' (Interview 55), here I read it as a right-wing party consolidating the neoliberal hegemony. In the 2000s, the AKP approached globalisation positively by institutionalising the market economy model and triggering international competitiveness in the global markets (Interview 55). It claimed that the state should support the competitiveness of SMEs in international markets (Interview 55; AKP, 2001: 18). In its 2002 election manifesto, the AKP defended EU membership as a 'primary objective' with the rationale that the possibility of membership would consolidate democracy and ensure economic development (AKP, 2002: 37). The party also considered the Customs Union positively for increasing exports and Turkish industry's international competitiveness (Interview 55). As the interviewee from the AKP put it, 'Turkish SMEs are content with the delocalisation of European production thanks to the Customs Union' (Interview 55). Although the AKP remained committed to reforms during the 2000s, the interviewee from the AKP noted that the EU had shown double standards and expected concessions regarding nationally sensitive issues like the Kurdish problem and Turkey's position in Cyprus in return for the EU's commitment to the reform process (Interview 55). The interviewee also stated that 'the EU's pull factor for membership is diminishing with the eurozone crisis as the EU could not keep the Maastricht criteria while xenophobia is increasing against Muslims and migrants in Europe, not to mention Europe's aging population and its incapability to generate political actorness in foreign affairs' (Interview 55). Nevertheless, 'the AKP has seen the EU as instrumental to developing standards and retaining EU membership as a goal' (Interview 55).

Opposition parties can be expected to be more critical of EU membership because their social base is mainly composed of workers, retirees, SMEs and farmers. However, contrary to this expectation, the opposition parties' interviewees stated that they support membership on the condition that Turkey's membership is on equal terms and conditions as for other EU members. Centre-left political parties – the CHP and the DSP – accepted globalisation as a fact. As they failed to provide an alternative to the market economy model, their critique of globalisation focused on social policy (Interviews 54, 56 and 64). Hence, during the 2000s the CHP and the DSP proposed, respectively, a 'social market economy' model and a 'societal competitive economy' (CHP, 2007: 24–25; Türker 2005: 3). Both models prioritised growth, competitiveness in global markets and low inflation, while incorporating a social dimension focused on employment, equal distribution of income and a functioning welfare state (CHP, 2010: 143–144). In short, they accepted that globalisation is irreversible, but believed it can be regulated (Interview 64). They thus promoted production for global markets with a social dimension and employment policy (Interviews 54 and 56).

Regarding EU membership, their position can be summarised as 'membership on equal terms and conditions' (Interview 54). They expected that membership would improve Turkey's economy by boosting production and exports, increasing the quality of goods and services, and enabling inward technology transfers (Interviews 54 and 58), while also improving social standards, enabling a more equal distribution of income and eliminating regional disparities (Interviews 54 and 56). They expected the EU's structural funds to compensate those groups disadvantaged by globalisation (Interview 58) and that membership would help Turkey realise its modernisation goal, originally set by Atatürk, 'to reach the level of contemporary civilisation' (Interviews 54 and 58). Finally, they expected EU membership to benefit Turkey's foreign policy by strengthening its regional power while eliminating risks from fundamentalist Islam and/or the dismemberment of Turkey (Interview 54). Their criticisms concerned political issues and national sensitivities. The first concerned the Cyprus problem. The CHP rejected negotiating Turkish membership in relation to the Cyprus problem (CHP, 2006: 20 and 119) and maintained the position that there are 'two separate, equal and independent states with equal sovereignty in Cyprus' (Interview 58; DSP, 2004: 12). The second issue was related to minority rights. Here, they criticised the EU for pursuing imperialist policies to divide and rule Turkey by asking it to officially recognise the Kurdish and Alevi populations as minorities as additional concessions 'specific' to Turkey's membership application (Interviews 54 and 58). Third, they condemned the EU for demanding that Turkey officially recognise the 'Armenian genocide' (Interview 58). Finally, they disapproved of any form of 'special status', privileged partnership, or any other discriminatory policies such as EU proposals to have permanent derogations regarding the free movement of labour and structural funds (Interviews 54 and 58; CHP, 2006: 5–7 and 234). Overall, the two social democratic parties were not against EU membership per se. Rather, they called for full membership status on equal terms and conditions, as neatly summarised by the title of a CHP booklet: *Yes to Full Membership, No to Special Status* (CHP, 2006: 9–10).

The MHP's position can also be summarised as 'honourable membership on equal terms and conditions' (Interview 59). The MHP read globalisation as a structural imperative that can only be taken advantage of by endorsing national champions (Interview 59). The party expected that EU membership would help Turkey become an actor in global markets by increasing the competitiveness of Turkish industry and achieving higher institutional standards (Interview 59). Their criticisms focused on national interests, such as permanent derogations or any form of privileged partnership (Interview 59). The MHP argued that the EU should not intervene in Turkey's domestic affairs, particularly by imposing conditions regarding Cyprus and Armenia

(MHP, 2007: 117). For the MHP, the EU's policies concerning the Kurdish problem threaten Turkey's unitary state structure (Interview 59). Finally, the party accused the EU of excluding Turkey from its security and defence initiatives (Interview 59).

Contrary to the above stated expectation, the 'emancipatory left' political parties supported membership during the 2000s for political reasons. Before the 1980s, membership of the EEC was assessed around the motto 'The Europeans are the partners and we are the market' (Interview 44). This stance changed with globalisation, which the parties considered an inevitable development and one that can only be tackled through internationalisation of the labour movement (Interview 44). For these parties, globalisation has worsened income disparities and other inequalities (Interview 60), although they also viewed globalisation as 'progressive' in stimulating information exchange and technological development, which have contributed to lessening the isolation of the Kurdish movement (Interview 60). Despite criticising the EU as a capitalist integration model (Interview 44), they supported membership for four reasons. First, globalisation has necessitated a struggle at the international level (Interview 44). Second, internationalisation and/ or supranationalism were needed for decentralisation, as these processes were expected to transfer power from national central authorities both to supranational and local levels, thereby opening space for the expression of ethnic and cultural rights (Interview 60). Third, membership would consolidate democracy while demilitarising politics and limiting the 'military's hegemony' in the political sphere (Interview 44). Fourth, the EU's regional funds were expected to improve the industrial infrastructure of eastern Anatolia, while free movement of workers was expected to help remedy the region's socio-economic problems (Interview 60). Hence, they support EU membership under the motto 'Another Europe is possible'.

Struggle in state institutions

In line with my hypothesis, the interviewees from state institutions related to the global economy, specifically the Central Bank, the Undersecretariat of Foreign Trade and the Ministry of Industry and Commerce, all favoured liberalisation and the economic implications of EU membership. The interviewee from the Ministry of Industry and Commerce considered liberalisation and free trade as 'progressive' for Turkey's industrialisation and industrial development (Interview 49). Thus, he argued that the Customs Union was decisive in making Turkish industry more competitive, increasing the quality of products (Interview 49). It was expected to consolidate Turkey's market economy model while maintaining its market share in Europe (Interview

47). As such, the EU and IMF were seen as double anchors providing macroeconomic stability (Interview 40). Yet, as the interviewee from the Secretariat General for EU Affairs highlighted, the Customs Union has never been perceived as an end in itself within the bureaucracy (Interview 57). Rather, it is a strategy to deepen integration with the final goal of membership (Interview 57). The prospect of EU membership has enabled price stability and macroeconomic development while keeping inflation low and increasing efficiency (Interview 40). Additionally, it was believed to provide standardisation in Turkey's production and to force Turkey to adapt international rules, which are two decisive factors in attracting FDI (Interviews 48 and 51). As such, the economic rationale for defending membership was in parallel with ideas articulated within the pro-membership project. Turkey's European orientation was also believed to be a state policy that has continued since the republic's establishment, and hence not easily changeable by any political party or government (Interview 47).

The interviewees from the Secretariat General for EU Affairs and Ministry for Foreign Affairs also adapted a pro-EU perspective regarding democratic consolidation and foreign policy. They considered Turkey's reform process essential to comply with international rules on human rights, democracy and the rule of law (Interview 46), given that EU norms are in line with the universal principles of the United Nations Convention and International Labour Organization (ILO) standards (Interview 46). They suggested that Turkey needs the prospect of EU membership to provide a 'stronger anchor' for consolidating democracy, given that Turkey's societal base is interpreted as weak to call for democratic reform (Interview 46). They predicted that EU membership can civilise domestic politics and make government more accountable and responsive to its citizens (Interview 46). The interviewees from the Ministry of Foreign Affairs considered membership as a 'strategic objective' for Turkey's Western orientation (Interviews 48 and 53).

However, the interviewees had two reservations related to foreign and security policy. First, regarding Cyprus, they criticised the EU for breaking the promise in the Annan Plan to end the isolation of the Turkish Republic of Northern Cyprus (Interview 48). They also criticised the EU's decision to give membership to the Republic of Cyprus as if it represented the whole island prior to any negotiated solution. This is considered 'unacceptable' because it de facto recognises Turkey as an occupying force on the island (Interview 53). Moreover, the EU's preconditions regarding the Additional Protocol related to Cyprus means that – technically speaking, at least – no negotiation chapters can be closed until this deadlock is resolved (Interview 53). The second main reservation concerns security. The interviewees accused the EU of downgrading Turkey's military position related to European Security and Defense Policy (ESDP) operations. As one interviewee pointed out, 'the EU fails to keep its promise to consult Turkey with regards to ESDP operations' (Interview 48). In line with the Berlin Plus formula, Turkey expects the EU to consult it over ESDP missions that use NATO assets (Interview 53). On 16 December 2002, NATO and the EU agreed that the EU can use NATO's military assets for its own crisis management operations if NATO declines to intervene. Because Turkey is the only non-EU NATO member, its main concern here relates to any potential EU mission regarding its conflict with the Republic of Cyprus and bilateral disputes with Greece (Interview 53). Although Turkey was assured in the Ankara Document that ESDP missions will not be directed against an ally and there will be cooperation with Turkey over the missions, the interviewee criticised the EU for not consulting Turkey (Interview 53).

In parallel with Cox's arguments regarding the internationalisation of the state, I predicted that representatives of state institutions not related to the international economy under the neoliberal form of state will be more critical of free trade and the market economy while being sidelined within the bureaucracy. Indeed, the interviewee from the Ministry of Labour and Social Security had a negative view of globalisation as a process generating de-unionisation and unemployment while worsening labour conditions. He also stated that 'globalisation is irresistible' (Interview 41). Similarly, the interviewee from the Ministry of Agriculture and Rural Affairs expected EU membership to increase the pressures of competitiveness on Turkey's agricultural structure, which is characterised by small, partitioned holdings (Interview 52). This means that 'there is not even a proper differentiation between farmers and peasants in Turkey, where most farmers are uneducated, their produce is of lower quality and they are inexperienced in marketing' (Interview 52). Consequently, it was anticipated that Turkish agriculture, especially livestock and dairy production, would not be able to compete with market-oriented larger European enterprises in the food industry (Interview No. 52). Despite such criticisms, these institutions either concurred with the neoliberal conception of the economy or accepted globalisation as 'irresistible'. For instance, contrary to Turkey's previous economic doctrine of a planned economy, now considered inefficient, the DPT adapted neoliberal economic policies and supported the neoliberal form of state that boosts the private sector and promotes international competitiveness (Interview 50). Similarly, the interviewee from KOSGEB stated that SMEs have already experienced the economic impact of EU membership after Turkey's market was opened to competition with European firms under the Customs Union (Interview 39). To quote the interviewee, 'There is no difference in EU membership from the Customs Union for SMEs' (Interview 39). In response, KOSGEB started to support an export-promotion strategy by improving export capacity and the international competitiveness of Turkey's SMEs (Interview 39).

Regarding EU membership, although the DPT took a negative stance towards the Customs Union in the 1990s due to concerns over the competitiveness of Turkey's industry, it reconsidered this stance in the 2000s (Interview 50). Hence, the DPT supported EU membership on the grounds that economic integration has already occurred through the Customs Union, so membership will benefit Turkey by enabling it to participate in EU decision making (Interview 50). KOSGEB expected EU membership to render Turkey's SMEs more competitive and improve the quality of products (Interview 39). The interviewee from the Ministry of Agriculture and Rural Affairs supported membership for providing access to the EU's agricultural support mechanisms and funds (Interview 52). More importantly, globalisation has already compelled Turkey to liberalise its agricultural regime, particularly by implementing a farmers' register system and direct income support in line with WB policies (Interview 52). The direct support mechanism provided support on the basis of land area, which was later criticised for discouraging agricultural production and opening up the market for international firms (Interview 52). In contrast, EU membership was expected to provide protectionism thanks to the EU policy of ensuring self-sufficiency (Interview 52). Similarly, the interviewee from the Ministry of Labour and Social Security highlighted that the association partnership through the Customs Union only entailed economic integration, whereas EU membership would incorporate the social dimension and improve democratisation (Interview 41). To quote the interviewee, 'Turkey should become a member as goods circulate freely whereas people cannot' (Interview 41). The interviewee also expected that the European Social Model will protect Turkey's workers against globalisation while strengthening trade unionism (Interview 41). The interviewee also defended social dialogue as a way to overcome class antagonism and ideological struggle while contributing to the democratisation of industrial relations (Interview 41).

Hence, contrary to my prediction, these interviewees viewed globalisation as irresistible and supported EU membership for its potential benefits, such as agricultural and structural funds, and improved working conditions due to the progressive European Social Model. They also endorsed EU membership on the basis that Turkey's market has already been integrated into Europe's via the Customs Union (negative integration), so EU membership is needed to add the social dimension (positive integration). However, they also stated that there has been very little internal debate in Turkey's state institutions regarding EU membership. Instead, it has been considered as a 'state policy' that is not open to discussion (Interviews 41 and 48). As one interviewee put it, 'There has never been any departure from the pro-membership perspective under any government despite political vacillations' (Interview 47).

Struggle in the social factory of capitalism

The struggles against the capitalist discipline over social reproduction had differing conceptions of globalisation. Interviewees from the women's rights/feminist movement read globalisation as a capitalist process that disproportionally impoverishes women (Interviews 43 and 61). Women are often the first to make sacrifices for their families, bear the brunt of unemployment or perform social services for free in parallel with social cuts, especially during economic crises (Interviews 36, 43 and 61). Globalisation also increasingly exploits women through flexible working conditions (Interviews 61 and 65). The interviewee from the Helsinki Citizens' Assembly argued that liberalisation led to human rights violations through privatisation of public services like health and education that excluded disadvantaged groups (Interview 62). Similarly, the interviewee from İHD claimed that the economic rules of neoliberalism cause human rights breaches by increasing inequality and unemployment while deepening poverty (Interview 37). Yet, although worsening economic conditions have increased the need for social policies, welfare states have withered away globally (Interview 37). Hence, 'rights' are replaced by 'social charity mechanisms' which contradict 'human dignity' and increase human rights violations (Interview 37). Noting that the current economic system causes environmental problems, the interviewee from Greenpeace Mediterranean criticised the dominant economic discourse of the 2000s that presents environmental precautions as 'economically costly' (Interview 63).

Activists from the ecological struggle[1] criticised globalisation for accelerating ecological destruction (Interview 97) – for instance, by destroying local seed production and making farmers dependent on the global seeds market (Interview 97). Nevertheless, they acknowledge that globalisation is a structural imperative (Interviews 97 and 98). Furthermore, it has some positive consequences. First, globalisation has increased agricultural diversity (Interview 97) – for instance, kiwi fruits are now being grown in Turkey (Interview 97). Second, it has advanced internationalism in civil society and increased awareness of 'globality' – i.e. the fact that humans live in a global world (Interviews 97 and 98). Both TEMA's and Doğa's membership reacted positively to adapting EU environmental legislation (Interview 98). During the 2000s EU reform process the two organisations worked closely with Turkey's Ministry of Agriculture to adjust to the European acquis (Interviews 97 and 98). Thanks to the EU reform process, Turkish state officials and civil society were able to familiarise themselves with European standards to protect the environment (Interview 98). Regarding globalisation's impact on migration, one interviewee noted that it has eased human mobility while making migration more visible (Interview 104). Another claimed that it has equally increased inequalities and generated another push factor for migration, especially towards developed countries (Interview 104). Third, globalisation was believed to open up political space for the gender struggle by accelerating internationalisation and international mobilisation (Interviews 36 and 65).

During the 2000s there has been no debate in Turkey on the overall economic effects of the Customs Union (Interviews 61 and 66). Instead, the women rights/feminist movement mostly discussed EU projects and financial support related to the economic dimension (Interview 66). For instance, the interviewee from Kamer referred to how EU financial assistance helped women in eastern and south-eastern Anatolia (Interview 66). Indeed, interviewees in the social factory of capitalism endorsed EU membership in relation to its political, social and cultural dimensions. First, they acknowledged that the EU offers a progressive model to improve women's conditions, given that European countries have been the first to implement positive discrimination and quotas (Interview 36). Second, Turkey's women's rights/feminist movement used the EU reform process strategically to institutionalise women's rights, especially following the 1999 Helsinki Council (Interviews 32 and 43). For example, the movement successfully lobbied to change Turkey's Civil Code and Criminal Code, taking European countries as a model (Interview 42). A particular achievement was that the state was declared as 'responsible for providing gender equality' (Interview 33). Another interviewee acknowledged that the EU reform process enabled this legislation to be finally passed in parliament in 2005, having first been proposed in 1992 (Interview 35). Here, the organic link was formed through the European Commission, which conferred with representatives of the women's rights/feminist movement and human rights groups prior to publishing its regular progress reports (Interviews 37 and 42). Third, interviewees from women's rights groups and human rights groups read the EU membership process as helping Turkey consolidate its democracy (Interviews 32 and 65). Here, they viewed the Turkish state as a 'strong state' – that is, one that curbs civil society to develop under the 'authoritarian republican oligarchy' and its 'military and bureaucratic tutelage' (Interviews 36, 37, 38, 62 and 65). The interviewees expected that the EU, as an international actor, could apply pressure to open up space for civil society, democracy and human rights (Interviews 32, 34, 36, 38, 62 and 65). Fourth, preparing for EU membership was also seen as a peace process to help Turkey solve its problems with Greece in the Aegean Sea (Interview 36) and find a peaceful solution to the Kurdish problem (Interview 66). The interviewee from İHD, for example, criticised the state's 'security doctrine' for 'inventing' internal and external enemies, whether Armenians, Greeks, Kurds, Alevis and human rights groups, in order to perpetuate the state's existence (Interview 37). Hence, the interviewee believed that the EU process can help in the search for a democratic solution to the Kurdish problem and contribute to constructing a cosmopolitan political culture that respects differences based on ethnicity, religion or sect (Interviews 37 and 38). Finally, the interviewee from the conservative Capital City Women's Platform highlighted that the EU process contributed to questioning Turkey's strict rules of 'state secularism', thereby generating more space for conservative segments to practice their religion (Interview 45).

However, Turkey's women's rights/feminist movements do not offer unconditional support (Interviews 32 and 42), criticising the EU on three grounds. First, the EU was seen as ignoring women's employment and rising flexible work among women (Interview 61) by allocating funds to 'female entrepreneurship' rather than 'women's employment' (Interviews 32 and 42). As the interviewee from the Socialist Feminist Collective put it, 'the EU ignored the instruments of patriarchal capitalism' (Interview 61). Second, the EU limited its consideration of the gender struggle to the public sphere in relation to equal pay (Interview 61). This reflected a limited understanding of the gender struggle concentrated on protecting the interests of employed white women while ignoring the exploitation of low-income women, migrant women, single mothers and undereducated women (Interview 61). Moreover, for the interviewees, the public and private spheres cannot be separated in the feminist struggle because women's labour encompasses 'emotional labour' and women's labour for their family (Interview 61). The EU should therefore widen its conception of women's labour to include women's unpaid household labour (Interview 61). Third, the interviewees highlighted that accessing EU funding was too bureaucratic and cumbersome (Interview 32). There are even private firms in Turkey that prepare proposals for the EU funds on behalf of women's groups, which distorts the way EU funds are used (Interview 43).

Why not a united front against neoliberal restructuring?

This section questions why social forces that have been disadvantaged by globalisation have been unable to form a united front to resist neoliberal restructuring and the discipline of capital around social reproduction. My empirical research uncovered three reasons why they have failed to establish relations of force to form an alternative historical bloc. First, the struggle at the economic level was already considered 'lost' in terms of developing an anti-globalisation movement, especially after participation in the Customs Union (Interview 37). Moreover, for these groups, the economy was of secondary importance. For instance, they mostly discussed EU membership in relation to social, political and cultural dimensions, viewing the Customs Union as a 'technical' issue that is only relevant to particular industrial sectors (Interviews 45, 62 and 65). This suggests that they have internalised neoliberal 'common sense', which assumes that the economy operates in an apolitical field. Hence, their criticisms of globalisation and neoliberal restructuring mostly remain issue-specific, with interviewees discussing them in relation to their separate effects on women, human rights and the environment. As a result, their structural critique remained weak, which resonates with criticisms of poststructuralism for simply sweeping the whole question of capitalism under the carpet (Wood, 1990: 79). Second, after the neoliberal turn in the 1980s, those struggles prioritised pluralism and criticised previous forms of organising within the class struggle and working-class movement for operating hierarchically. In doing so, however, they embraced political liberalism while ignoring economic liberalism, thereby failing to problematise the structure of capitalist social relations, making it more difficult to develop an anti-capitalist agenda structurally through forming relations of force. Although they acknowledged that neoliberalism generated depoliticisation after the 1980s, they embraced it to open up space for democratisation and critical thinking (Interview 65). Indeed, pluralism and autonomy from class politics were welcomed for widening the political space to articulate struggles around gender, human rights and the environment (Interview 65). An example of this transition is the women's rights/feminist movement. Before the 1980s, this movement was organised under class politics with the assumption that women would be emancipated by overthrowing the capitalist system (Interview 34). After the 1980s, however, influenced by neoliberal restructuring and the second-wave feminist movement, they adapted a pluralist struggle. Thus, my interviewees claimed that women's rights/feminism should not be 'secondary' or 'subordinated' to the working-class movement and contended that women's problems go beyond the economy (Interview 36). They internalised the motto that 'Women are not only economically exploited but politically and socially oppressed' (Interview 65). As one interviewee put it, 'I got divorced from Marxism' because 'sexual hierarchy is just as important as class hierarchy' (Interview 36). Their criticism of class struggle was that 'feminism should not be reduced to conducting politics for women' (Interview 61). Rather, feminism should be maintained as an ideology that designates women as a subject in politics while defining the main contradiction as 'gender equality' (Interview 65). Similarly, the interviewee from İHD argued that the primary struggle is adapting the 'universal language of human rights and freedoms', and that this should not be considered secondary to the working-class struggle (Interview 37). The interviewee from Doğa defines the struggle as 'changing the distorted relation between nature and humans who perceive themselves hierarchically on top of all the species, as if humans are at the centre of the universe with nature perceived as a "resource" to be exploited' (Interview 99). So, she claimed, 'Doğa defends the rights of nature' (Interview 99). This resonates with Mouffe's (1993: 1) conception of the 'explosion of particularisms' and 'emancipation(s)' (Laclau, 1996: vii). My empirical research showed that emancipation is now defined in a pluralist way as a struggle against gender inequality in political representation (Interview 33), gender-based violence and honour killings (Interview 66), and gender inequality in education and employment (Interview 35).

Third, those involved in these struggles have developed an alternative conception of political praxis. Here, they criticise the mass movement rhetoric which prioritises organising around classical institutions of representative democracy, such as trade unions and political parties. The interviewees instead emphasised social movement rhetoric and small, horizontally organised groups, mostly founded in a flexible, ad hoc manner (Interviews 36 and 66). The interviewees mentioned taking roles in rotation to avoid leadership in the movement (Interview 36). As one interviewee admitted, 'We even suppressed particular women who demanded leadership and manifested leadership potential' (Interview 36). These groups have also turned to alternative, postmodern forms of struggle, such as the internet (Interview 33).

Most of the interviewees from the women's rights/feminist movement no longer believe that political parties can articulate their interests in the political sphere. They therefore prefer to remain independent from political parties, claiming that this has prevented the movement from becoming an instrument of any particular political party (Interviews 34, 36, 61, 63 and 66). They have also abandoned the idea of 'structural emancipation' and the assumption that revolution will emancipate women from the patriarchy (Interviews 36 and 43). As an interviewee put it, 'The collapse of the capitalist system was articulated as the solution to patriarchy before the 1980s, which was an illusory argument' (Interview 36). The representatives from organisations that address the ecological crisis also argued that they prefer to maintain 'political neutrality', especially given the current political polarisation (Interviews 97 and 98). Given that their volunteers have different political affiliations, some might abandon the movement if TEMA or Buğday takes a contrary political stance (Interviews 97 and 98). Similarly, the interviewee from Team International Assistance for Integration (TIAFI) highlighted that the organisation does not discuss politics as it might polarise people, whereas

TIAFI's major aim is to help refugees socially integrate in Turkey (Interview 101). As the interviewee from TEMA pointed out, their objective is not to do politics but to work on the soil and environment (Interview 98).

Conclusion

This chapter extended the debate regarding the struggle for hegemony between social forces to political and civil society. There are two aims behind such an endeavour. The first was to question to what extent the ruling class can articulate its economic vested interests embedded within the neoliberal pro-membership project in universal terms in political and civil society. The second was to uncover whether the alternative class strategies – introduced in Chapter 3 – can form a united front with disadvantaged groups and struggles against the expansion of the discipline of capital in the sphere of social reproduction by presenting their project on a universal terrain. On the one hand, in line with my hypothesis, representatives of state institutions related to the global economy favoured EU membership because they believe it can increase Turkish industry's competitiveness while attracting FDI and consolidating democracy. On the other hand, contrary to my prediction, representatives of those state institutions that develop policies for groups disadvantaged by globalisation, such as labour, the agriculture sector and SMEs, also supported membership. However, their rationale was different from that of social forces within the pro-membership project. More specifically, they expected EU membership to provide protectionism from the negative effects of globalisation while supporting disadvantaged groups through the EU's structural funds and social policy. They also argued that because market integration has already been consolidated via the Customs Union (negative integration), Turkey should complete membership to benefit from the social dimension (positive integration).

The analysis then concentrated on political parties, approached as representing class struggle in relation to their social base. First, I read the ruling AKP as a conservative right-wing party that was backing the pro-membership project in line with its support for globalisation and neoliberal restructuring. Second, and contrary to my expectation, representatives of opposition parties also supported membership, whether to gain membership on equal terms and conditions, or on the grounds that economic integration has already been consolidated through the Customs Union and membership will help Turkey to struggle against globalisation through internationalism at the regional level. Then I examined the struggles of women's rights/feminism, human rights and environmental groups as a class struggle in the sphere of social reproduction against the discipline of capital. Again, contrary to my expectation, these groups support EU membership in relation to its political and social policy dimensions.

The empirical data revealed that the pro-membership project was indeed hegemonic in the 2000s because it was supported by various social forces in Turkish political and civil society. In the previous chapter I argued that the pro-membership project was pioneered by internationally oriented capital and adapted by SMEs. Similarly, state institutions linked to the global economy endorsed EU membership to increase competitiveness, consolidate democracy and attract FDI. Concurrent with Cox, European integration constitutes 'a microcosm of the larger internationalising process' (Cox, 1987: 259). The interviewees from state institutions referred to EU membership as a regionalisation model that can help Turkey comply with the international rules of the global economy and international standards regarding human rights and the rule of law. Hence, they viewed Turkey's EU reform process and its neoliberal content as 'progressive' despite uncertainty about the country's prospects of attaining membership status. Although the AKP identifies its social base as SMEs, farmers and artisans, its social purpose in pioneering the pro-membership project in the 2000s was to consolidate the neoliberal transition. The AKP government considered EU membership a 'primary objective' for competitiveness and democratisation. However, rather than seeing membership as the ultimate goal, the AKP perceived membership as instrumental for Turkey to catch up with international standards and development.

Rather than one project supporting and one project opposing EU membership, there were two rival class strategies in the 2000s contesting pro-membership in the Turkish context: neo-mercantilism and Ha–vet (No–Yes), neither of which constituted an overall counter-hegemonic historical bloc. The neo-mercantilist bloc was supported by nationally oriented labour and centre-left political parties. During the 2000s, Turkey's centre-left political parties (the CHP and DSP) failed to develop an alternative economic model to the market economy and accepted globalisation as a fact. Instead, they aspired to develop social policy within the market economy, neatly summarised by the 'societal competitive economy' and 'social market economy'. Accordingly, they adapted the economic rationale behind the pro-membership project and supported EU membership as a way to boost production, improve social policy and compensate disadvantaged groups through EU structural funds. Their only critique derived from political concerns related to the EU's demands regarding the Cyprus problem, the Kurdish and Armenian issues and the possibility of only offering Turkey a privileged partnership status, thereby excluding it from structural funds and preventing free movement of Turkish workers. Hence, their position can be neatly summarised as 'membership on equal terms and conditions' and they can be analysed within the neo-mercantilist rival class strategy.

Ha–vet was underpinned by internationally oriented labour, emancipatory left political parties and struggles within the social factory of capitalism. Although the emancipatory left political parties criticised the EU as a capitalist integration model, they endorsed membership in order to struggle with globalisation at the international level, demilitarise politics and consolidate democracy. The interviewees involved in struggles over gender, the environment and human rights were concerned that globalisation will exacerbate the ecological crisis, expand flexible work for women and engender further privatisation of public services, which should be accessible for all as a human right. However, they also believed that struggle in the economic sphere was already lost with the completion of the Customs Union. Hence, they endorsed EU membership for political, social and cultural reasons – to open up space for civil society, civilise politics and consolidate democracy, contribute to attaining a peaceful solution to the Kurdish problem and construct a cos-mopolitan culture. The following chapter investigates the struggle around EU membership in the 2010s within the context of rising populism and economic crisis. It uncovers the position of social forces in the 2010s and reconsiders the hegemonic struggle during this period.

Note

1 I interviewed three institutions related to the struggle against the ecological crisis. The first institution is TEMA (Turkish Foundation for Combating Soil Erosion, Reforestation and the Protection of Natural Habitats). It was formed in 1992 to combat deforestation and maintain natural habitats. It prioritises five working areas: reforestation, education programmes and ecological literacy, environmental policy and international relations, rural development and volunteerism (Ataç, 2022a). It aspires to increase public awareness and knowledge related to deforestation and natural habitats, which will in return increase the pressure on the political authority 'to save Turkey from desertification' (Ataç, 2022a). As of 2022, TEMA has filed almost three hundred lawsuits against state regulations related to the environment (Ataç, 2022b). TEMA educates almost 60,000 children on sustainability each year (Ataç, 2022b). The second institution, Buğday (Wheat) Movement (Buğday Ekolojik Yaşamı Destekleme Derneği) was founded in 1990 by Victor Ananias, who opened a restaurant in Bodrum called Buğday Vegetarian Restaurant that endorsed healthy nutrition through unprocessed, local and seasonal food (Buğday, 2023). In 2002, it became an association, the Buğday Association for Support-ing Ecological Living, of environmentalist volunteers and members supporting sustainability, ecological living and local, healthy and environmentally friendly food production (Buğday, 2023). It aims to increase awareness about an ecological

life, create solutions for ecological problems and to promote ecological life. It supports 'ecological, healthy, fair and sustainable' food production with various projects, such as establishing local food chains in Turkey, the Seed Exchange Network and the No Pesticides on my Plate campaign (Buğday, 2023). The third institution is Doğa Derneği, founded in 2002 to struggle to preserve biodiversity, nature conservation, educating the population regarding the environment struggle and conserving birds and their habitats. On its website, its mission is stated as 'defending the rights of nature in all its forms including its processes, which are necessary for persistence of life on earth' (Doğa Derneği, 2023). It identifies itself as a grassroots organisation providing community-based solutions for the conservation of species and habitats based on scientific research (Doğa Derneği, 2023).

5

Deglobalisation? Reconsidering the struggle under authoritarian neoliberalism

This chapter discusses how social forces have repositioned themselves in the hegemonic struggle over the last decade. Since the Great Recession of 2008, the pull factors of EU membership have lost credibility while enlargement has been taken off the agenda in EU politics. There have also been talks on deglobalisation and rising protectionism with references to the geostrategic rivalry between the US and China, the COVID-19 pandemic and the war in Ukraine. Regarding European politics, the EU has failed to generate economic convergence among member states, as was revealed during the eurozone crisis and by continued socio-economic disparities between the EU's core and periphery. The credibility of European integration has also been weakened by Brexit and discussions around other member states potentially leaving, not to mention the rise of far-right politics in Europe. Meanwhile, in Turkish politics, the EU membership perspective has lost popularity while EU–Turkey relations have fluctuated in parallel with populist politics. Within such a historical context, this chapter investigates how social forces within the pro-membership project have continued to defend membership. Is pro-membership still hegemonic? How have social forces within Ha–vet and neo-mercantilism revisited their position in the last decade? Can they form an alternative within the context of crises of liberalism?

The lost battle for hegemony? Pro-membership social forces revisiting the struggle within the context of crises of liberalism

Despite talks on deglobalisation, representatives of internationally oriented capital note that they have not experienced protectionism in the last decade (Interviews 90 and 92). Instead, globalisation is being replaced with geostrategic priorities, nearshoring and deepening regionalisation (Kaslowski, 2022). For instance, there is a recent trend to increase intra-trade in the Pan-European Mediterranean Cumulation of North Africa and Eastern Europe, with Algeria, Tunisia, Morocco and Turkey (Interview 91). Regarding the global supply chain, the COVID-19 pandemic has led to social change due to four reasons. First, due to geostrategic rivalry, Western countries are devising policies to decrease their dependence on China (Interview 87). Second, representatives of internationally oriented capital highlight that Chinese wages are no longer that advantageous. To quote the interviewee, 'as Chinese GDP increased, wages have steadily increased as well' (Interview 87). Equally, China has started to focus on high-value-added products while cheap production is delocalised to Vietnam, Korea or the Philippines (Interview 87). As the interviewee from the electronic sector noted, 'Turkey has turned out to be a preferred destination in the current deglobalisation era because it is geographically close to Europe, it is a more trustable partner, and wages are cheaper than China' (Interview 95). According to the interviewee, monthly wage costs, which were around £300 in Turkey and £65 in China at the beginning of the 2000s, increased to around £400 in Turkey and £550 in China and by 2020 (Interview 95). Third, when faced with disruptions during the pandemic, companies developed policies to diversify suppliers of particular key products, either through onshoring, nearshoring or relocating production, to eliminate vulnerabilities to global risks (Interviews 87 and 92). Fourth, the ecological crisis and greater carbon footprint makes trade with distant geographies irrational (Interview 91). According to the interviewee from the textile sector, for example, 'in contrast to the globalisation period, the carbon footprint and the European Green Deal have accelerated trading nearshore, and we are expecting an increase of Turkey's share in European exports' (Interview 91). Indeed, several interviewees noted that Turkey's exports started to increase during the COVID-19 pandemic (Interviews 87, 90 and 92). For instance, due to nearshoring, whereas Turkey was the third or fourth largest provider of textile and garment goods to the European market in the early 2010s, it becomes the second largest in 2023 (Interview 90). Similarly, the interviewee from the OSD stated that Turkish suppliers increased their share of automotive exports to the EU from 35 per cent to 42 per cent during the COVID-19 pandemic (Interview 92).

Representatives of internationally oriented capital have not changed their position vis-à-vis EU membership, although they acknowledge that the pull factors for membership have decreased with the EU being preoccupied with its own problems and failing to generate a powerful political voice internationally (e.g. Kaslowski, 2020). Moreover, Turkey has criticised EU migration policies as 'selective humanitarianism', given that the EU has reacted differently to the needs of Syrian and Ukrainian migrants (Interview 87). Yet, as former TÜSİAD president Simone Kaslowski argues, 'the current stalemate and freezing of the membership negotiations cannot and shall not be permanent' (Kaslowski, 2020). As one interviewee put it 'political relations may become fierce in this populist era, however trade always continues without disruptions'

(Interview 91). They defend membership by referring to four main liberal arguments. The first is the economic argument that the EU is the primary trading partner for Turkey and a global economic actor that sets international standards. The interviewee from TÜSİAD argued that the capacity of Turkish companies to export to the EU market indicates that they meet international standards, thereby increasing the global competitiveness of Turkish goods (Interview 87). As the interviewee noted, 'even if Turkey does not become a member, the EU provides leverage for Turkish industry' (Interview 90). Second, the EU continues to be a model for democracy and human rights (Kaslowski, 2022; Özilhan, 2020). According to former TÜSİAD president Erol Bilecik, developments in Turkey's economy already demonstrate that economic growth cannot be sustained without consolidating democracy (Bilecik, 2018). Hence, Turkey has to revitalise its EU-related reform agenda regarding democracy, human rights and freedoms (Bilecik, 2018). Third, they also defend the pro-membership perspective arguing that membership would be the result of two hundred years of Turkey's modernisation project (Kaslowski, 2020). Fourth, they see the EU anchor as essential for establishing a rules-based international system in foreign affairs. They portray Turkey's strategic priority as strengthening relations with the West through European integration, while being guided by international law and agreements, and emphasising diplomacy and cooperation in international affairs (TÜSİAD, 2021a: 23).

Additionally, representatives of internationally oriented capital refer to two new arguments in defending membership in the hegemonic struggle. First, regarding the ecological crisis, the EU is seen as a key anchor for Turkey to comply with the Green transition (Interview 87). They propose a circular economy model as an alternative to the current linear 'take-make-consume-waste' economic model (TÜSİAD, 2021b: 8). In contrast, the circular economy model recycles commodities by keeping them continuously flowing between producers and users (TÜSİAD, 2021b: 8), thereby reducing waste, managing resources efficiently and promoting sustainable policies for development and competitiveness (TÜSİAD 2021b: 8). In Turkey's case, the circular economy is expected to increase efficiency and decrease dependence on imports of interim goods (TÜSİAD, 2021b: 17). More specifically, according to TÜSİAD's report on the circular economy, interim goods account for 42.2 per cent of imports since 2016 (TÜSİAD, 2021b: 17). Applied in Turkey, this model could decrease waste, stimulate domestic savings and enable Turkey to meet international standards and UN Sustainable Development Goals (TÜSİAD, 2021b: 17). The İKV, the civil society organisation analysed in the fourth chapter as having organic links with capital, has also lobbied for Turkey's compliance with the European Green Deal. For instance, before Turkey signed the Paris Convention, İKV general secretary, Çiğdem Nas, invited the government to sign it so that Turkey would not be excluded from the transition to a Green economy (Nas, 2021). Yet, in addition to the need for a sustainable future, the capital groups' demands for Turkey to comply with the Green Deal also reveal their vested economic interests. In particular, an important risk that they perceive for Turkey's economy is carbon taxes being levied on goods produced in countries that do not comply with Green Deal environmental standards (Yenel, 2020). Moreover, according to TÜSİAD's Head of Industrial Policies, Fatih Ebiçlioğlu, although the EU has signed free trade agreements with Latin American and Asian countries, a switch to a Green economy will benefit Turkey because of the higher carbon emissions from long-distance trade (Ebiçlioğlu, 2020). For instance, compared to Turkey, transporting a container from Mexico or Vietnam to the EU market produces, respectively, 1.6 and 1.8 times more carbon emissions (Ebiçlioğlu, 2020).

The second new argument in supporting the membership perspective concerns the perception of the EU as a model for digital transformation. As the interviewee from TÜSİAD argued, the EU aspires to become a global leader in artificial intelligence and industrial automation (Interview 87). Similarly, TÜSİAD member Hakan Bulgurlu claims that the EU plays a pivotal role for global business in the digital transformation (Bulgurlu, 2021). More specifically, EU legislation provides an anchor to boost new job opportunities and upgrade skills in digital economies while establishing a digital ecosystem (Bulgurlu, 2021). Turkey will also need to comply with EU data standards, such as data storage (Bulgurlu, 2021). Here, the European Data Governance Act provides a model to generate trust in data sharing while providing transparency and equal access for everyone (Bulgurlu, 2021). Digitalisation also goes hand in hand with the struggle to overcome the ecological crisis. For example, referring to one of Turkey's major multinational companies, Bulgurlu (2021) notes that 'Arçelik is now using 50 per cent less energy in its production in Romania thanks to progressive manufacturing and digitalisation.' Representatives from internationally oriented capital defend digitalisation with the expectation that Industry 4.0 will boost productivity and investment, which in return creates employment (TÜSİAD, 2016: 14). As one interviewee noted, both larger enterprises and multinational companies have started lights-out manufacturing (Interview 92).

Regarding SMEs, the interviewees acknowledged that the global supply chain is now concentrating production in near geographies while protectionism between regional blocs is rising (Interview 88, MÜSİAD, 2022: 6). This is for two reasons. On the one hand, there is increasing mistrust of China due both to the disruptions it caused within the global supply chain during the COVID-19 pandemic and growing global economic competition between the US and China (MÜSİAD, 2022: 9). On the other hand, the ecological crisis and the issue of transport-related carbon footprints are pushing countries to nearshoring (Interview 88). Hence, Turkish SME exports to the European market have increased in the last decade (Interview 88). According to MÜSİAD president Mahmut Asmalı, the pandemic did not negatively impact SMEs thanks to the government's policy of 'keeping industry's wheels turning under lockdown' (Asmalı, 2022a). Indeed, according to Asmalı, Turkey has become a major procurement and production hub for the European market since the COVID-19 pandemic by successfully filling the gap generated by China's disruptions to the global supply chain (MÜSİAD, 2022: 10). This is particularly because Turkey is geographically close to the European market and can quickly fulfil orders from Europe (Asmalı, 2022b). For instance, SMEs in MÜSİAD can deliver orders to Europe within a month rather than five to six months for orders from China (Asmalı, 2022b). Moreover, Turkish goods are now preferred in the European market due to their high quality and because Turkey complies with international production standards (Asmalı, 2022b). In 2022, two further factors encouraged a rise in Turkey's SME exports. First, Turkish goods have become relatively cheaper than those of its international competitors due to exchange rate parity (Asmalı, 2022b). Second, the EU's energy crisis due to the war in Ukraine meant that European firms increased their investments in Turkey, thereby stimulating FDI inflows (Asmalı, 2022b).

Hence, among Turkey's SME representatives there has been no change in their support for the pro-membership project. As TOBB resident Rıfat Hisarcıklıoğlu stressed, the EU is Turkey's largest trading partner while Turkey is the EU's sixth largest trading partner (Hisarcıklıoğlu, 2021). Moreover, 62 per cent of Turkey's FDI originated from the EU market in 2021 (Hisarcıklıoğlu, 2021) and SMEs perceive the membership perspective as indispensable for Turkey to attract FDI (Interview 82). The EU membership process has also helped Turkey consolidate a competitive industrial structure and a functioning market economy (Hisarcıklıoğlu, 2021) while its SMEs are already integrated institutionally with Europe (Interview 82). For instance, Rıfat Hisarcıklıoğlu has acted as the Eurochambres' vice president. Although SME representatives are concerned about the Green Deal and the EU's Carbon Border Adjustment Mechanism (Interview 88), they are preparing themselves because the EU plans to implement a carbon tax after October 2023 for six selected sectors (aluminium, fertilisers, iron, steel, electricity and cement) (Interview 88). As the interviewee from the İstanbul Chamber of Industry put it, 'whereas the argument among Turkish manufacturers vis-à-vis the EU's environment acquis was pre-eminently "economically costly" in the 2000s, this is no longer relevant due to the carbon tax. It is essential for Turkey's industry to adapt the Green Deal' (Interview 88). Accordingly, MÜSİAD announced a 'Climate Manifesto' in 2021 and set itself the goal of preparing Turkey's SMEs for the circular economy model (MÜSİAD, 2021). According to Hisarcıklıoğlu, the Green economy model is a new development strategy for Turkey (Hisarcıklıoğlu, 2022). As Hisarcıklıoğlu (2022) put it, 'Development was associated with only economic growth. Yet in this new era of ecological crisis, the carbon footprint has to be included in discussions around development.'

In adapting the European acquis for social policy, the interviewee from MÜSİAD acknowledged that SMEs may encounter costs (Interview 70). Another interviewee claimed that Turkey's SMEs will not adapt social acquis until Turkey gains EU membership because doing so will increase production costs for SMEs while decreasing their competitiveness (Interview 82). Another socio-economic issue concerns refugees, who provide an important reserve army in the labour market for Turkey's SMEs. According to a MÜSİAD report on Syrian refugees, contrary to the pre-eminent prejudices that refugees are an economic burden, they contribute considerably to the economy by increasing the labour force. This has facilitated production by turning 'industry's wheels', solved recruitment problems for unskilled jobs and reduced labour costs while creating demand in the economy (MÜSİAD, 2018: 4). The MÜSİAD report highlights that Syrian refugees decrease employers' costs as refugees are willing to accept unskilled jobs for lower wages, especially in construction, seasonal agriculture and various other industrial sectors (MÜSİAD, 2018: 10).

Representatives of internationally and nationally oriented capital are not convinced by recent debates around shifting Turkey's Western orientation and foreign policy axis (Interview 87). Given that the EU remains Turkey's primary market, they interpret the growing anti-European discourse as political and conjunctural within the current populist era (Interviews 70 and 88). Similarly, they do not believe that alternative regionalisation models, such as the Shanghai Cooperation Organisation, or strengthening relations with Russia or Iran, can provide a realistic alternative to the EU (Interview 87). These countries are geographically too distant from Turkey, rendering trade more difficult (Interview 67). Moreover, neither business nor the bureaucracy has done any preliminary work to establish economic links with alternative geographies (Interview 69). Nevertheless, they acknowledge that in this conjuncture of populism and economic crisis, the EU has adapted a 'transactional' approach to Turkey, which aims to maximise short-term benefits through issue-specific cooperation (Interview 87).

Meanwhile, until a more conducive political climate emerges, representatives of capital argue that Turkey should further integrate with the EU by reforming the Customs Union or through security or energy cooperation (Bilecik, 2018). For instance, the head of İKV, Ayhan Zeytinoğlu, stated that 'revising and modernising the Customs Union is essential for the Turkish economy'

(Zeytinoğlu, 2020). There are four key issues for representatives of capital. First, Turkey faces difficulties in renegotiating its own free trade agreements once the EU has signed bilateral agreements with third countries (Zeytinoğlu, 2020). This generates asymmetries as goods entering the European market from these countries can also circulate freely in the Turkish market. This causes trade deflection as Turkey's products cannot circulate until the EU free trade agreement with the third party is also signed with Turkey (Interview 91). Second, representatives of capital expect the Customs Union to include additional sectors, particularly agriculture, services, transportation and public procurement (Interview 69). Third, a dispute settlement mechanism is needed (Zeytinoğlu, 2020). Fourth, the power relationship is also asymmetrical because Turkey does not participate in EU decision-making procedures despite being committed to the EU's foreign trade regime (Interview 67).

The struggle under conditions of authoritarian neoliberalism: the position of labour

Regarding the position of Turkish labour, interviewees from both internationally and nationally oriented labour described the conditions of the global working class in the 2010s as further deteriorating (Interview 89). Several factors were identified. First, globalisation has structurally failed to generate wealth while making distribution of income more unequal (Irgat, 2023), thereby worsening the working class's socio-economic conditions globally (DİSK, 2020: 3). Following the 2008 Great Recession, capital groups have implemented more aggressive policies vis-à-vis labour, which have prevented the latter from receiving a fair share of global wealth (Interview 89), resulting in increasing inequalities and an erosion of the middle classes (DİSK, 2020: 3). As Pevrul Kavlak, general secretary of Türk-İş put it, 'Globalisation promised heaven with wealth, employment, freedom and justice but transformed the lives of the working class into hell' (Kavlak, 2016). Second, neoliberalism has failed to consolidate democracy and develop human rights because it runs counter to organised societies (Kavlak, 2016). To directly quote the interviewee 'globalisation and labour movements are on the opposite sides as the former pursues labour exploitation while the latter works to construct organised societies' (Interview 30). Moreover, more authoritarianism is required to enforce market rule (DİSK, 2020: 3). Third, the COVID-19 pandemic negatively impacted labour, particularly as the interviewee from DİSK noted 'the COVID-19 pandemic did not generate a crisis for Turkey's manufacture in line with the decision of capital groups and the AKP government to keep industry's wheels turning under the lockdown' (Interview 89). Hence, whereas health and safety conditions forced a halt to production in developed countries, developing countries continued industrial production with the state resorting to its coercive mechanisms (Interview 89). In Turkey, for instance, employment during the COVID-19 pandemic increased by 20 per cent in factories where the United Metalworkers' Union is organised (Interview 89). The United Metalworkers' Union publicly announced how many workers were infected with COVID-19, thereby revealing that the numbers announced by the Ministry of Health did not reflect the actual numbers of infected people (Interview 89). Fourth, irregular migration has further worsened working standards. Syrian refugees in Turkey are mostly employed in the informal economy below the minimum wage and in unsafe conditions (Türk-İş Editorial, 2016). This not only generates unfair competition among labour groups inside Turkey but also causes unrest between unemployed and employed workers (Türk-İş Editorial, 2016). Capital groups have also used the presence of Syrian workers as leverage to downgrade social conditions and reduce real wages (Interviews 68 and 94). Meanwhile nearshoring has accelerated investments, particularly in eastern Anatolia, as enterprises employ migrant workers in the informal economy (Interview 89). Fifth, global capital groups have acquired power over national policies thanks to globalisation and they used this power to prevent Turkey from improving its public services, opening space for privatisation (Interview 96). Health and education should be 'public services' offering equal opportunity of access to each citizen (Interview 96). However, in cooperation with certain national capital groups, global capital first cut the resources of state hospitals, then declared that they were 'unproductive, ineffective and cumbersome' to open the way for privatisation (Interview 96). That is, in the last decade, thanks to globalisation, health and education have become new spheres for profiting (Interview 96). Globalisation has also negatively impacted agriculture, which has been dominated by large corporations, leaving smaller Turkish farmers unproductive (Interview 96). As one interviewee put it, 'globalisation replaced productive farmers with productive companies' (Interview 96). Despite these negative conditions, however, Turkey's labour movement has so far remained sidelined without developing the necessary capacity to produce an alternative (Irgat 2023). In addition, dissent at the societal level in Turkey is fractured by conservative policies as well as ethnic and identity politics (Irgat 2023).

Internationally oriented labour continues to defend its struggle at the international level (DİSK 2020: 4). Accordingly, there has not been any change in its representatives' position vis-à-vis membership – namely defending 'Labour's Europe' (Interview 89). There are three main reasons for this. First, thanks to its social dimension, the EU is still the only region-alisation model where income is more evenly distributed (Interview 68). One interviewee noted that 'the EU as a regionalisation model is the best so far in terms of rights acquired by the working class' (Interview 73), and continued by asking 'Why should Turkey take the Shanghai Coopera-tion Organisation as a model, a region where workers get $15 per day?' (Interview 73). Hence, for these representatives, the EU's socio-economic model constitutes a viable path for Turkey (Interview 68). Second, the EU provides an indirect mechanism to force Turkish employers to comply with social standards as European distributers require a value tag from Turkish producers (Interview 94). This requires Turkish employers to comply with various social standards, such as not abusing child labour and not harming nature or using particular chemicals (Interview 94). Although employers in Turkey often fire workers simply for unionising, those producing for European firms cannot do so due to European standards (Interview 73). As one interviewee put it, 'Ironically, Turkish employers comply with these standards so long as they are threatened with losing exports to the European market' (Interview 94). Third, the EU is an important reference point for consolidating Turkey as a secular and social state that respects the rule of law (Interview 71). Fourth, Turkish workers expect that free movement of workers in Europe will provide them with the possibility to migrate and find employment in European countries (Interview 94), which are preferred destinations due to better salaries and decent work conditions (Interview 94).

On the other hand, the interviewees from internationally oriented labour were also sceptical about EU membership on three grounds. They mostly compare Turkey's situation with Europe's periphery and the socio-economic conditions of the last EU enlargement wave. First, as the interviewee from Birleşik Metal-İş pointed out, 'there is a different European model in Eastern Europe' where wages and socio-economic conditions remain below the EU average (Interview 89). This refutes the argument that membership will improve Turkey's social standards (Interview 94). Second, defending EU membership on the expectation that it will consolidate democracy in Turkey has also lost ground (Interview 94). As one interviewee put it: 'Turkey has adapted the acquis and did not apply it. The EU has no sanction mechanism for non-compliance.' (Interview 89). Third, the expectation that 'enlargement will consolidate democracy, rule of law and human rights' has evaporated because these values are not consolidated even in some member states, such as Hungary or Poland (Interview 94). According to the interviewee from Türk Metal, the union prioritises internationalism, which is not limited to the EU (Interview 73) For instance, Türk Metal's president is also president of the International Eurasian Metal Workers Federation (IEMF), which represents fifteen million workers from fifty-six unions across twenty countries in Eurasia as of March 2020 (IEMF, 2022).

Representatives of nationally oriented labour continue to support EU membership with a discourse of an 'honourable membership perspective' (Interviews 76, 78 and 96). The EU is still an important reference for universal rights and Turkey has to reach this level of civilisation (Interview

76). EU membership is expected to improve the rule of law, human rights and democracy (Interview 78), while enterprises producing for the European market have to comply with social standards related to social dumping and/or firing workers for unionising (Interview 76). The reform process has also helped Turkey to systematise and institutionalise its agricultural regulations while EU membership could enable Turkey to become self-sufficient (Interview 78). However, this support is conditional, with the interviewees criticising the EU on three grounds. First, the EU reform process has not so far improved working conditions for labour, so the expectation that EU membership will improve social standards has vanished (Interviews 76 and 80). Indeed, delocalisation of production from the EU has actually reduced real wages in Turkey, not only in industrial sectors but also in public services with the 'Chinese growth model based on cheap labour' impacting all economic sectors and downgrading real wages in Turkey (Interview 96). Meanwhile, public services are increasingly privatised and subjected to market conditions, thereby worsening equal access (Interview 80). As one interviewee complained, 'Turkey should not be a centre of cheap labour for European capital' (Interview 96). Second, EU reform has changed the form but not the content of democracy in Turkey. In other words, the reforms have remained on paper without being implemented in practice (Interview 80). According to one interviewee, 'Democracies cannot be consolidated through international mechanisms such as the EU, but by national/domestic indicators' (Interview 96). That is, democracies can only be consolidated through organised and unionised societies (Irgat 2019). Third, the interviewees criticised EU policies vis-à-vis the Syrian refugee crisis as 'inhumane' in pushing people escaping from civil war away from Europe's borders (Irgat 2023). Moreover, according to the interviewee from Türk-İş, if relations with the EU remain limited to economic integration without the membership perspective and the social dimension, the stance of workers will become negative (Interview 76). Here, the interviewees from nationally oriented labour referred to internationalism rather than the EU per se. For instance, Türk-İş chairs the Turkish delegation on Labour 20, a platform uniting the trade unions of G20 countries to promote decent work throughout supply chains and ensure fair income distribution (Türk-İş Editorial, 2015).

Debate within political society: political parties and state institutions

Following its acceptance in the referendum on 16 April 2017, Turkey switched to a Turkish-type presidential regime run by a governing coalition called the People's Alliance, which was established in 2018 as an electoral alliance between the AKP and the MHP. The AKP defines Turkey's foreign policy as 'Turkey-centred, multidimensional and multilateral' while aspiring to make Turkey a 'global and regional actor' (AKP, 2018: 288; AKP, 2022). Within this strategy, it characterised EU membership as a 'strategic goal' (AKP, 2018: 295; AKP, 2022), while viewing European integration as a successful project for generating 'peace, economic prosperity and solidarity' (AKP, 2022).

However, the belief that Turkey will join the EU as a full member has evaporated as the AKP has become more sceptical of the EU. According to the AKP's Brussels representative, Ruhi Açıkgöz, 'the EU distracts attention' with the idea of full membership although he believes the EU will 'never' accept Turkey because it is 'too crowded, too Muslim and too poor' (Açıkgöz, 2020). The AKP also accuses the EU of failing to keep its promises regarding free movement of people and elimination of visa restrictions (Interview 81). It criticises the EU for failing to sympathise with Turkey after the 15 July 2016 coup attempt and for its complaints about democracy in Turkey during the state of emergency (Interview 81). The interviewee from the AKP also argued that the EU can neither formulate a common foreign policy nor become a global economic actor challenging China (Interview 81). However, the AKP remains committed to the EU reform process as 'Ankara standards' are 'instrumental' to reaching universal standards rather than making EU membership a goal in itself (AKP, 2022). Yet Turkey's foreign policy remains 'Turkey-centred' while the EU perspective should not hinder strategic cooperation with the US and Russia (AKP, 2018: 295–296). Moreover, it serves Turkish national interests to further develop its relations with near neighbours like Russia and other regional blocs, such as the Shanghai Cooperation Organisation, or other regionalisation models in the Middle East, Balkans and Caucasus (Interview 81). Turkey's foreign policy has to be multilateral through cooperating with Balkan countries, Turkish Republic of Northern Cyprus, Ukraine, the Caucasus, North Africa, Middle East, Latin America and Turkic Republics in Central Asia (AKP, 2018: 289–290). Meanwhile, Turkey can develop its cooperation with the EU on a selective basis, such as regarding migration, economics, transport and energy (AKP, 2018: 289).

The main opposition to the ruling People's Alliance is known as the Nation Alliance, composed of six parties – namely the CHP, Good Party (İyi Parti), Felicity Party, Democrat Party, Future Party and Democracy and Progress Party (DEVA). The Nation Alliance announced a common vision criticising Turkey's new presidential regime for fostering arbitrary governance centred around the President that has caused both economic and political crises (Nation Alliance, 2023: 11). Instead, they propose to revert to a strong parliamentary system that will consolidate participatory legislation, a transparent executive and an independent judiciary with strong checks and balances (Nation Alliance, 2023: 11 and 13). The new political vision aspires to upgrade Turkey's economy through digital and Green transitions and a sustainable development strategy (Nation Alliance, 2023: 75). Foreign policy will be reoriented around Atatürk's principle of 'peace at home, peace in the world' by emphasising dialogue, mutual respect for neighbours' territorial integrity and non-interference in their domestic affairs (Nation Alliance, 2023: 229). Foreign policy will no longer be used or abused for domestic and ideological political competition (Nation Alliance, 2023: 229). The opposition defines Turkey's EU membership perspective as a common goal while emphasising dialogue, equality and justice in Turkey–EU relations (Nation Alliance, 2023: 230). Finally, the alliance proposes that Turkey should join the European Digital Single Market and comply with the European Green Deal (Nation Alliance, 2023: 105 and 230).

Because the voting share of four parties in the Nation Alliance falls below three per cent, this study only analyses the views of the CHP and İyi Party (Cumhuriyet, 2023). In its 'Call for the Second Century', the CHP aspires to present a new vision for Turkey. It criticises the AKP's economic model for turning Turkey into a hub of 'cheap labour' producing low quality products while concentrating wealth around rentier groups (CHP, 2022: 55). As CHP general secretary Selin Sayek Böke describes it, 'This rentier economic model slaughters the climate and impoverishes society' (CHP, 2022: 55). The CHP also claims to save Turkey from the trap of premature deindustrialisation (CHP, 2020: 76). To do so, it proposes a new economic model, the 'New Age Development Strategy', with three priorities: technology, ecology and employment security (CHP, 2022: 10 and 56). This model will respect the Green transition, provide social justice, generate stable employment relations and adapt to the circular economy (CHP, 2022: 13 and 55). It equally calls for a return to orthodox economic policies, such as central bank independence, macroeconomic stability and low inflation (CHP, 2022: 11). Regarding foreign policy, the CHP criticises the AKP's approach towards Syria and Libya as 'interventionist and adventuresome' (CHP, 2020: 269). In addition, it claims that the new presidential system has created 'one-man' diplomacy while eroding established foreign affairs institutions and instrumentalising foreign policy for domestic political competition (CHP, 2018: 27). The CHP proposes instead to organise Turkey's foreign policy around four principles: respecting international law; prioritising citizens' wealth and security; multilateralism; integration and cooperation with global and regional blocs (CHP, 2018: 118–119). The CHP equally criticises AKP policies vis-à-vis the EU for constraining Turkey's membership perspective to a 'migration deal' and for generating unprecedented crises with European countries due to its 'aggressive and inconsistent' policies (CHP, 2018: 28; CHP, 2020: 271). There is still a consensus within the CHP that favours EU membership (Interview 79). Hence, the party has called for a revitalisation of accession talks and the reform process (CHP, 2018: 120; CHP, 2020: 271). An interviewee from the CHP believes that EU membership will generate economic growth, consolidate democracy and improve social standards (Interview 79). There is no alternative regionalisation for Turkey given its trade deficits with both Russia and China, while its initiatives in the Middle East have been unsuccessful (Interview 79). At the same time, however, the CHP also reiterates its concerns regarding national positions, such as the need for EU recognition of Turkish Cypriots' rights (CHP 2018: 120).

The İyi Party announced its party programme, named 'Turkey will be made good by the Good Party'. Its policies are centred around 'restoring liberalism' by returning to orthodox economic policies and strengthening the parliamentary regime. The party proposes a new 'stability and inclusive growth' model to reduce inflation, provide price stability and strengthen foreign reserves by guaranteeing central bank independence (İyi Party, 2022; İyi Party, 2023: 40). It emphasises inclusiveness while criticising AKP policies for generating 'social assistance addiction', particularly among lower income groups (Yılmaz, 2022). The İyi Party also acknowledges the transition within the global economy, highlighting that trade and finance are concentrated among countries that share similar political, economic and legal systems (İyi Party, 2022: 25). In this new global setting, Turkey's primary partner is the EU, so there is a need to revitalise the Customs Union while Turkey should adapt the European Green Deal and the digital transition (İyi Party, 2022: 25 and 26). The party also proposes legal guarantees for investors by restoring the rule of law (İyi Party, 2023: 41), and calls for the re-establishment of the parliamentary regime to safeguard checks and balances, the separation of powers and independence of the judiciary (İyi Party, 2023: 5). In foreign policy, it calls for multilateralism and emphasises Atatürk's principle of 'peace at home and peace abroad' (İyi Party, 2023: 62). The party sees Turkey as a 'lonely' country in its foreign policy while becoming closer to a 'Middle Eastern' country (İyi Party, 2023: 62). This will be corrected by developing relations with the EU and cooperating with Asia-Pacific countries (İyi Party, 2023: 62).

A third electoral alliance, the Labour and Freedom Alliance, was founded in August 2022 between the People's Democratic Party (HDP), TİP, Labour Party (EMEP), Labourist Movement Party (EHP), Social Freedom Party (TÖP), Party of the Greens and Left Future (YSGP) and Federation of Socialist Assemblies (SMF). The first major priority the alliance identified in its manifesto for the 2023 elections concerned the economic and social destruction of labour groups, farmers, peasants and artisans (Labour and

Freedom Alliance, 2023). It accuses the AKP of accumulating wealth for the capitalist class composed of participant enterprises and construction firms while reducing labour's share of national wealth (Labour and Freedom Alliance, 2023). Instead, the alliance proposes a 'decent economy model' to improve wages and working conditions for labour, support vulnerable groups through a 'social rights programme' and nationalise services to provide public services for all (Labour and Freedom Alliance, 2023). The second priority is ending 'one-man rule' by restoring democracy and strengthening the parliamentary regime and local administrations (Labour and Freedom Alliance, 2023). The third priority concerns the Kurdish problem. Accusing the AKP of securitising the Kurdish question, the alliance proposes to replace the government's 'denial and oppression' approach with a policy centred on finding a democratic solution for peace through dialogue (Labour and Freedom Alliance, 2023). More widely, the alliance aspires to promote peace among peoples by resisting the interests of imperialists and their domestic collaborators, ending expansionist military operations in Turkey's neighbourhood and adapting a peaceful foreign policy based on principles and equality for all peoples (Labour and Freedom Alliance, 2023). It proposes to finalise the readmission agreement, restore peace in the region for refugees who want to return to their countries and offer migrant status to refugees who prefer to stay in Turkey (Labour and Freedom Alliance, 2023). Regarding the EU membership perspective specifically, the HDP's İzmir deputy, Kürkçü, noted that the party's position has not changed (Kürkçü, 2017). That is, the HDP continues to support 'Labour's Europe' and to refer to internationalism in creating a Social Europe that respects human rights and supports the coexistence of the Kurdish population in Turkey through a peaceful solution (Kürkçü 2017). The membership perspective is still seen as providing decisive leverage to consolidate democracy and internalise the principles and institutions of human rights and the rule of law (Kürkçü 2017). The TİP, however, has developed a more critical tone. In its Revolution Programme, it considers the EU an imperialist power and proposes to resist any regional or global imperialist military and political ambitions of the EU, NATO and the US (TİP 2023).

As far as state institutions are concerned, those that are closely linked with the global economy continue to defend globalisation and EU membership. For example, the interviewee from the Central Bank considered globalisation as an inevitable 'evolution' in history (Interview 72). He pointed out that 'Globalisation has engendered a process in which competitive entrepreneurs were upgraded by integrating with the global supply chain while uncompetitive ones perished' (Interview 72). If countries reject globalisation, he argued, they would 'imprison their citizens to inefficient and expensive products' due to being stuck with goods only produced in the domestic market (Interview

No. 72). Yet in the 2010s, global trade has contracted with rising protectionism and political developments such as terrorism and the securitisation of border controls (Tüfenkçi, 2017). Nevertheless, Turkey continues to implement an export-promotion strategy and supports further liberalisation of global trade (Tüfenkçi, 2017). The 2010s were equally challenging for global politics as uncertainties have increased due to the COVID-19 pandemic and political and economic crisis (MFA, 2023). Conflicts and rivalry among states accelerated along with an erosion of multilateral institutions and respect for universal rights and principles (MFA, 2023). Within this historical context, the MFA prescribes Turkey's foreign policy in the 2010s as 'entrepreneurial and humanitarian' (MFA, 2023).

Regarding Turkey's EU membership bid, the interviewees acknowledged that the arguments in support of it have weakened in the last decade. For instance, there is no longer an expectation that membership will consolidate democracy in Turkey (Interview 75), while the fact that membership has not consolidated democracy in Poland and Hungary has further weakened the democratisation argument (Interview 100). Enlargement has not been on the European agenda with the EU preoccupied by internal problems following the eurozone crisis (Interview 75). Turkey–EU relations stagnated after the 2013 Gezi Park protests and 2016 coup attempt in Turkey (Interview 100) and were further damaged by the 15 July 2019 EU Council Decision, which suspended high-level political dialogue, and the Association Council meetings following an escalation of tensions with Greece related to Turkey's drilling activities in the Eastern Mediterranean (Interview 100). Consequently, Turkey's bureaucracy lost its pro-European mood and motivation (Interview 75). For instance, the interviewee from the Central Bank argued that the EU has neither the political vision nor the economic capability to enable Turkey's accession (Interview 72). To refer to the interviewee: 'The EU is outdated. Economically, it has even failed to save Greece with a population of eleven million, so I do not think the EU can contribute to the Turkish economy or politics' (Interview 72). Meanwhile, in global politics, the EU equally failed to react effectively to important foreign policy issues or define the main parameters of its relations with Russia and China (Interview 72). Other interviewees described Europe as an old continent that could no longer provide solutions to the world's current problems (Interviews 72 and 75).

The interviewees nevertheless acknowledged that there has been no change in Turkey's pro-membership perspective. Despite the negative political conjuncture, Turkey–EU relations have always continued at the institutional level without any rupture (Interview 75). According to the interviewee from the Directorate for EU Affairs, however, the EU suspended its rules-based institutional-structural dialogue with Turkey following the 15 July 2019 Council Decision, and instead uses 'ad hoc mechanisms' with high-level political leaders when needed (Interview 100). This redefines the EU's approach to Turkey as 'transactional' rather than on membership per se (Interview 100). This 'transactional approach' is related to the development of high-level political dialogue limited to particular policies prioritised by the EU, such as health, migration, agriculture, climate change and/or digitalisation (Interview 100). There is a tendency in the European bureaucracy to situate Turkey as a strategic partner or neighbour rather than as a candidate for full membership (Interview 100). However, the Ministry for Foreign Affairs still defines Turkey's EU membership perspective as a 'strategic priority' (MFA 2023), referring to EU norms and values, as well as the potential benefits of EU membership for Turkey. First, the EU acquis is still perceived in Turkey's bureaucracy as setting the stage for Turkey to comply with international norms and universal standards (Interviews 75 and 100). Second, Turkish entrepreneurs and representatives of capital will not give up on the European market because the two markets are so highly integrated (Interview 74). The EU is seen as a 'regulatory power' for setting standards internationally. Hence, compliance with European standards will increase Turkey's global economic competitiveness (Interview 100). For instance, Turkey has to comply with the Carbon Border Adjustment Mechanism and social standards in order to be competitive in international markets (Interview 100). Third, membership will bring political stability, which is an important anchor to attract FDI for Turkey (Interview 74). Fourth, the EU membership project is seen as part of a Westernisation project that should not be abandoned (Interview 75). Faruk Kaymakçı, Deputy Minister of Foreign Affairs and Director for EU Affairs, expects a positive agenda to update the Customs Union and Turkey's membership perspective while enhancing cooperation over migration, with the struggle against terrorism, and foreign affairs issues such as Cyprus, Syria, the South Caucasus and Libya (Kaymakçı, 2021). According to Gonca Işık Yılmaz Batur, Deputy Minister of Trade, the Customs Union should incorporate e-commerce, digitalisation and free movement of services (Batur, 2021). Turkey should benefit from EU funds related to the transition to Green economies and a circular economic model in line with the European Green Deal (Batur, 2021). Hüsnü Dilemre, former deputy undersecretary of the Ministry of Economics, also acknowledged that deepening the Customs Union through liberalising public procurements, services and agriculture will benefit Turkish entrepreneurs (Dilemre, 2017).

Those ministries that are developing policies for vulnerable groups take a more critical stance regarding globalisation and EU membership. Yet their critical stance is in line with the current populist conjuncture because their nodal point is nationalism and the role of the nation-state rather than improving the socio-economic conditions of vulnerable groups. For example, the former Minister of Agriculture and Forestry, Bekir Pakdemirli, claimed that globalisation threatens Turkey's agricultural self-sufficiency and creates monopolies in global trade, with just ten firms controlling 90 per cent of trade in agricultural products and 73 per cent of the seed market (Pakdemirli, 2021b). Moreover, historical developments in the 2010s, such as the COVID-19 pandemic, the ecological crisis and the war in Ukraine, show that agriculture is a strategic sector and that countries have to ensure food security for their populations (Interview 103). Countries have changed their policies to protectionism in trade, providing self-sufficiency and supporting local production (Pakdemirli, 2022). In March 2023, Turkey initiated legal changes in agriculture to support planned production and contract farming in order to guarantee sustainability and food security (Interview 103). Future projections are not promising as the global population and demand for agricultural products are expected to increase by 60 per cent whereas agricultural land area will remain constant (Pakdemirli, 2020, Interview 103). There is also the problem of scarce water resources, given that Turkey is categorised as a 'water stressed country' (Interview 103). Under these conditions, Pakdemirli predicts an increase in agricultural nationalism, self-sufficiency and local production and short-distanced supply chains (Pakdemirli 2020). Similarly, the Minister of Labour and Social Security, Vedat Bilgin, argued that globalisation and its neoliberal assumptions collapsed following the 2008 economic crisis (Bilgin, 2022). While capital mobility and technological developments continued in the 2010s, nation-states remain the main actors in the current conjuncture of geostrategic rivalry (Bilgin, 2022). Bilgin reads the conjuncture of the 2010s as the rise of the East with China and the Asian Tigers and the declining power and crisis of Western imperialist powers (Bilgin, 2023a). Within such a context, Western countries have returned to their former classical imperialist policies to restore their hegemony, such as provoking civil wars, sectarian conflicts and military coups, and weakening democracies (Bilgin, 2022; 2023a). Turkey is not exempt from such imperialist ambitions and it should resist Western imperialist policies in all its forms for the sake of its national interests (Bilgin 2022 and 2023a).

Those ministries that are developing policies for vulnerable groups also developed a more sceptical stance towards Europe, with imperialism as a nodal point. For instance, the Minister of Labour and Social Security, Vedat Bilgin, cannot see any long-term perspective for labour to improve deteriorating working standards and falling real wages due to soaring inflation in Turkey. Instead, he suggests short-term remedies, such as workers taking severance pay directly and eliminating the age requirement for retirement (Bilgin, 2023c). He articulates dissent with a nationalist rhetoric that emphasises the Western countries' imperialist policies while highlighting the 'greatness' of Turkey's economic and political developments: 'The Western countries are "irritated" by Turkey's 'economic miracle', democratisation and development in the defense industry under its new presidential system and it is currently "out of control" from Western imperialist influence' (Bilgin, 2023b). Thanks to Turkey's military drone technology, it is no longer only dependent on the 'residuals' of NATO assets militarily (Bilgin, 2023b). Similarly, the Deputy Minister of Environment, Urbanisation and Climate Change, Mehmet Emin Birpınar, also bases his criticism on imperialism and the environmental impact of Western modernisation. According to Birpınar, the West exploits developing countries through its imperialist policies, and abuses nature: 'The Industrial Revolution envisaged a development model that exploited air, water and soil savagely and mercilessly' (Birpınar, 2021a). Hence, the West cannot offer a model for Turkey; rather, it is the core of the problem (Birpınar, 2021a). Birpınar also refers to climate injustice by noting that developed countries have been the world's main polluters through historic greenhouse gas emissions, yet it is the developing countries which are expected to be hardest hit by the ecological crisis (Birpınar, 2021b). Birpınar suggests that 'Turkey needs to remember its own history when Turkey's older generations were not aware of the concept of "ecological literacy", but they were literate in ecology and lived in an environmentally friendly way without greed' (Birpınar 2021a).

However, this critique fails to provide a credible alternative. For instance, Pakdemirli endorses a liberal regime promoting Turkey's agricultural exports and searching for new regional and global markets (Pakdemirli, 2021a). Despite his criticisms of Western modernisation and its brutal environmental exploitation, Birpınar states that Chapter 27 on the environment within Turkey's EU accession negotiations remains open, and that Turkey has already aligned with sixty regulations (Birpınar, 2021c). Moreover, the EU's Green transition is in line with the double transitions to a cyclical economy and sustainable development (Birpınar, 2021b). The interviewee from TZOB acknowledged that if Turkey becomes an EU member or if the Customs Union is revised to include agriculture, then Turkish dairy and livestock farmers will be unable to compete with their North European competitors and will go bankrupt, whereas nut and fig farmers will do better (Interview 83). Most developing countries have to make concessions regarding their agricultural production in return for cultivating their manufacturing sector (Interview 77). Moreover, they also support EU membership to attract FDI and consolidate democracy (Interview 83). Although some Turkish farmers may be negatively impacted, EU membership will eventually help Turkey to modernise its agriculture while creating a register system and improving renovation (Interview 77). The interviewee from the Ministry of Agriculture and Forestry acknowledged that the EU's latest enlargement wave towards the Balkans was not promising for agricultural production (Interview 103). For instance, Polish agricultural production and farmers' welfare declined after Poland's accession (Interview 103). Hence, Turkey should not bear the burden of adapting to the Common Agricultural Policy without benefitting from structural funds and the free movement of people (Interview 103).

Struggles against the discipline of capital in the social factory of capitalism

Struggles in the social factory of capitalism have been negatively impacted by deglobalisation in the last decade. Despite debates over deglobalisation, global capital remains mobile whereas nation-states constrain labour mobility through nationalist policies and securitisation discourse (Interview 102). Meanwhile, the struggle for women's rights and feminism in Turkey experienced setbacks during the 2010s. For instance, Turkey withdrew from the Council of Europe, İstanbul Convention on Violence against Women with a presidential decree on the grounds that it normalises homosexual rights, which is supposedly incompatible with the country's traditional family and social values. These setbacks were reflected during the interviews. According to the interviewee from Kamer, for example, the public authorities have become less willing to listen to their concerns (Interview 84) while research grants for gender studies have declined at the European level (Interview 85). As the interviewee put it, 'women constitute one of the first categories to make sacrifices in times of crisis' (Interview 85).

The interviewee from the Human Rights Association highlighted that human rights was instrumentalised globally in the 2010s, with nation-states negotiating and making concessions regarding norms, institutions and human rights principles in return for boosting their national interests (Interview 102). For instance, although the International Criminal Court accused the Russian President Vladimir Putin of war crimes, Russia still retains its veto right in the UN Security Council (Interview 102). Regarding democratisation, Syria's civil war and the collapse of the Kurdish peace process both negatively impacted democratisation in Turkey (Interview 102), with freedom of expression, freedom of the press and the right to protest all being constrained (Interview 102). Meanwhile, Turkey's current economic crisis has further damaged socio-economic rights (Interview 102). These conditions are expected to trigger nationalism and empower the representatives of radical Islam in Turkish politics (Interview 102). One interviewee defined the current conjuncture as a 'period of uncertainty' because the rule of law has been discarded, with Turkey's executive now controlling the judiciary and weakening checks and balances while mostly relying on the will of the President (Interview

102). As the interviewee put it, 'The presidential regime has converted the state to a party-state', signifying the concentration of power in the executive (Interview 102).

Interviewees from organisations struggling for human rights referred to two important negative repercussions of neoliberalism that became increasingly clear in the 2010s. First, globalisation has triggered depoliticisation of society and eroded the public sphere and citizenship rights (Interview 105). The rights previously offered to citizens in the public sphere on an equal basis through rights-based politics have been transformed into 'social charity and social assistance mechanisms' that generate dependency on the political regime (Interview 102). Second, civil society has also developed in the private sphere, such that various activists now perceive themselves as professionals interested in improving their curriculum vitae rather than working for the public interest. Neoliberal policies since the 1980s have eroded the public sphere and commons, and encircled and transformed civil society, especially in the 2010s (Interview 105). As Bal (2022b: 490) notes: 'Turkish human rights CSOs [civil society organisations] have been neoliberally restructured and reproduced along with the new funding priorities, which turned solidarity into competition.' The interviewee from the Helsinki Citizens' Assembly expressed this point as follows:

> Turkey evolved into a 'consumer society' after the 2000s, which transformed every segment from space to ethics. The Gezi Park protests signified the citizens' efforts at defending the public space (the commons) but it was lost. The 'state' has started to be governed as a 'corporation'. Civil society is not exempt from this transition. However, this transition is contradictory to the spirit of civil society, which can only exist in the public sphere. I cannot believe how it is possible for a human rights association to conceive of people as a 'resource' to use, which shows us that managerialism has been internalised in civil society as well as a capitalist economic sector. However, the Helsinki Citizens' Assembly continues to resist working as a corporation and adapting managerialism (Interview 105).

The interviewees speaking about ecological struggle observed that they were marginalised in the 2010s. As the interviewee from Doğa put it: 'The state started to exclude civil society actors on the environment that raise ecological concerns related to state-funded or supported construction projects' (Interview 99). For instance, Doğa initiated its 'Stop Ilısu Dam, Save Hasankeyf' campaign in 2008 to save the archaeological site and increase public awareness to stop the dam project, which would flood the area in southeast Turkey. After the campaign's success in getting international financial donors to withdraw from the project, Prime Minister Erdoğan publicly linked Doğa with terrorism. Doğa's cooperation and dialogue with state officials was then ended while its membership started to decrease (Interview

99). Another milestone was the Gezi Park protests. As one interviewee put it, 'After Gezi, the government started to discredit civil society actors on the environment by describing them as "Chapulling (çapulcu in Turkish)", which translates approximately to looters or marauders' (Interview 99). Meanwhile, Doğa stopped its political activism and continued its struggle for nature through legal platforms (Interview 99). The political atmosphere in the 2010s also worsened the conditions facing migrants. The interviewee from TIAFI also criticised the EU approach to project management for being too professional and bureaucratic (Interview No. 101). It thus fails to develop an efficient approach to address real concerns of refugees and to empower them economically and socially (Interview 101). Since the 2010s, the anti-refugee atmosphere in Turkey has increased (Interview 106). During this populist era, the narrative that refugees are uneducated and a burden on European societies has spread (Interview 101). The current economic crisis and rising inflation in Turkey are worsening economic conditions for both migrants and poorer segments (Interview 106).

There is still support for EU membership among these interviewees. They argue that EU membership should be supported because of EU norms and values like democracy, humanitarian and universal rights (Interview 85). In particular, women's rights campaigners and feminist activists view the legal achievements related to gender struggle in the 2000s as a key reference, even if the government has neglected them in the last decade (Interview 84). For example, the EU reform process is appreciated for gender mainstreaming (i.e. incorporating a gender perspective in designing, implementing and monitoring policies to combat discrimination) (Interview 85). As the interviewee noted: 'Women's struggle in Turkey had a concrete achievement thanks to the EU reform process so that a gender perspective is incorporated into public policies and administrative structures institutionally' (Interview 85). The EU reform process has also generated a 'collective consciousness and a memory' related to gender (Interview 85). As the interviewee noted: 'This memory and legacy will not disappear although we have experienced an erosion in women's achievements globally' (Interview 85). Civil society actors related to migration had a positive stance regarding EU membership perspective because they expect that it will provide funding for migration (Interview 104). Turkey has also been accepted as a strategic partner in Europe's periphery protecting borders from mass flows. However, EU membership will make Turkey an equal member participating in the decision making without needing to sign a readmission agreement (Interview 104).

Yet these interviewees raised five main criticisms of the EU. First, they considered the EU as acting instrumentally and turning a blind eye to the democratic backlash in Turkey in return for Turkey acting as a buffer zone to keep refugees outside EU territory (Interviews 84 and 102). As mentioned below, there is no longer an expectation that EU membership will consolidate democracy in Turkey (Interview 86). In particular, the EU has not yet developed a mechanism for non-compliance with democratic standards (Interview 86). Moreover, political parties in EU countries are also being defeated by right-wing politics and populism alongside the erosion of the European public space (Interview 105). Second, the EU has turned a blind eye to women's employment in Turkey (Interview 86). As the interviewee noted: 'We have to be critical of the EU as well. Women's employment is around 75 per cent in the EU and 30 per cent in Turkey and the EU has failed to make it a priority' (Interview 86). The third criticism concerns the environment and imperialism. As the interviewee from Doğa put it: 'In addition to the EU's norms and values which are progressive, the EU has a dark side related to imperialism. The Ilısu Dam that destroyed Hasankeyf was financed by an Austrian firm' (Interview 99). Similarly, the interviewee from TEMA stated that:

> Multinational firms are two-faced because they have to respect environmental standards in their home country whereas they benefit from poor and flexible legislation on the environment in developing countries. I remember that a multinational firm was advertising Turkey on its website as a 'low-cost mining country' in exploiting resources while neglecting environmental standards. (Interview 98)

Fourth, the interviewee from the Buğday Movement criticised the Common Agricultural Policy for threatening local production in developing countries while prioritising European agricultural self-sufficiency (Interview 97). Moreover, the European model is based on a poor agricultural paradigm (Interview 97) because it is an outcome of the Green Revolution, which established modern industrial agriculture through standardisation, marketisation and mechanisation of production while promoting hybrid seeds (Interview 97). This model has enhanced the role of private firms while proletarianising farmers (Interview 97). More importantly, the Green Revolution conceives of soil as just a 'medium' that has to be planted using chemicals, pesticides and fertilisers (Interview 97). This model is disturbing the country's ecology, increasing the carbon footprint and disregarding the ecosystem (Interview 97).

According to one interviewee, the COVID-19 pandemic revealed that industrial agriculture cannot produce nutritious food, so humans need to take supplementary food in pill form from pharmacies (Interview 97). This paradigm should be replaced with regenerative agriculture (Interview 97). Within the Brown Revolution, a new agricultural paradigm is being constructed worldwide to repair soil by treating it as a living eco-system that has to be nurtured and protected, including its biology and micro-organisms (Interview 97). Regenerative agriculture buries carbon in the soil and concentrates on protecting the soil's micro-organisms (Interview 97). As the interviewee noted, 'human beings are not planting the soil, we are repairing its eco-system, which will then produce agricultural products naturally without the need for chemicals or fertilisers' (Interview 97). Furthermore, regenerative agriculture cannot improve health while protecting the environment and biodiversity (Interview 97).

Fifth, the interviewee from TIAFI[1] argued that Europeans have ignored the overall Syrian migration question while focusing on 'keeping Syrian refugees away from European territory' (Interview 101). During the 2000s, the EU shifted from a 'global approach to international migration' to a 'securitised approach' to control and protect Europe's borders while cooperating with countries in its near geographies to push mass flows on the periphery through readmission agreements in the 2010s (Interview 104). According to the same interviewee, although the developed countries' imperialist policies deepen inequalities and promote civil wars in developing countries, thereby triggering forced migration, these same developed countries, which generally benefit from migration flows, complain about forced migration when they cannot control it (Interview 104). As the representative from International Blue Crescent put it:

> International migration impacts the Global North and Global South differently. The Global North is taking advantage of its imperialist policies. They extract products in developing countries by ignoring environmental standards and benefitting from cheap labour for cheaper prices in global market. Yet developing countries will be hit more by ecological crises, and we will have climate migration in the future (Interview 106).

The interviewee from TIAFI also criticised the EU projects for being too professional and inefficient to empower refugees (Interview 101). As the interviewee put it:

> International organisations are not aware of the real conditions at the grassroots as they are mostly interested in collecting data, presenting data on migration in fancy hotels and spending their money for their salaries and research visits. They seem to be more interested in empowering their CV rather than refugees (Interview 35).

Conclusion

The social forces supporting pro-membership continue to defend EU membership. Turkey's internationally oriented capital still pioneers the EU membership perspective by repeating economic and political arguments in support of membership. In particular, they expect EU membership to consolidate the market economy and democracy in Turkey. However, they also refer to two new arguments by presenting the EU as a model for Turkey to join the Green transition and digitalisation. They note that market integration between Turkey and the EU was not disrupted by deglobalisation or the COVID-19 pandemic. Instead, the pandemic and disruptions to the global supply chain from China, coupled with rising wages in China, have consolidated Turkey's trade dependence on the EU market. Furthermore, nearshoring has been promoted by the West's geostrategic rivalry with China and new carbon taxes, which the representatives of Turkish capital expect to further stimulate EU–Turkey trade. Turkey's SME representatives also agree that trade with the EU market has accelerated in the last decade due to the AKP government's policy of 'keeping industry's wheels turning under lockdown' during the COVID-19 pandemic and the effects of nearshoring on the global supply chain. They continue to defend EU membership as a form of leverage to encourage Turkish SMEs to comply with international standards. Turkish SME representatives have changed their discourse regarding environmental standards from claiming that they were economically costly during the 2000s to a policy of complying with the European Green Deal due to European carbon taxes on the border. However, they are not willing to comply with EU social standards unless Turkey gains EU membership. The ruling AKP regime has become more critical of the EU in the last decade, particularly accusing the EU as insincere regarding Turkey's membership bid. Nevertheless, the party still sees membership as a strategic goal at the discursive level. Representatives from state institutions linked to the global economy continue to claim that globalisation is inevitable and therefore see EU membership as a strategic goal to enable Turkey to comply with international standards. They have become more sceptical, however, in tandem with the EU's rising protectionism and securitisation politics. They criticise the EU for losing in the global competition and for failing to develop a strong voice in global politics. And they also criticise the EU's approach to Turkey as transactional, particularly for downgrading Turkey's prospects from full EU membership to a strategic partnership to only cooperate regarding certain strategic policies, such as migration, health and agriculture. Nevertheless, these representatives also acknowledge that the bureaucracy has not yet abandoned the membership perspective.

Labour has been negatively impacted by the Great Recession, the COVID-19 pandemic, the migration crisis and the war in Ukraine. Economic crisis and rising authoritarianism have prevented labour from gaining a fair share of global wealth, leading to widening inequality. The interviewees criticised the AKP government's policy of 'keeping industry's wheels turning' under lockdown. Meanwhile, irregular migration has created a larger reserve army of labour, thereby increasing the pressure on labour to accept poorer working standards and wages. Within such a context, labour representatives have become more critical of EU membership, although they continue to come up with two alternative class strategies in the open-ended struggle. The social forces within Ha–vet still defend 'Labour's Europe' and internationalism, referring to the expectation that the EU's social model will produce better working standards if Turkey gains EU membership. Moreover, Turkish enterprises already producing for the European market have to comply with international labour standards, which representatives of labour can use to corner capital groups. They also expect the EU model to help Turkey consolidate its secular regime and social state. However, they also criticise the socio-economic conditions of Eastern Europe, highlighting that democratic credentials and working standards have not improved in recently acceded member states, particularly Poland and Hungary. The interviewee from Birleşik Metal-İş put it bluntly: 'there is another European model in Eastern Europe' (Interview 89). Hence, the expectation that membership can consolidate democracy in Turkey has evaporated. Indeed, the EU turned a blind eye to the democratic backlash in Turkey in return for Turkey keeping refugees away from Europe's borders. The position of Turkey's emancipatory left is seen in the Labour and Freedom Alliance, which considers the EU as providing significant leverage for democratisation and human rights. The TİP, however, describes the EU as an imperial power and calls for an end to the EU–Turkey readmission agreement.

Regarding neo-mercantilism as a rival class strategy, nationally oriented labour's EU perspective is based on the idea of 'honourable membership'. Its representatives acknowledge that the EU is a model for democracy, human rights and social standards. Furthermore, the EU reform process has helped Turkey systematise its agricultural production. However, they have also been critical of the EU, particularly because the EU reform process has not improved socio-economic conditions for Turkish labour with particular industrial sectors in Turkey implementing the Chinese growth model on cheap labour. They also question the assumption that the EU can consolidate democracy in Turkey. Instead, they argue that democracies can only be improved through organised societies and internal dynamics. In addition, they criticise the EU's migration policy as 'inhumane' in pushing Syrian and other refugees away from Europe's borders. Indeed, the Türk-İş representative was openly negative about EU membership unless it enabled Turkey to benefit from the EU's social standards, regional and structural funds and free movement of workers. Turkey's main political opposition group, the Nation Alliance, also supports EU membership, emphasising the need for Turkey to comply with the Green Deal and the digital transition. However, they also want to revitalise Turkey's membership bid through further dialogue conducted on an equal and just basis.

Note

1 TIAFI (Team International Assistance for Integration) was founded in 2017 as a non-profit grassroots organisation in İzmir. It opened a large community centre in Tepecik to increase self-sufficiency, empowerment and integration for vulnerable Syrian and Turkish families. It started by providing physiotherapy for disabled refugee children from war-torn Syria. It currently provides a wide range of services, such as free hot lunches, helping refugees familiarise themselves with Turkey's asylum system, health and school services, exercise programmes for children with disabilities and skill-development activities for women and children. For more information, please see https://tiafi.org.

Conclusion

The Political Economy of Turkey's Integration into Europe: Uneven Development and Hegemony aimed to analyse Turkey–EU relations as an instance of class struggle within the uneven and combined geographical expansion of capitalist accumulation. It embarked on historical materialism with an emphasis on two analytical categories: hegemony and uneven and combined development. As such, it aspired to fill two gaps in the literature in particular. First, existing studies fail to situate Turkey's European membership trajectory within the structural dynamics of globalisation. However, Turkey stands on the periphery of Europe and its trajectory of integration with the global political economy can hardly be read independently from its integration with Europe. Turkey's elimination of trade protectionism through the Customs Union is not only related to reducing trade protectionism vis-à-vis European products but encompasses liberalisation for global trade, given that Turkey complies with the EU's common external tariff. During the 1990s, Turkey also implemented macroeconomic policies under EU and IMF guidance and surveillance, with the EU playing a decisive role in ensuring Turkey's compliance with structural adjustment policies. Second, the pre-eminent tendency in Turkey–EU relations is to analyse political decisions without an emphasis on how social forces in Turkey position themselves vis-à-vis globalisation and EU membership perspective. This book aimed to fill these gaps through generating primary data collected from interviewees representing social forces regarding their positions vis-à-vis globalisation and Turkey's EU membership perspective during the 2000s and 2010s. The analyses were presented as a hegemonic struggle to problematise ongoing power relations and the socio-economic content of integration of Turkey to European structures without limiting the debate to the question of whether Turkey will become a full member or not.

The book discussed whether there was a hegemonic pro-European project in the 2000s that pioneered EU membership negotiations and, if so, who were the social forces behind it. It then considered the social forces disadvantaged by globalisation with the potential to form an alternative historical bloc opposing EU membership and neoliberal restructuring. I examined whether these social forces could form a united front and, if not, why there was no alternative to neoliberal restructuring. The book then analysed the position of these social forces during the 2010s in a historical conjuncture characterised by deglobalisation and authoritarian neoliberalism. It investigated how pro-membership social forces have continued to defend the pro-membership project within a historical context identified with crises of liberalism and questioned whether the critical tone of these disadvantaged groups has intensified to develop an alternative in the current populist conjuncture.

In the book, representatives of capital and labour are analysed in relation to international and nationally oriented fractions. Despite rising FDI stocks as a share of GDP in Turkey, especially after the 2000s, trade remains the main mechanism of Turkey's integration with globalisation. Accordingly, in Chapters 3 and 5, I discussed class struggle in relation to internationally and nationally oriented fractions of capital and labour. Textile and automotive industries were examined as internationally oriented given their privileged position within Turkey's exports while the SMEs, the agriculture sector and public sector were considered as nationally oriented. Though I expected internationally oriented forces of labour and capital to support an open economy and EU membership, nationally oriented capital and labour are supposed to be more critical due to pressures over competitiveness and their preference for protectionism and national subsidies. Transnationalisation rose in the 2010s, with the ratio of FDI stock to GDP increasing from 15 per cent in 2010 to 27 per cent in 2019. However, FDI inflows fluctuated because of speculative capital. Hence, in Chapter 5, intra-class struggle in the 2010s was also discussed in relation to internationally and nationally oriented forces of capital and labour. Yet class struggle is not limited to particular industrial sectors. It was conceived in the social factory of capitalism and struggles around identity politics were approached as class struggle as well. Here, I drew on van der Pijl's claim that 'the issue is no longer that "capitalism" is showing signs of collapse … What is failing today is not capital but the capacity of society and nature to support its discipline' (van der Pijl, 1998: 48). Accordingly, I inserted struggles around patriarchy, the environment, migration and human rights into the research design as instances of class struggle against the discipline of capital in the field of social reproduction. These social forces were expected to contest Turkish membership of the EU and neoliberal restructuring.

In approaching the state, I criticised the pre-eminent tendency in the Turkish political science literature of treating it as a *sui generis* entity of the 'strong state' tradition (Buğra, 1994; Heper, 1985; Keyder, 1987). This, in my view, is problematic for three reasons. First, the strong state tradition treats the state as having a rationality and 'substantive ends' of its own (Yalman, 2009: 160 and 200). Second, it depicts the main struggle in society as one of elites versus people (in a populist sense), which masks class struggle. Third, it treats the state and civil society as well as politics and economics as external to and autonomous from one another. This takes the state as a 'black box' beyond human agency, while identifying civil society as a progressive sphere for democratisation. However, as discussed in Chapter 3, civil society also works as 'fortresses and earthworks' (Gramsci, 1971: 238), which has helped Turkey's ruling class to transcend their vested economic interests and present their project on a universal terrain by gaining consent from the subordinate classes in society around the pro-membership project. As debated in Chapter 3, although the interviewees from civil society claimed to present 'expert' opinions as independent knowledge, these institutions have organic links with capital. Yet they contribute to present neoliberal restructuring as 'common sense' with the social function of presenting ideas associated with membership as universal. Hence, they can be considered as 'trench-systems' in the war of position. Conversely, in Chapters 4 and 5, I argued that women rights/feminist, environmental and human rights struggles in civil society have the potential to develop a counter-hegemonic historical bloc.

In the Introduction, I reviewed the literature on Turkey–EU relations to highlight three specific gaps. First, previous studies have limited the debate to the form of EU enlargement, neglecting the socio-economic content and failing to problematise the power relations of Turkey's ongoing integration into European structures. Second, the literature is compartmentalised in that the European studies literature ignores the structural dynamics of globalisation whereas the political economy literature mostly considers structural change without integrating Europe into Turkey's neoliberal restructuring. Third, the literature mostly relies on political decisions without generating empirical data while the labour perspective is completely neglected. To fill these gaps, the book presented a critical political economy perspective by drawing on historical materialism with reference to two analytical categories: hegemony and uneven and combined development. This approach has the merits of integrating the structure into analysis, considering the socio-economic content of Turkey's ongoing integration with Europe, and presenting the struggle over the trajectory of Turkey's membership bid as an instance of class struggle.

This book did not confine its consideration of class struggle to the forces of capital and labour in Turkish society. As explained in Chapter 1, the crux of the issue is to integrate struggles of political recognition within identity politics such as gender, the environment and human rights into the research design. This is also related to the theoretical discussion within Marxism. Is historical materialism class reductionist and economic essentialist, as critiqued by post-Marxist and poststructural research? Does historical materialism fail to explicate political struggles following social changes like advanced capitalism, deindustrialisation, post-industrial societies and rising individualism? Chapter 1 engaged in a dialogue between historical materialism and Laclau and Mouffe's *Hegemony and Socialist Strategy* (1985) and Hardt and Negri's *Empire* (2000). In *Hegemony and Socialist Strategy*, Laclau and Mouffe accuse historical materialism of class reductionism and economic essentialism. They aspire to go beyond historical materialism by radicalising hegemony in order to integrate plural and radical forms of social antagonisms in society around the project of radical democracy. This political praxis of radical and plural democracy, they claim, can encompass struggles for both economic 'redistribution' and political 'recognition' within Leftist politics (Laclau and Mouffe, 1985: xv and xviii). Similarly, in *Empire* (2000), Hardt and Negri assert that 'postmodernisation of the global economy' requires a rethinking about political subjectivity, with industrial labour being replaced with immaterial labour and multitude in information economies (Hardt and Negri, 2000: 28 and 29; 2004).

In Chapter 1, I criticised post-Marxist research for five reasons. First, concurrent with Wood (1981: 70), post-Marxism and poststructuralism take capitalism's structured separation of economics and politics for granted, which in turn 'de-socialises the material'. The neglect of the material from postmodernist critical thought results in a 'theoretical retreat from the problem of domination within capitalism' and strategically fails to repoliticise capitalism (Žižek, 2000: 97). Second, I noted that the Gramscian notion of the integral state and ethical state not only captures the role of the capitalist state per se in the struggle over hegemony, but conceives of civil society as a sphere where hegemony is both contested and consolidated. In contrast, *Hegemony and Socialist Strategy* undertheorises the state and fails to contest neoliberal civil society. Coupled with Laclau and Mouffe's separation of politics and economics, their analyses operate within the neoliberal order's separation of the state and civil society. My third criticism concerned the status of the 'international' sphere in the hegemonic struggle. In the post-Marxist conception of hegemony, the international sphere is not salient in the hegemonic struggle. Contrarily, historical materialist scholarship not only considers class struggle within the uneven and combined development of capitalism but also discusses the struggle over hegemony in the national context within the context of the international. My fourth objection was related to historicism. By claiming a break with past forms of industrial society, Laclau and Mouffe eliminate the possibility of analysing capitalist development historically. Finally, post-Marxism conceives of structure as hindering freedom and emancipation while articulating particularisms within identity politics. Yet, they completely turn a blind eye to social totality and the capitalist discipline. Concurrent with Sim (2000: 31) authority is confused with authoritarianism. Moreover, in agreement with Wood (1995: 1) this closes the possibility of countering the totalising power of capitalism.

Based on these theoretical objections, I argued that historical materialism does not necessarily exclude struggles of political recognition. The research then adopted Bieler and Morton's ontology of internal relationship in conceptualising the international sphere, which allowed me to integrate the contradictions around patriarchy, the environment and human rights as instances of class struggle in the nexus of the extended social factory (Bieler and Morton 2018: 133–134). Similarly, van der Pijl argues that it is the 'discipline of capital over the entire reproductive system' and its 'exploitation of the social and natural substratum' that has to be resisted (van der Pijl, 1998: 36 and 47). Federici (2012: 7) describes the social factory as the extension of capitalist discipline to such an extent that 'the distinction between society and factory collapses, so that society becomes a factory and social relations *directly become relations of production*' (emphasis in original). Accordingly, the current struggle over Turkey's EU membership bid is observed as resistance to the forms of social reproduction imposed by capitalist discipline. Understanding the struggle as such paved the way to include struggles around patriarchy, the environment, migration and human rights as an instance of class struggle in the social factory of capitalism.

Chapter 2 then provided the historical background for the following empirical analyses of the positions of different social forces regarding globalisation and Turkey's EU membership perspective. It discussed Turkey's state–society relations by situating it within the country's integration into the global political economy, focusing on the main coordinates of the class struggle during three periods: the Fordist period of the 1960s and 1970s; the neoliberal turn in the 1980s; and the post-2008 authoritarian neoliberal period. In the 1960s and 1970s, Turkey adapted the ISI model in tandem with Fordist accumulation and a developmentalist state. I characterised Turkey–EU relations at this time as a tug of war due to the controversy regarding the envisaged trade liberalisation with the EEC versus industrialisation and development under the ISI model. Concurrent with Yalman (2009: 30), Turkey's transition to neoliberalism in the 1980s is read as a passive revolution. In the absence of a bourgeoisie to provide moral and intellectual leadership for the neoliberal accumulation strategy based on export promotion, the military coup was instrumental in containing labour and limiting its resistance to liberalisation. In 1987, Turkey applied for full EU membership and began tariff reductions for European products. I argued that the neoliberal hegemony was strong enough to endorse completion of the Customs Union as a prelude to membership. Turkey's neoliberal restructuring encompassed financial liberalisation in the 1990s, paving the way for inflow of speculative short-term capital followed by vicious cycles of growth, crisis and adjustment, with the Turkish economy suffering from crises in 1994, 1999 and 2001.

Then I read AKP's hegemony as an instance of *trasformismo* – the 'formation of an ever more extensive ruling class' (Gramsci, 1971: 58), which I supported with two reasons. First, this hegemony extended the ruling class by integrating SMEs, and has consolidated neoliberal restructuring through financialisation, despite presenting itself as a rupture from previous corrupted right-wing governments. Second, the AKP disarticulated dissent by appealing to those social forces in society disadvantaged by globalisation. To do so, it adopted a populist discourse that presented the main division as centred on identity politics – namely 'the people' versus 'the Kemalist bureaucratic and military elite'. In line with Cox's claim that *trasformismo* works 'to co-opt potential leaders of subaltern social groups' (Cox, 1983: 166–167), the AKP regime has co-opted those social forces disadvantaged from globalisation with the potential to come up with a progressive alternative to the neoliberal project. However, the chapter concluded that the AKP has not developed a political agenda to institutionally improve labour conditions. Furthermore, it has aligned itself with social mechanisms around charities, in line with a hyperliberal form of state that prioritises individualistic welfare mechanisms.

I then considered the 2010s in terms of rising authoritarian neoliberalism following the Great Recession and growing contradictions of accumulation based on financialisation in the global economy and the growth strategy of emerging markets. Globalisation and financialisation accelerated inequalities as mobility and liberalisation for capital reduced corporate taxes while putting labour movements into competition with each other to attract investments. I noted that Gramscian historical materialist scholars read the period following the Great Recession as authoritarian neoliberalism and a crisis of neoliberal hegemony. During this period, a significant segment of social forces withheld consent for neoliberalism while capital groups were unable to provide moral and intellectual leadership around neoliberal hegemonic projects due to neoliberalism's contradictions. Instead, the neoliberal form of state resorted to coercive mechanisms with the ruling class less willing to take consent from subordinate forces and instead marginalising them (Bruff, 2014: 113). As van der Pijl (2019: 257) argues, populist leaders rely on a politics of fear by misrepresenting and distorting facts, simply because they cannot offer any material rewards for the majority in society.

Turkey's state–society relations in the 2010s are also identified as authoritarian neoliberalism with rising contradictions in the growth pattern and the state's coercive mechanisms following the Gezi Park protests, the 15 July 2016 coup attempt, and the change to a presidential regime. I particularly referred to three contradictions of dependent financialisation – namely the pattern of 'jobless growth' and declining real wages, dependence of growth on demand from core capitalist countries and the structural demand-gap due to wealth concentrations and rising inequalities. Concurrent with Bedirhanoğlu et al. (2020: 3) the state form is characterised by 'the privatisation and personification of state power, the rise of coercion, discretionary economic management, and the crippling of basic modern state institutions through processes such as deconstitutionalisation and Islamisation'. During the 2010s, the social forces underpinning the AKP regime dissolved as large and medium-sized enterprises abandoned the bloc because of the government's unorthodox economic policies, while liberal intellectuals also withdrew their support. At this point, the AKP formed a coalition with the nationalist MHP, named as the People's Alliance. As Marois (2019: 132) remarks, financialisation disadvantages the popular classes and labour groups. Indeed, Turkey is one of the worst ten countries for workers (ITUC, 2023). Labour conditions further deteriorated after the COVID-19 pandemic with the capitalist classes realising that the changing global supply chain provided an 'opportunity' to attract investments into Turkey through a low-wage policy. Yet, despite deteriorating socio-economic conditions, the popular classes and particular labour groups have continued to support the AKP regime. This is explicated with reference to coping mechanisms, such as AKP's neoliberal form of social policy that substitutes the welfare state with welfare governance, its assistance programmes, populist politics around identity politics and AKP's financial inclusion policies. Here, I particularly referred to Uzgel (2020: 66) who reminds us that 'after all, neoliberalism is not only about the markets and the states, but also about how to administer a society that lives with declining wages, higher consumerism and a huge increase in consumer debt'.

The following three chapters presented my empirical findings. Chapters 3 and 4 framed the struggle in the 2000s around three projects. There is not a single pro-membership project and a single alternative project (as presumed by the hypothesis). Instead, the contours of Turkey's struggle were much more complex: while the pro-membership project was hegemonic in the 2000s, it was contested by two rival class strategies: namely neo-mercantilism and Ha–vet. The pro-membership project was supported by internationally oriented capital, SMEs, the AKP and state institutions related to the global economy. In line with the hypothesis, internationally oriented capital led the pro-membership perspective. Its representatives expected EU membership to stimulate exports and economic growth, provide competitiveness, enable technology transfer and safeguard a functioning market economy and macroeconomic stability – which were seen as decisive factors in stimulating FDI. They welcomed the neoliberal turn in European integration that revisits social policy by prioritising the workplace around social partnership and the conditioning of employment to economic growth.

Contrary to the hypothesis, representatives of nationally oriented capital – SMEs and the agricultural sector – also supported membership. They read globalisation as inevitable, suggesting a strategy of creating internationally competitive 'national champions' as the only viable strategy for survival under globalisation. They have already become integrated with the transnational production structure via outsourcing and contract manufacturing, in parallel with the delocalisation of production. This resonates with the argument of Robinson, who notes that transnationalisation is a process of decentralisation and fragmentation of transnational production, and that it operates through 'multilayered networks of outsourcing, subcontracting, collaboration, and so on, that increasingly link local and national agents to global networks' within which agents either 'globalise or perish' (Robinson, 2004: 14, 15, 19 and 20). I observed that nationally oriented capital has already experienced the effects of liberalisation engendered by the Customs Union – either through bankruptcy or by adapting to new conditions. Hence, they were no longer concerned about integration into the EU's Internal Market. So, they also saw the membership perspective as a process that could help Turkey's nationally oriented sectors adapt to international rules and standards. This industrial disciplining would enable them to operate competitively in international markets. There was a fraction within the agriculture sector, however, which adapted a critical stance because they believed Turkish farmers would be unable to compete with European competitors, leading to the closure of many small farms, thereby creating impoverishment and unemployment. However, such a perspective was marginalised. In the 2000s, the AKP government also defended the pro-membership project for providing economic development and consolidating democracy. In line with Cox's analysis on the 'internationalisation of the state', those state institutions closely linked to the global economy – such as the Central Bank, Ministry of Commerce and Industry, the Ministry of Foreign Affairs, and the Secretariat General for EU Affairs – defended the membership perspective to consolidate the market economy model and guarantee compliance with international rules, while maintaining security for Turkish markets – all key factors to attract FDI. These interviewees also believed that the EU membership perspective has been a state policy since the republic's establishment and throughout its modernisation project. They also argued that the EU provided a 'stronger anchor' for consolidating democracy given that Turkey's own societal base is too weak to ensure it.

Chapter 3 also concluded that pro-membership was hegemonic in the 2000s. Gramsci conceives of hegemony as a moment when the ruling class transcends its economic-corporate interests and takes on a role of 'moral and intellectual leadership' by posing the questions on a 'universal plane' (Gramsci, 1971: 181–182). I argued that pro-membership was hegemonic in the 2000s on two grounds. On the one hand, the project was no longer debated in relation to the narrow economic interests of the dominant class and/or class fraction. Social forces transcended their vested economic interests in defending the membership perspective, successfully articulating a hegemonic world view by delivering persuasive ideas covering a wide range of issues, including social policy, foreign policy, democratisation and modernisation. They have done so to such an extent that the reform process was carried out in the 2000s without explicitly focusing on actually attaining membership status. It was possible to observe this hegemonic position in the AKP policy of the 2000s vis-à-vis the reform process codified as 'turning Copenhagen criteria into Ankara criteria', signifying that it was in the interests of Turkey to carry out the EU reforms, even though Turkey would not become a full member in the future. On the other hand, the hegemonic status of pro-membership became further apparent in civil society, where particular institutions played a decisive role in presenting ideas associated with membership as 'universal', while cultivating 'objective and scientific' knowledge claiming their independence due to being financially independent from state. However, I read this process as providing the 'fortresses and earthworks' (Gramsci, 1971: 238) for the hegemonic project. That is, these civil society institutions opened particularly sensitive issues up to public debate by asking 'experts' – 'traditional intellectuals' in a Gramscian sense – to write opinion papers. These institutions presented the membership perspective as progressive – a process that consolidates democracy and civilises politics by moving it away from the conception of the 'strong state'.

I then argued in Chapters 3 and 4 that the pro-membership project was contested by two rival class strategies in the 2000s: neo-mercantilism and Ha–vet. Although they were critical to particular aspects of EU membership, neither offered an overall alternative. Neo-mercantilism ended up supporting 'membership on equal terms and conditions', while Ha–vet articulated a struggle at the European level – a position that can be neatly summarised with its motto: 'Another globalisation and Europe is possible'.

The Ha–vet was underpinned by internationally oriented labour, emancipatory left-wing political parties and struggles against capitalist discipline in the extended social factory. In line with the hypothesis, internationally oriented labour representatives (the textile and automotive industries and DİSK) supported membership, though with a different rationale from those social forces underpinning the pro-membership project. They criticised globalisation for generating de-unionisation and flexible work. Yet internationally oriented labour was not concerned with the pressures of competitiveness from joining the EU's Internal Market. Rather, globalisation was taken as a 'fact' that has undermined – 'dynamited' even – the struggle at the national level (Interview 15). Hence, the only viable strategy for struggling against globalisation was defending the internationalisation of labour. They also supported Social Europe as a regionalisation model for turning globalisation to the benefit of workers. Moreover, as the economic effects of participating in the Internal Market had already been experienced under the Customs Union, the economic struggle was already lost. Thus, they interpreted the EU membership perspective in terms of issues around social policy and democratisation. The representatives of internationally oriented labour argued that the European Social Model was progressive in contributing to improving working conditions in Turkey. Additionally, they expected EU membership to strengthen civil society and democratisation by constraining the mechanisms of the 'strong state'. European integration was also seen as a 'peace project' that could help Turkey solve problems in Cyprus, mend its relationship with Greece, and better address the Kurdish and Armenian questions.

Contrary to my hypothesis, social democratic parties and Kurdish political parties, which I analysed as the 'emancipatory left', also supported Ha–vet during the 2000s. While this fraction criticised globalisation for generating inequality and income disparity, they also accepted it as a fact to be resisted through a struggle at the international level. Kurdish political party representatives also supported membership in the expectation that regional funds and the free movement of workers could help Turkey's eastern region solve its economic problems. They also expected that democratisation through EU reforms would help Turkey to scrutinise human rights violations, while membership would decentralise politics, shifting state power to supranational and local levels. Contrary to expectation, representatives from the struggles against the capitalist discipline, such as human rights, patriarchy and the environment, supported EU membership on political grounds. They expected membership to improve the conditions of women and human rights and consolidate democracy through strengthening civil society, while curbing the strong state and its 'military tutelage'. They also supported the EU's role in helping to find a democratic solution to the Kurdish problem.

During the 2000s, the pro-membership perspective was contested by another rival class strategy – neo-mercantilism – led by nationally oriented labour analysed through Türk-İş, the agriculture sector and public employees, and supported by centre-left political parties and state institutions developing policies for disadvantaged groups. It is only the representatives of nationally oriented labour who were concerned about the repercussions of integrating with the Internal Market and criticised globalisation on the grounds of deindustrialisation. However, they were divided on the socio-economic consequences of EU membership. While some representatives expected protection from globalisation through the EU's structural funds, others expected further liberalisation through EU membership. They also claimed that the European Social Model would place labour under the tutelage of capital and operate as a mechanism justifying imperialist exploitation. In this view, workers in developed and developing countries cannot cooperate as long as imperialism endures. They also did not see that EU membership would consolidate democracy in Turkey because democracies can only be consolidated by domestic dynamics. The centre-left political parties could not come up with an alternative economic model other than a form of social market economy. That is, they have internalised competitiveness as essential for economic growth while promoting policies for alienating distortions of the market economy, such as employment, equal income distribution and the welfare state. Accordingly, they supported EU membership for stimulating competitiveness and facilitating technology transfer. They also referred to probable contributions of the European Social Model as well as regional and structural funds to improve socio-economic conditions in Turkey. Thence, criticisms of social forces within neo-mercantilism were constrained to national sensitivities – including the Cyprus problem, and the Kurdish and Armenian questions – as well as any suggestion of a 'special status or privileged partnership' for Turkey. Here, they accused the EU of discriminating against Turkey and asking for unilateral concessions that damaged Turkey's national interests. They saw the EU as an imperialist bloc trying to dismember Turkey and articulated the nation-state as a viable site for the struggle against imperialism. They offer conditional support for EU membership, provided it provides 'membership on equal terms and conditions' whereby Turkey benefits from structural funds and the free movement of workers.

Chapter 4 also investigated whether social forces disadvantaged by globalisation could come up with a united stance against the discipline of capital, and highlighted three reasons why they could not. First, their representatives considered the economic aspect of the struggle lost, with the anti-globalisation movement fading after the 1990s. In the case of Turkey–EU relations, interviews argued, the economic dimension of the struggle had already been lost after Turkey joined the Customs Union. Moreover, interviewees from struggles around patriarchy, human rights and the environment conceived the economy as secondary. Almost all of the interviewees from these struggles interpreted the Customs Union as a 'technical' issue. Their structural critique to capitalist power remained weak, which was theoretically in line with the critical stance of post-Marxism and poststructuralism to the material sphere, as discussed in Chapter 1. For instance, the former president of Kesk even argued that 'workers will automatically be emancipated in Turkey when a democratic and peaceful solution to the Kurdish problem is founded' (Interview 80). Second, interviewees criticised previous forms of organising within the labour movement as hierarchical, while prioritising pluralist forms of struggle. As such, they internalised political liberalism while ignoring economic liberalism, and failed to problematise the structure of capitalist social relations, making it more difficult to develop a structural anti-capitalist agenda. As one interviewee put it, 'I got divorced from Marxism' because 'sexual hierarchy is just as important as class hierarchy' (Interview 36). Third, they distanced themselves from the rhetoric of organising around a mass movement based on classical institutions of representative democracy, such as trade unions and political parties. Rather, they prioritised a social movement rhetoric and small, horizontally organised groups, mostly founded in a flexible, ad hoc manner.

Chapter 5 reconsidered the struggle among Turkey's social forces in the 2010s in a historical conjuncture of crises of liberalism, rising populism and far-right politics. My empirical research uncovered that there has been no change in the position of social forces supporting the pro-membership perspective. Representatives from internationally oriented capital continue to defend membership, with arguments that EU membership will increase competitiveness, consolidate democracy, establish rules-based foreign policy, and that membership is the end-state of Turkey's two hundred years of modernisation project. However, I argued that pro-membership is no longer hegemonic. Social forces supporting the pro-membership hegemonic project encounter difficulties in providing 'moral and intellectual leadership' for subordinate social forces in society. The arguments that membership will consolidate democracy and open up space for civil and political liberties in Turkey are not convincing with the rise of the far-right in European politics. Here, interviewees particularly mentioned the argument that newly acceding member states from Central and Eastern European countries could not consolidate their democracies, referring to populist leaders such as Victor Orbán. The argument that the EU could help Turkey to consolidate a peaceful foreign policy based on rules and dialogue is unconvincing, with the rising nationalism and war in Europe. Hence, pro-membership arguments focus on the economic vested interests of the capitalist class. Actually, representatives of internationally oriented capital have developed two new arguments in the 2010s in defending membership. On the one hand, they present the EU as a model for the Green transition to tackle the ecological crisis by replacing the linear economy with a circular economic model. On the other hand, they see the EU as an anchor for digital transformation. Yet these arguments cannot go beyond the economic-corporate phase and defend membership at a universal level. They are far removed from providing moral and intellectual leadership by projecting a model encompassing different dimensions – from ecology to agriculture, foreign policy to migration.

Indeed, the pro-membership project encounters difficulties in presenting the struggle in political society with convincing arguments that are able to transcend the economic-corporate phase to the complex superstructural level in the hegemonic struggle. To quote Bates, hegemony is a form of rule by a particular class which is able to convince society about the validity of its world view (Bates, 1975: 352 and 355). On the one hand, the AKP no longer promotes the membership perspective although it still keeps EU membership as a strategic priority in its official documents. Instead, especially following the 15 July 2016 coup attempt, its representatives criticise the EU on the grounds of acting insincerely and breaking its promises regarding Turkey's membership, particularly the free movement of people and visa liberalisation. For instance, the AKP's Brussels representative Ruhi Açıkgöz argued that the EU would not take Turkey as a full member as Turkey is 'too crowded, too Muslim and too poor' (Açıkgöz, 2020). The EU is also seen as failing to become a global foreign policy actor. On the other hand, representatives from the state institutions closely linked with the global economy uncovered that they cannot convince social forces to comply with the EU acquis. Although these state institutions continue to see EU membership as a strategic priority, they acknowledge that arguments in favour of member-ship have weakened. As an interviewee put it, 'there is only one argument that is convincing for social forces to comply with EU acquis which is that the EU norms and rules are significant to set the stage for Turkey to comply with international standards' (Interview 100).

Yet the structural power of capital provides the opportunity for pro-membership social forces to determine the main coordinates of Turkey–EU discussion with two pioneering arguments: the EU is the main market for Turkish exports; and the EU anchor is needed for international competitive-ness. Representatives from internationally oriented capital noted that they have not experienced deglobalisation or protectionism. On the contrary, trade with the EU has increased in parallel with China's decreasing role in the global supply chain, policies prioritising nearshoring due to geostrategic rivalry with China and consideration of the environmental crisis and the greater carbon footprint of trading with distant geographies. They also referred to falling real wages in Turkey, especially after the COVID-19 pandemic. Representatives from nationally oriented capital also acknowledged that trade with the EU has accelerated in the last decade due to disruptions from China in the global supply chain and larger carbon footprints from long-distance trade. They argue that the EU is Turkey's principal export market and source of FDI inflows. Moreover, Turkey's SMEs have become institutionally integrated with the European structure. For instance, TOBB president Rıfat Hisarcıklıoğlu is also Eurochambres' vice president. Although

SME representatives are concerned about the EU's Carbon Border Adjustment Mechanism, they have revised their earlier view that 'the EU's environment acquis is economically costly'. Now they have adapted a new strategy acknowledging the need to align with the Green Deal.

Regarding the position of social forces supporting rival class strategies during the 2010s, representatives from both internationally and nationally oriented labour argued that labour conditions have worsened due to capital's more aggressive strategies following the 2008 economic crisis, rising inequality and labour failing to gain its fair share from income. The COVID-19 pandemic further deteriorated labour conditions. To quote the interviewee from DİSK: 'The COVID-19 pandemic did not generate a crisis for Turkey's manufacturers in line with the decision of capital groups and the AKP government to keep industry's wheels turning under the lockdown' (Interview 89). Irregular migration has also negatively impacted Turkey's labour due to the informal employment of migrants below the minimum wage, and increasing labour unrest while enlarging the reserve army. Despite these deteriorating conditions, dissent has been sidelined and fractured through identity politics in the populist era.

There has not been an overall alternative to the pro-membership project in the 2010s either. To recall Yalman (2021: 16) on alternatives to neoliberal restructuring, the crisis did not generate a crisis of hegemony because of the absence of a systemic alternative challenging pre-eminent power blocs and hegemonic class forces, particularly from the working classes. Social forces within Ha–vet and neo-mercantilism maintain their support for membership. However, they increase their critical tone to the European project related to modernity, ecology, individualism, economic disparities and/or the democratic credentials of European countries. The representatives from labour are more critical about the economic and social repercussions of EU membership. Referring to the last EU enlargement wave, they highlight that socio-economic conditions and wages in eastern Europe have not improved with membership. The interviewee from Birleşik Metal-İş claimed that 'there is a different European model in eastern Europe' (Interview 89). Interviewees from nationally oriented labour acknowledged that the EU reform process has not improved wages or the socio-economic conditions of labour in Turkey. Instead, it triggered the privatisation of public services and suppressed wages. As one interviewee noted, 'Turkey should not be a centre of cheap labour and a hub of procurement for European capital' (Interview 96). Moreover, rising socio-economic disparities between northern and southern members of the EU, as well as the failure of the EU project to generate economic convergence among member states, cause Turkish labour to increase its critical tone regarding the economic arguments for membership.

The political argument for EU membership is also unconvincing. The interviewees acknowledged that the democratisation argument evaporated after Turkey adapted, but did not implement, the acquis related to the rule of law and democracy. Moreover, the experience of democratisation through EU reforms demonstrates that democracies can only be consolidated through domestic societal dynamics, rather than through an international anchor like the EU. The representatives from struggles in the social factory of capitalism were also more critical of the EU, especially for ignoring Turkey's democratic backsliding as long as Turkey acts as the EU's buffer zone for refugees. Representatives from struggles against patriarchy accused the EU of ignoring women's low employment level in Turkey. The interviewees talking about ecological struggle highlighted that ecological crisis is an outcome of European modernity. Moreover, individualism and greed are embedded within European capitalist societies. To quote the interviewee from TEMA: 'Multinational firms are two-faced because they have to respect environmental standards in their home country whereas they benefit from poor and flexible legislation on the environment in the developing countries' (Interview 98). The interviewee from Buğday argued that Europe has a poor agricultural paradigm based on modernisation, standardisation, marketisation and a conception of soil as a 'medium' to be planted with chemicals and pesticides. This model is causing an ecological crisis and has to be replaced with a regenerative agricultural paradigm which will repair the soil and improve the ecological system. According to the Deputy Minister of Environment, Urbanisation and Climate Change, Mehmet Emin Birpınar, 'the Industrial Revolution envisaged a development model that exploited air, water and soil savagely and mercilessly since modernisation' (Birpınar, 2021a). Interviewees also criticised the EU on migration policy. They noted how the EU's migration policy has shifted from a global approach to a securitised approach focused on controlling its borders. Moreover, they claimed that the imperialist countries, including European member states, caused the migration problem by promoting civil wars, and that they benefit from migration flows, although they only complain about uncontrolled migration.

Ha–vet is far from providing an alternative to the pro-membership project. It can hardly transcend its economic-corporate phase and present a universally appealing bloc. Indeed, social forces underpinning the Ha–vet strategy end up supporting membership in the absence of an alternative regionalisation model. Their representatives continue to defend Labour's Europe and struggle at the international level. They see Europe as the best example of regionalisation in terms of equal distribution of income and its social policies. As one interviewee put it: 'Why should Turkey take the Shanghai Cooperation Organisation as a model, a region where workers get $15 per day?' (Interview 73). Moreover, workers employed in enterprises exporting to the EU benefit from the EU's value tag, which forces Turkish enterprises to comply with its social standards. To refer to the interviewee from Tekstil-İş: 'Ironically, Turkish employers comply with these standards so long as they are threatened with losing exports to the European market' (Interview 94). The membership perspective is also supported for free movement of workers and to consolidate a secular regime in Turkey. Regarding 'emancipatory left' political parties, the Labour and Freedom Alliance has not changed its membership stance and defends Labour's Europe. It sees EU membership as a leverage to consolidate democracy and help find a peaceful solution to the Kurdish problem. The TİP, however, conceives of the EU as an imperialist bloc, calling to resist any regional association with the EU, NATO or the US.

Representatives from struggles against the discipline of capital in the social factory of capitalism acknowledged setbacks in women rights and human rights, with worsening socio-economic conditions and the government being less willing to listen to their concerns. For example, representatives from environmental struggles highlighted that they were marginalised following the Gezi Park protests. Representatives from human rights groups acknowledged that human rights, as a category, has been instrumentalised in the 2010s, with nation-states giving concessions from international rules and norms while negotiating in their national interests. Conditions for human rights in Turkey deteriorated following the Syrian civil war and the collapse of the Kurdish peace process. Moreover, the rising economic crisis in Turkey is likely to further damage socio-economic rights. The interview from İHD defined the current political conjuncture as a 'period of uncertainty' with the political authority discarding the rule of law within the context of concentration of power around the executive (Interview 102). Moreover, neoliberalism, that has been implemented in the last four decades, has constrained the public sphere, the commons and transformed civil society in the private sphere. It has also promoted depoliticisation, substituting rights offered to citizens on an equal basis with social assistance mechanisms. Conditions for struggles around migration also worsened in the 2010s within a context of populism, the politics of fear and rising alienation of migrants. However, they maintain their support for EU membership for its norms and democratisation. For example, interviewees combatting patriarchy perceive the EU as setting international standards to improve women's conditions, with the EU reform process contributing to gender mainstreaming in Turkey. Representatives from struggles around migration expect funding from the EU.

Regarding social forces within neo-mercantilism, they also end up levelling their support to membership 'on equal terms and conditions' during the 2010s. EU membership is expected to improve democracy and social standards while helping Turkey to reach to the level of contemporary civilisation, a goal set by Atatürk during the founding of the Republic of

Turkey. Neo-mercantilism does not stand as an alternative either. As a rival class strategy, its ideas concerning economic and social policy echo a long defeated Keynesian welfare regime, in which the priorities are protecting national industries, tripartism and moderate income redistribution under state supervision. Social forces supporting neo-mercantilism are structurally disadvantaged within the neoliberal world order. As they articulate corporatism and forming alliances with nationally oriented capital, they are further defeated by the inclusion of nationally oriented SMEs within the transnational production structure. This defeat has constrained opposition to national interests – meaning it focuses on issues such as discrimination against Turkey regarding Cyprus, Greece, and the Kurdish and Armenian issues – and protests against privileged partnership.

Turkey is on the periphery of Europe and its integration into European structures constitutes an example of the uneven and combined development of capitalism. It's unevenness stems from market integration through the Customs Union which has opened Turkish market to European firms without any social dimension such as free movement of workers, structural and/or regional funds. In a nutshell, unevenness is generated through the pre-eminence of negative integration (market liberalisation) without positive integration (any integration pattern to ameliorate the negative consequences of market liberalisation). In the 2010s, the uneven and combined nature of Turkey's integration with Europe was consolidated. As the interviews revealed, global supply chain disruptions and geostrategic rivalry with China have encouraged nearshoring, which has increased Turkey's production during the COVID-19 pandemic and the AKP government's decision to 'keep industry's wheels turning' even under lockdown. Interviews uncovered that declining real wages and deteriorating social standards have been significant for Turkey to substitute China as a more trustable partner in the global supply chain.

Yet the analytical category of uneven and combined development is not limited to understanding the origins of capitalism and can be extended to uncovering the dynamics of social class relations in the global political economy. Here there was uneven and combined development in the management of migration for the labour market in the 2010s between Turkey and the EU. The inflow of a highly skilled labour force is a priority for European business. For instance, BusinessEurope published a position paper on 'The Future of EU Migration Policy' stating that it aims to develop 'A European migration policy that facilitates the recruitment and retention of skilled third country nationals' (BusinessEurope, 2019: 1). They defend it for the future of the Digital Single Market and tackling the ageing labour force in Europe. The report presents some demographic highlights such as the projection that people in Europe over 65 would increase to 51 per cent of the population and that the EU population would decrease to around 60 million by 2060 (BusinessEurope, 2019: 3). The BusinessEurope paper differentiates between EU policies for refugees and the integration of highly skilled labour force. It states that 'the migration of skilled workers and the integration of refugees are separate issues and need to be viewed separately' (BusinessEurope, 2019: 2). Accordingly, the Blue Card is promoted as a major positive driver to attract skilled labour to be employed in the Single Market. However, the EU has developed policies to externalise immigration to non-member third countries through policies such as stricter border management and visa policies as well as readmission agreements when faced with increasing migration pressures from irregular migrants and asylum seekers following the mid-2000s (Yıldız, 2016: 1). To quote Yıldız (2016: 204), 'the EU's externalisation of its immigration policy is more likely to be perceived as shifting the burden of keeping unwanted migrants onto non-member transit countries, rather than sharing the burden with them'.

In recent years, the brain drain from Turkey and youth emigration has been a major issue. In the Turkish Youth Study 2023, researchers questioned 2,140 young people aged between 18 and 25 located in sixteen provinces all around Turkey (Turkish Youth Study, 2023). One of the significant findings of the study is that 63 per cent of participants said that they preferred to live abroad, with 47 per cent of respondents mentioning better living conditions and 20 per cent mentioning freedoms (Turkish Youth Study, 2023: 7). The number of migrants from Turkey increased by 62 per cent compared with 2021, and reached 466,914 in 2022 (TUIK 2024). Almost half of these migrants are between 20 and 30 years old (TUIK 2024). Doctors emigrating from Turkey is notable, following the privatisation of health, rising precarious conditions in the health sector and deteriorating working conditions under the COVID-19 pandemic. For instance, a report published by İstanbul Policy Centre highlights that the Ministry of Health does not publish numbers of doctors emigrating, though doctors who apply for 'good standing certificates' from the Turkish Medical Association uncover their intention to move abroad (Güzel, 2024: 2). Applications for these certificates increased by 91 per cent from 2022 to 2023, with the number of Turkish medical doctors in Germany increasing from 995 in 2015 to 2,160 in 2022 (Güzel, 2024: 3).

It is also plausible to conclude that the 2010s has proved liberalism wrong in the sense that market freedoms through economic neoliberalism has not consolidated democracy and/or improved political liberties. Turkey, as one of the pioneering countries adapting neoliberal restructuring as a passive revolution in the 1980s in the peripheral context, and experiencing neoliberalism and market freedoms through political Islam and populist politics since the 2000s, is not an exemption. Moreover, Turkish enlargement constitutes an example of the limits of formal democracy and how the

EU reform process has not contributed to consolidating democracy in a candidate country. These observations resonate with the writings of scholars affiliated to the critical political economy literature related to the relationship between democracy and capitalism. According to Ayers and Saad-Filho (2015: 602), democracy and capitalism are incompatible simply because capitalism generates economic disparities constraining political democracy. As such, neoliberalism sterilises democracy and constrains it to elections as a result of the depoliticisation of socio-economic struggles (Ayers and Saad-Filho, 2015: 604). Indeed, Ayers and Saad-Filho (2015: 603) argue that only 'formal democracy' can prevail under neoliberalism. Similarly, Munck (2005: 66) names democracy under neoliberalism as 'thin and anaemic' while 'politics is marketed like any other commodity'. Crouch identifies the current era as post-democracy as the political sphere has been preoccupied by a group of privileged and corporate elites, which is similar to the pre-democratic period (Crouch, 2004: 6 and 104). Moreover, the digitalisation and surveillance capacities of the state have contributed to oppressing dissent.

Yet the future trajectory is uncertain considering that 'hegemony is never constant but always contested' (Bieler, 2005: 466). However, it is possible to observe certain coordinates that provide hints for the future dynamics of class struggle. Capital may prefer to maintain the current status quo, whereby open trade is guaranteed by the Customs Union while avoiding the costs associated with implementing European social standards. My interviews revealed that a consensus remains among both fractions of capital that the EU is an important reference point for Turkish capital's compliance with international rules and standards. Moreover, they have become integrated with the European market without shouldering the economic burden of aligning with the European Social Model. The SME representatives openly stated that they would not align with the EU's social policy without Turkey becoming an EU member state. This is why they defend adaption of the social acquis conditional on Turkey gaining EU membership. Yet the social forces underpinning rival class strategies increased their critical stance vis-à-vis membership in the 2010s. The EU's stance is transactional, which prioritises particular strategical policies such as migration to cooperate with Turkey. Labour groups have also raised criticisms following the experience that membership has not improved social standards in eastern European member states. Social forces within neo-mercantilism have already declared that they consented to the process on the condition of benefitting from agricultural and structural funds and the free movement of workers. In the absence of a social dimension, they may oppose the membership perspective. Ultimately, it is the future coordinates of the global political economy and class struggle which will determine the future of Turkey–EU relations.

The local elections of March 2024 generated hope for the opposition. The AKP lost its majority as it acquired 35 per cent of votes, while the CHP won 37 per cent. The CHP won the largest three cities – İstanbul, Ankara and İzmir – and acquired a majority in the metropolitan councils. Moreover, elections tripled female majors from 4 to 11 out of 81 provinces and female candidates won in 64 districts out of 922 (Karataş, 2024). Although women's rights and the feminist movement has been negatively impacted by both neoliberal restructuring and conservatism under political Islam, especially in the last two decades, rising female leadership in the political sphere is generating hope. Moreover, there is more criticism of the AKP presenting itself as a complete break from previous corrupt right-wing governments. As Buğra and Savaşkan (2014: 195) discuss, the Islamic economic development model differentiates itself from the Western capitalist system, which is criticised as 'individualistic' and 'selfish' in terms of its motive of accumulation. The *homo Islamicus* is supposed to be different from Western *homo brutalism* with an emphasis on Islamic ethical norms and informal mechanisms of solidarity and philanthropy (Buğra and Savaşkan, 2014: 195). This societal vision envisages that Islamic moral principles would guarantee 'fair treatment' to workers while invalidating 'Western' institutions such as collective bargaining and/or class struggle (Buğra and Savaşkan, 2014: 197). However, rising wealth concentration, disparities in the distribution of income and deteriorating economic conditions, especially for middle and lower income groups, coupled with high inflation, are all putting the relationship between capitalism and political Islam into question. As Samir Amin (2007) reminds us, 'Political Islam is not anti-imperialist, even if its militants think otherwise.' The pre-eminence of culture and religion in the political sphere has helped to conceal the structural power of the ruling class and the problem of domination within capitalism. Rising criticisms may open more space for repoliticising socio-economic struggles and capitalist discipline as well as discussing alternatives in the future coordinates of class struggle.

Interviews

Interview 1: Former consultant of Press and Public Relations of Türk-İş (1995–2000 and 2002–07); Ankara, 28 January 2008.

Interview 2: Former president of Hak-İş between 1995 and 2011; Ankara, 29 January 2008 (author and Prof. Dr. Mustafa Türkeş).

Interview 3: Former international coordinator of TÜSİAD between 2008 and 2016; former general secretary, Turkish Industry and Business Association (TÜSİAD); telephone interview, 2 April 2010.

Interview 4: Former chair of External Relations and EU Affairs Committee, Turkish Industry and Business Association (TÜSİAD) and adviser to chair of the Administrative Board of Doğan Holding; İstanbul, 9 April 2010.

Interview 5: Former deputy secretary general and coordinator to EU Affairs, Independent Industrialists and Businessmen Association (MÜSİAD); İstanbul, 12 April 2010.

Interview 6: Former president, Textile Workers' Union (Tekstil-İş), former president of DİSK (1994–99) and former deputy from the Democratic Left Party (DSP); İstanbul, 13 April 2010.

Interview 7: Former chair of the Industry, Services and Agriculture Committee, Turkish Industry and Business Association (TÜSİAD) and vice president of Kibar Holding; İstanbul, 19 April 2010.

Interview 8: Former president of the Confederation of Progressive Trade Unions of Turkey (DİSK) between 2000 and 2011; İstanbul, 20 April 2010.

Interview 9: Secretary general, İstanbul Chamber of Industry; İstanbul, 20 April 2010.

Interview 10: Secretary general, OSTİM Industrial Zone; Ankara, 29 April 2010.

Interview 11: Assistant to president of Hak-İş, responsible for international relations; Ankara, 5 May 2010.

Interview 12: Former chief adviser of Türk-İş, responsible for international relations (1993–2003), former alternate member of Executive Board of European Trade Union Confederation (ETUC), former director of education of Trade Union for Road, Building and Construction Workers (YOL-İŞ); Ankara, 7 May 2010.

Interview 13: President, Textile, Knitting, Clothing, and Leather Industry Workers' Union of Turkey (Teksif); Ankara, 7 May 2010.

Interview 14: Specialist, Research, Education and Foreign Affairs, Turkish Confederation of Employer Associations (TİSK); Ankara, 10 May 2010.

Interview 15: Former Brussels representative, Confederation of Progressive Trade Unions of Turkey (DİSK) and former coordinator for EU–Turkey Trade Union Coordination Committee; Ankara, 10 May 2010.

Interview 16: Chair of Eczacıbaşı Holding and TÜSİAD honorary chair, former member of European Roundtable of Industrialists (ERT); interview by e-mail; 20 May 2010.

Interview 17: Former president, Öz İplik-İş (Real Trade Union for Workers in Weaving, Knitting and Garment Industry affiliated to Hak-İs); Ankara, 15 December 2010.

Interview 18: Former general education secretary, Real Trade Union for Workers in Food and Tobacco and Beverages Industry (Öz Gıda İş – affiliated to Hak-İs); Ankara, 16 December 2010.

Interview 19: President, Türk Tarım Orman-Sen (Union of Public Employees in Agriculture and Forestry of Turkey); general secretary for foreign affairs, Confederation of Unions of Public Employees of Turkey; Ankara, 20 December 2010.

Interview 20: Former deputy secretary general, Union of Turkish Agricultural Chambers; Ankara, 22 December 2010.

Interview 21: Former international relations expert, Eğitim Sen (Education and Science Workers' Union); Ankara, 23 December 2010.

Interview 22: Former president, Birleşik Kamu-İş (Confederation of United Public Workers' Unions); Ankara, 24 December 2010.

Interview 23: Former president, Real Trade Union for Workers in Agriculture, Land and the Water Industry (Öz Tarım-İş); Ankara, 28 December 2010.

Interview 24: Former president, Confederation of Unions of Public Employees of Turkey; Ankara, 29 December 2010.

Interview 25: Former secretary for Press and Public Relations, Memur-Sen (Confederation of Public Servants Trade Unions); Ankara, 30 December 2010.

Interview 26: Former general secretary, Automotive Manufacturers Association; İstanbul, 7 January 2011.

Interview 27: Former expert, Statistics and Research, Turkish Textile Employers' Association; İstanbul, 7 January 2011.

Interview 28: Former deputy director general, Turkish Exporters Assembly (TİM); İstanbul, 10 January 2011.

Interview 29: President, Birleşik Metal İş (United Metalworkers' Union affiliated with the DİSK); İstanbul, 11 January 2011.

Interview 30: Former president of Confederation of Public Employees Trade Unions (Kesk); İstanbul, 11 January 2011.

Interview 31: Expert, responsible for press, TOBB, telephone interview, 28 April 2011.

Interview 32: Former president of Ka-der; İstanbul, 14 April 2010.

Interview 33: Former member of executive committee, Ka-der; İstanbul, 21 April 2010.

Interview 34: Member of former Leftist Progressive Women's Association, former president of Ka-Der; İstanbul, 21 April 2010.

Interview 35: Former president of ÇYDD (Association for Modern Living); İstanbul, 22 April 2010.

Interview 36: Radical feminist, founder of Ka-der, former president of Purple Roof Women's Shelter Foundation; 27 April 2010.

Interview 37: Former president of Human Rights Association (İHD); Ankara, 27 April 2010.

Interview 38: Former president of Mazlumder; Ankara, 27 April 2010.

Interview 39: Former head of department of EU and Foreign Relations, KOSGEB; Ankara, 29 April 2010.

Interview 40: Former director of research and currency policy, Central Bank of Turkey; Ankara, 30 April 2010.

Interview 41: Expert, EU Coordination Department, Ministry of Labour and Social Security; Ankara, 3 May 2010.

Interview 42: Member of consultation board of Ka-der and member of executive committee of European Women's Lobby; Ankara, 4 May 2010.

Interview 43: Member of Ka-der and European Women's Lobby (EWL) coordinator for Turkey; Ankara, 4 May 2010.

Interview 44: Former member of parliament from Peace and Democracy Party; Ankara, 5 May 2010.

Interview 45: Religious/conservative feminist, Capital City's Women's Platform; Ankara, 6 May 2010.

Interview 46: Former director, Directorate for Political Affairs, Secretariat General for EU Affairs; Ankara, 11 May 2010.

Interview 47: Former director, Directorate for Single Market and Competition, Secretariat General for EU Affairs; and former director in Undersecretariat of Foreign Trade; Ankara, 11 May 2010 (Author and Prof. Dr. Mustafa Türkeş).

Interview 48: Former deputy director general for EU, Ministry of Foreign Affairs; Ankara, 13 May 2010.

Interview 49: Former deputy director general for industry, Ministry of Industry and Commerce; Ankara, 13 May 2010.

Interview 50: Former president of State Planning Organisation (DPT); Ankara, 13 May 2010.

Interview 51: Expert, Office of Relations with the European Union, Central Bank of Turkey; Ankara, 13 May 2010.

Interview 52: Former chief of the section responsible for the EU, Ministry of Agriculture and Rural Affairs; Ankara, 14 May 2010.

Interview 53: Expert, section for EU Affairs, Ministry of Foreign Affairs; Ankara, 14 May 2010.

Interview 54: Former secretary general, Democratic Left Party; Ankara, 14 December 2010.

Interview 55: Co-founder, former board member and former deputy chair (administrative and financial affairs), Justice and Development Party; Ankara, 22 December 2010.

Interview 56: Former deputy chair responsible for elections and legal affairs, Republican People's Party; Ankara, 22 December 2010.

Interview 57: Former head of the Directorate of Single Market and Competition, Secretariat General for EU Affairs; Ankara, 28 December 2010.

Interview 58: Former deputy chair between 2003 and 2010, Republican People's Party; Ankara, 29 December 2010.

Interview 59: Former deputy of İzmir and deputy chair of the National Action Party (MHP); Ankara, 30 December 2010.

Interview 60: Former coordinator and member of Foreign Affairs Commission, Peace and Democracy Party (BDP); Ankara, 30 December 2010.

Interview 61: Feminist activist, Socialist Feminist Collective; İstanbul, 11 January 2011.

Interview 62: Project coordinator, Helsinki Citizens' Assembly; İstanbul, 12 January 2011.

Interview 63: Former unit-head of campaigns, Green Peace Mediterranean; İstanbul, 13 January 2011.

Interview 64: Former deputy chair responsible for administration and finance, Republican People's Party; İstanbul, 14 January 2011.

Interview 65: Woman activist, former scholar and co-director of Women's Studies and Implementation Centre of İstanbul University; İstanbul, 12 January 2011.

Interview 66: President of Kamer; London, 10 February 2011.

Interview 67: Former general secretary, Automotive Manufacturers Association (OSD), İstanbul, 14 November 2016.

Interview 68: Former general secretary, DİSK Tekstil İşçileri Sendikası, İstanbul, 15 November 2016.

Interview 69: Former general secretary, Turkish Exporters Assembly, İstanbul, 22 November 2016.

Interview 70: Expert, coordinator of Economic Research, MÜSİAD, İstanbul, 22 November 2016.

Interview 71: Former president of DİSK, İstanbul, 23 November 2016.

Interview 72: Director of research and currency policy, Central Bank of Turkey, Ankara, 30 January 2016.

Interview 73: President of Türk Metal, Ankara, 1 February 2017.

Interview 74: Director, Directorate of Economic and Financial Policies, Secretariat General for the EU Affairs, Ankara, 1 February 2017.

Interview 75: Former director, Directorate for Accession Policy, Secretariat General for EU Affairs, Ankara, 1 February 2017.

Interview 76: Former adviser to president, Türk-İş, 2 February 2017, Ankara.

Interview 77: Coordinator, Directorate General of European Union and International Relations, Ministry of Food Agriculture and Livestock, Ankara, 2 February 2017.

Interview 78: President, Türk Tarım Orman-Sen, 6 February 2017, Ankara.

Interview 79: Former deputy from İzmir between 2002 and 2014, Republican People's Party, Ankara, 6 February 2017.

Interview 80: Former president, Kesk, Ankara, 7 February 2017.

Interview 81: Former head of economic affairs, Justice and Development Party, Ankara, 7 February 2017.

Interview 82: Expert, Department of the European Union, Union of Chambers and Commodity Exchanges of Turkey (TOBB), Ankara, 8 February 2017.

Interview 83: Adviser to president, Union of Turkish Agricultural Chambers (TZOB), Ankara, 10 February 2017.

Interview 84: President of Kamer, telephone interview, 30 May 2019.

Interview 85: Former head of İstanbul University Centre for Women's Studies, member of Women's Library and Information Centre Foundation Board, telephone interview, 12 June 2019.

Interview 86: International relations coordinator, Women's Coalition Turkey, telephone interview, 21 June 2019.

Interview 87: Leader of roundtable global relations and the EU in Turkish Industry and Business Association (TÜSİAD), TÜSİAD board member, online interview, 29 July 2022.

Interview 88: General secretary, İstanbul Chamber of Industry, online interview, 1 August 2022.

Interview 89: General secretary of Confederation of Progressive Trade Unions of Turkey (DİSK) and president of Birleşik Metal-İş (United Metalworkers' Union), online interview, 5 August 2022.

Interview 90: Deputy general secretary, Turkish Textile Employers' Association (TTSIS), online interview, 15 August 2022.

Interview 91: Head of research department, Turkish Textile Employers' Association (TTSIS), online interview, 15 August 2022.

Interview 92: General secretary, Automotive Manufacturers Association (OSD), online interview, 19 August 2022.

Interview 93: Coordinator for global and European Union affairs, Automotive Manufacturers Association (OSD), online interview, 19 August 2022.

Interview 94: Tekstil İşçileri Sendikası, DİSK-Tekstil, online interview, 8 December 2022.

Interview 95: Chief executive officer, LUNA Electric Electronics, online interview, 7 March 2023.

Interview 96: Former president, Birleşik Kamu-İş, telephone interview, 22 March 2023.

Interview 97: Member of strategic board, Buğday Association for Supporting Ecological Living, online interview, 29 March 2023.

Interview 98: Chairperson of the board of directors, TEMA, online interview, 14 April 2023.

Interview 99: Chairperson of the board of directors, Doğa, online interview, 25 April 2023.

Interview 100: Expert, Directorate for EU Affairs, Ministry of Foreign Affairs, online interview, 19 May 2023.

Interview 101: Founder, TIAFI, Team International Assistance for Integration, İzmir, 20 May 2023.

Interview 102: Former co-chair, Human Rights Association (İnsan Hakları Derneği İHD), online interview, 25 May 2023.

Interview 103: Expert, Directorate General for European Union and Foreign Relations, Ministry of Agriculture and Forestry, online interview, 7 June 2023.

Interview 104: Academic staff on international migration, Department of International Relations, Yaşar University, 14 June 2023, online interview.

Interview 105: Co-executive coordinator, Helsinki Citizens' Assembly, online interview, 15 June 2023.

Interview 106: Partnership manager, International Blue Crescent, online interview, 22 June 2023.

Interview 107: Former Brussels representative, Economic Development Foundation (İKV); Brussels, 21 April 2008.

Interview 108: Founding member, former programme director of good governance, Turkish Economic and Social Studies Foundation (TESEV); İstanbul, 14 January 2011.

Interview 109: Former international relations expert, Turkish Forestry, Soil, Water, Agriculture and Agricultural Workers Trade Union (Tarım-İş); Ankara, 17 January 2011.

Bibliography

Acemoğlu, D. and Autor, D. (2010) *Skills, Tasks and Technologies: Implications for Employment and Earnings*, NBER Working Paper 16082, Cambridge, MA: National Bureau of Economic Research.

Açıkgöz, R. (2020) *Brüksel 2018* [Brussels 2018], Skylive, available at: www.youtube.com/watch?v=x3QTLmeK4mA&list=PLIoZEdpULeHngpsiAQj WtDyqSQZv_bRnr (accessed on 24 February 2023).

Ahmad, F. (1993) *The Making of Modern Turkey*, London: Routledge.

AKP (2001) *AK Parti Kalkınma ve Demokratikleşme Programı* [Justice and Development Party programme for development and democratisation], available at: https://acikerisim.tbmm.gov.tr/items/4baa7399-15a8-44bb-88ce-abf5519b6183 (accessed on 10 September 2024).

AKP (2002) *Seçim Beyannamesi: Her Şey Türkiye İçin* [Election manifesto: everything is for Turkey], Ankara: AKP, available at: https://acikerisim.tbmm.gov.tr/handle/11543/954 (accessed on 24 February 2023).

AKP (2007) *Seçim Beyannamesi: Nice Ak Yıllara, Güven ve İstikrar İçinde Durmak Yok Yola Devam* [Election manifesto: many more good years ahead – keep moving forward with no let-up on security and stability], Ankara: AKP.

AKP (2018) *Güçlü Meclis, Güçlü Hükümet, Güçlü Türkiye: Cumhurbaşkanlığı Seçimleri ve Genel Seçimler Seçim Beyannamesi* [Strong parliament, strong government, strong Turkey: declaration for presidential and general elections], Ankara: AKP, available at: www.akparti.org.tr/media/quhdqtia/24-haziran-2018-cumhurbaskanligi-secimleri-ve-genel-secimler-secim-beyannamesi-sayfalar.pdf (accessed on 14 February 2023).

AKP (2022) *2023 Siyasal Vizyon* [2023 political vision], available at: www.akparti.org.tr/parti/2023-siyasal-vizyon/dünya/ (accessed on 20 February 2023).

Akyüz, Y. (2012) *The Rise of the South and New Paths of Development in the 21th Century, The Staggering Rise of the South?*, Background Paper 1, Geneva: UNCTAD, South Centre.

Akyüz, Y. (2013) *Waving or Drowning: Developing Countries after the Financial Crisis*, Research Papers 48, Geneva: South Centre.

Akyüz, Y. (2017) *Playing with Fire: Deepened Financial Integration and Changing Vulnerabilities of the Global South*, Oxford: Oxford University Press.

Akyüz, Y. (2018) 'Crisis alla Turca', Inter Press Service News Agency, 28 August 2018, available at: www.ipsnews.net/2018/08/crisis-alla-turca/ (accessed on 22 July 2023).

Akyüz, Y. (2020) 'Crisis alla Turca II – From Currency Crisis to Debt Crisis?', Inter Press Service News Agency, 29 October 2020, available at: www.ipsnews.net/2020/10/crisis-alla-turca-ii-currency-crisis-debt-crisis/ (accessed on 24 July 2023).

Akyüz, Y. and Boratav, K. (2003) 'The Making of the Turkish Financial Crisis', *World Development*, 31 (9), pp. 1549–1566.

Albo, G. and Fanelli, C. (2014) *Austerity Against Democracy, An Authoritarian Phase of Neoliberalism?*, Socialist Interventions Pamphlet 13, Toronto: Centre for Social Justice.

Altınörs, G. and Akçay, Ü. (2022) 'Authoritarian Neoliberalism, Crisis, and Consolidation: The Political Economy of Regime Change in Turkey', *Globalisations*, 19 (7), pp. 1029–1053.

Amin, S. (2007) 'Political Islam in the Service of Imperialism', *Monthly Review*, 1 December, available at: https://monthlyreview.org/2007/12/01/political-islam-in-the-service-of-imperialism/ (accessed on 16 April 2024).

Anderson, P. (1976) 'The Antinomies of Antonio Gramsci', *New Left Review*, 100 (1), pp. 5–78.

Anderson, P. (1998) *The Origins of Postmodernity*, London: Verso.

Anievas, A. and Nişancıoğlu, K. (2015) *How the West Came to Rule?: The Geopolitics Origins of Capitalism*, London: Pluto.

Aronowitz, S. (1986–87) 'Theory and Socialist Strategy', *Social Text*, 16, pp. 1–16.

Asmalı, M. (2022a) 'MÜSİAD Genel Başkanı Mahmut Asmalı, Gündemdeki Ekonomik Gelişmeleri Değerlendirdi' [MÜSİAD President Mahmut Asmalı assesses current economic developments], webinar, available at: www.youtube.com/watch?v=bqvi-l3wpYE (accessed on 16 December 2022).

Asmalı, M. (2022b) 'MÜSİAD Genel Başkanı Mahmut Asmalı, TV Net Makroskop Programında Değerlendirmelerde Bulundu' [MÜSİAD President Mahmut Asmalı in TV Net Makroskop], webinar, available at: www.youtube.com/watch?v=NFzGrbHGujo (accessed on 16 December 2022).

Ataç, D. (2022a) 'TEMA Vakfı'nın Güncel Projeleri ve Faaliyet Alanları' [TEMA's current projects and activities], webinar, available at: www.youtube.com/watch?v=Ni2Rstosq8o (accessed on 14 March 2023).

Ataç, D. (2022b) 'TEMA Vakfı'nın Sürdürülebilirlik Çalışmaları ve Sürdürülebilirlik Tavsiyeleri' [Actions and recommendations related to sustainability of the TEMA Foundation], webinar, available at: www.youtube.com/watch?v=Z-t7IaVoHBI&t=136s (accessed on 13 April 2023).

Aydın, M. and Açıkmeşe, S. A. (2007) 'Europeanization Through EU Conditionality: Understanding the New Era in Turkish Foreign Policy', *Journal of Southern Europe and the Balkans*, 9 (3), pp. 263–274.

Aydın, S. and Keyman, F. (2004) *European Integration and the Transformation of Turkish Democracy*, EU–Turkey Working Papers-CEPS 2, Brussels: Centre for European Policy Studies.

Aydın, Z. (2005) *The Political Economy of Turkey*, London: Pluto Press.

Aydın-Düzgit, S. (2016) 'De-Europeanisation Through Discourse: A Critical Discourse Analysis of AKP's Election Speeches', *South European Society and Politics*, 21 (1), pp. 45–58.

Ayers, A. J. and Saad-Filho, A. (2015) 'Democracy against Neoliberalism: Paradoxes, Limitations, Transcendence', *Critical Sociology*, 41 (4–5), pp. 597–618.

Babacan, E., Kutun, M., Pınar, E. and Yılmaz, Z. (eds) (2021) *Regime Change in Turkey: Neoliberal Authoritarianism, Islamism, Hegemony*, London: Routledge.

Bakırezer, G. and Demirer, Y. (2009) 'AK Parti'nin Sosyal Siyaseti' [Social policy of the AKP], in İ. Uzgel and B. Duru (eds), *AKP Kitabı: Bir Dönüşümün Bilançosu* [The book on AKP: balance sheet of a transformation], Ankara: Phoenix, pp. 153–178.

Bal, S. (2022a) 'The EU's Civil Society Conditionality in Turkey, Applying a Gramscian Lens to Procedural Diffusion', in C. Çakmak and A. O. Özçelik (eds), *EU Conditionality in Turkey: When Does It Work? When Does It Fail?*, London: Lexington Books, pp. 129–152.

Bal, S. (2022b) 'EU Financial Assistance to Civil Society in Turkey: Shrinking the Political Space in the Post-Gezi Process?', *Alternatif Politika*, 14 (3), pp. 486–518.

Bates, T. R. (1975) 'Gramsci and the Theory of Hegemony', *Journal of the History of Ideas*, 36 (2), pp. 351–366.

Batur, G. I. Y. (2021) 'AB-Türkiye Yüksek Düzeyli İş Diyaloğu, [Turkey–EU high-level business dialogue meeting]', webinar, available at: www.youtube.com/watch?v=CUx1Nv2_eD8 (accessed on 22 December 2022).

Baysan, T. and Blitzer, C. (1990) 'Turkey's Trade Liberalization in the 1980s and Prospects for its Sustainability', in T. Arıcanlı and D. Rodrik (eds), *The Political Economy of Turkey: Debt, Adjustment and Sustainability*, Basingstoke: Macmillan, pp. 9–36.

Becker, J. and Jäger, J. (2010) 'Development Trajectories in the Crisis in Europe'. *Debatte: Journal of Contemporary Central and Eastern Europe*, 18 (1), pp. 5–27.

Bedirhanoğlu, P. (2020) 'Social Constitution of the AKP's Strong State Through Financialization: State in Crisis, or Crisis State?', in P. Bedirhanoğlu, Ç. Dölek, F. Hülagü and Ö. Kaygusuz (eds), *Turkey's New State in the Making: Transformations in Legality, Economy and Coercion*, London: Zed Books, pp. 23–40.

Bedirhanoğlu, P., Dölek, Ç., Hülagü, F. and Kaygusuz, Ö. (2020) 'Introduction: Putting the AKP-Led State Transformation in its Neoliberal Historical Context', in P. Bedirhanoğlu, Ç. Dölek, F. Hülagü and Ö. Kaygusuz (eds), *Turkey's New State in the Making: Transformations in Legality, Economy and Coercion*, London: Zed Books, pp. 1–19.

Bellamy, R. (1990) 'Gramsci, Croce and the Italian Political Tradition', *History of Political Thought*, 11 (2), pp. 313–337.

Bhattacharya, T. (2017) 'Introduction: Mapping Social Reproduction Theory', in T. Bhattacharya (ed.), *Social Reproduction Theory: Remapping Class, Recentring Oppression*, London: Pluto, pp. 1–21.

Bieler, A. (2000) *Globalisation and Enlargement of the European Union: Austrian and Swedish Social Forces in the Struggle over Membership*, London: Routledge.

Bieler, A. (2005) 'European Integration and the Transnational Restructuring of Social Relations: The Emergence of Labour as a Regional Actor?', *Journal of Common Market Studies*, 43 (3), pp. 461–484.

Bieler, A. (2006) *The Struggle for a Social Europe: Trade Unions and EMU in Times of Global Restructuring*, Manchester: Manchester University Press.

Bieler, A. (2013) 'The EU, Global Europe, and Processes of Uneven and Combined Development: The Problem of Transnational Labour Solidarity', *Review of International Studies*, 39 (1), pp. 161–183.

Bieler, A. and Lindberg, I. (eds) (2011) *Global Restructuring: Labour and the Challenges for Transnational Solidarity*, London: Routledge.

Bieler, A., Lindberg, I. and Pillay, D. (eds) (2008a), *Labour and the Challenges of Globalisation: What Prospects for Transnational Solidarity*, London: Pluto.

Bieler, A., Lindberg, I. and Pillay, D. (2008b) 'What Future Strategy for the Global Working Class? The Need for a New Historical Subject', in A. Bieler, I. Lindberg and D. Pillay (eds), *Labour and the Challenges of Globalisation: What Prospects for Transnational Solidarity*, London: Pluto, pp. 264–285.

Bieler, A. and A. D. Morton (eds) (2001) *Social Forces in the Making of the New Europe: The Restructuring of European Social Relations in the Global Political Economy*, London: Palgrave.

Bieler, A. and Morton, A. D. (2004) '"Another Europe is Possible"? Labour and Social Movements at European Social Forum', *Globalisations*, 1 (2), pp. 305–327.

Bieler, A. and Morton, A. D. (2008) 'The Deficits of Discourse in IPE: Turning Base Metal into Gold?', *International Studies Quarterly*, 52 (1), pp. 103–128.

Bieler, A. and Morton, A. D. (2018) *Global Capitalism, Global War, Global Crisis*, Cambridge: Cambridge University Press.

Bieling, H.-J., Jager, J. and Ryner, M. (2016) 'Regulation Theory and the Political Economy of the European Union', *Journal of Common Market Studies*, 54 (1), pp. 53–69.

Bilecik, E. (2018) 'TÜSİAD 48. Olağan Genel Kurul Toplantısı' [TÜSİAD's 48th general assembly meeting], webinar, available at: www.youtube.com/watch?v=ChD3qhW5Mss&list=PLYykt1nmIGoH2O0L-JAR9DV04i6ZNlBGp&index=10 (accessed on 16 December 2022).

Bilgin, V. (2022) 'Bakan Bilgin, Ülke TV Canlı Yayınında Küresel Dönüşüm Sürecini ve Türkiye'nin Rolünü Değerlendirdi' [Minister Bilgin evaluated the global transformation process and Turkey's role on Ülke TV live broadcast], webinar, available at: www.youtube.com/watch?v=qR0YSoii57U (accessed on 2 May 2023).

Bilgin, V. (2023a) 'Bakan Bilgin, Türk Metal Sendikasının 17. Olağan Genel Kurulu'na katıldı' [Minister Bilgin attended the 17th ordinary general assembly of the Turkish Metal Union], webinar, available at: www.youtube.com/watch?v=A9_o5lcz4EM (accessed on 30 April 2023).

Bilgin, V. (2023b) 'Bakan Bilgin, Bengü Türk TV Canlı Yayınında Gündeme İlişkin Soruları Yanıtladı' [Minister Bilgin answered questions on the current agenda in Bengü Türk TV live broadcast], webinar, available at: www.youtube.com/watch?v=0CJKgT8do7k (accessed on 1 May 2023).

Bilgin, V. (2023c) 'Bakan Bilgin, TRT Haber Canlı Yayınında Çalışma Hayatı ve Gündeme İlişkin Soruları Yanıtladı' [Minister Bilgin answered questions on working life and current affairs on TRT News live broadcast], webinar, available at: www.youtube.com/watch?v=LpTLtyUQ5ts (accessed on 2 May 2023).

Birpınar, M. E. (2021a) 'MÜSİAD Vizyoner Zirvesi 21 – Basın Lansmanı' [MÜSİAD visionary summit 21], webinar, available at: www.youtube.com/watch?v=vZTxBq HNLbw&list=PLC7MJYgTOFYTVeA-CisyqOf3mwOflo_m8&index=3 (accessed on 15 December 2022).

Birpınar, M. E. (2021b) 'Avrupa Yeşil Mutabakatı ve Türkiye: Nötr Bir İklime Doğru' [The European Green Deal and Turkey: towards a neutral climate], webinar, available at: www.youtube.com/watch?v=tgSds2i_zTE&t=7948s (accessed on 2 May 2023).

Birpınar, M. E. (2021c) 'Urbanization and Climate Change, KEYEM Kent Söyleşileri, Çevre ve İklim Politikalarının Geleceği' [KEYEM city talks, future of environment and climate policies], webinar, available at: www.youtube.com/watch?v=RJ1aJh2vJAs (accessed on 3 May 2023).

Bohle, D. (2006) 'Neoliberal Hegemony, Transnational Capital and the Terms of the EU's Eastward Expansion', *Capital and Class*, 30 (1), pp. 57–86.

Bonefeld, W. (2015) 'European Economic Constitution and the Transformation of Democracy: On Class and the State of Law', *European Journal of International Relations*, 21 (4), pp. 867–886.

Boratav, K. (1990) 'Inter-Class and Intra-Class Relations of Distribution under "Structural Adjustment": Turkey During the 1980s', in T. Arıcanlı and D. Rodrik (eds), *The Political Economy of Turkey: Debt, Adjustment and Sustainability*, Basingstoke: Macmillan, pp. 199–229.

Boratav, K. (2003) *Türkiye İktisat Tarihi, 1908–2002* [Economic history of Turkey, 1908–2002], Ankara: İmge.

Boratav, K. (2005) *1980'li Yıllarda Türkiye'de Sosyal Sınıflar ve Bölüşüm* [Social classes and distribution of income in the 1980s in Turkey], Ankara: İmge.

Boratav, K. (2007) 'Net Resource Transfers and Dependency: Some Recent Changes in the World Economy', in A. H. Köse, F. Şenses and E. Yeldan (eds), *Neoliberal Globalisation as New Imperialism: Case Studies on Reconstruction of the Periphery*, New York: Nova Science Publishers, pp. 1–19.

Bozkurt, U. (2013) 'Neoliberalism with a Human Face: Making Sense of the Justice and Development Party's Neoliberal Populism in Turkey', *Science and Society*, 77 (3), pp. 372–396.

Bozkurt, U. (2021) 'State–Bourgeoisie Relations under Neoliberalism with Turkish Characteristics', *Historical Materialism*, 29 (4), pp. 1–41.

Bozkurt-Güngen, S. (2018) 'Labour and Authoritarian Neoliberalism: Changes and Continuities Under the JDP Governments in Turkey', *South European Society and Politics*, 23 (2), pp. 219–238.

Bruff, I. (2014) 'The Rise of Authoritarian Neoliberalism', *Rethinking Marxism: A Journal of Economics, Culture and Society*, 26 (1), pp. 113–129.

Buci-Glucksmann, C. (1980) *Gramsci and the State*, trans. David Fernbach, London: Lawrence and Wishart.

Buğday (2023) *The Buğday Movement*, available at: www.bugday.org/blog/the-bugday-movement/ (accessed on 28 March 2023).

Buğra, A. (1994) *State and Business in Modern Turkey: A Comparative Study*, Albany, NY: State University of New York Press.

Buğra, A. and Savaşkan, O. (2014) *Türkiye'de Yeni Kapitalizm: Siyaset, Din ve İş Dünyası* [New capitalism in Turkey: the relationship between politics, religion and business], İstanbul: İletişim.

Bulgurlu, H. (2021) 'TÜSİAD Digital Turkey Conference', 27 January, webinar, available at: www.youtube.com/watch?v=QNzH33CvM7k (accessed on 28 March 2021).

BusinessEurope (2019) *Position Paper: The Future of EU Migration Policy*, 24 September, available at: www.businesseurope.eu/sites/buseur/files/media/position_papers/social/2019-09-24_future_migration_policy.pdf (accessed on 28 June 2023).

Buttigieg, J. A. (2005) 'The Contemporary Discourse on Civil Society: A Gramscian Critique', *Boundary 2*, 32 (1), pp. 33–52.

Buzan, B. and Diez, T. (1999) 'The European Union and Turkey', *Survival*, 41 (1), pp. 41–57.

Cafruny, A. W. and Ryner, M. (eds) (2003) *A Ruined Fortress?: Neoliberal Hegemony and Transformation in Europe*, Oxford: Rowman & Littlefield.

Çakır, R. (2008) 'Interview with Şerif Mardin: Neighbourhood Pressure, What did I mean?', 29 May, available at: www.rusencakir.com/Prof-Serif-Mardin-Mahalle-Baskisi-Ne-Demek-Istedim/2028 (accessed on 27 February 2018).

Callinicos, A. (2010) 'The Limits of Passive Revolution', *Capital & Class*, 34 (3), pp. 491–507.

Callinicos, A., Kouvelakis, S. and Pradella, L. (2021) 'Introduction', in A. Callinicos, S. Kouvelakis and L. Pradella (eds), *Routledge Handbook of Marxism and Post-Marxism*, New York: Routledge, pp. 1–22.

Callinicos, A. and Rosenberg, J. (2010) 'Uneven and Combined Development, the Social-Relational Substratum of "The International"? An Exchange of Letters', in A. Anievas (ed.), *Marxism and World Politics: Contesting Global Capitalism*, Oxfordshire: Routledge, pp. 149–182.

Çarkoğlu, A. and Rubin, B. (eds) (2003) *Turkey and the European Union: Domestic Politics, Economic Integration and International Dynamics*, London: Frank Cass.

Çelik, A. (2013). 'Trade Unions and Deunionisation during Ten Years of AKP Rule', *Heinrich Böll Stiftung Turkey Representation*, 3, pp. 44–48.

Çelik, A. (2015) 'Turkey's New Labour Regime under the Justice and Development Party in the First Decade of the Twenty-First Century: Authoritarian Flexibilization', *Middle Eastern Studies*, 51 (4), pp. 618–635.

Central Bank (2001) *Transition to a Stronger Turkish Economy*, available at: www.tcmb.gov.tr/wps/wcm/connect/c1e0d048-983a-4a2a-a2b5-a0c24089be91/strengteningecon.pdf?MOD=AJPERES&CACHEID=ROOTWORKSPACE-c1e0d048-983a-4a2a-a2b5-a0c24089be91-m4ucbm9 (accessed on 23 July 2023).

Checkel, J. T. (2001) 'Social Construction and European Integration', in T. Christiansen, K. E. Jorgensen and A. Wiener (eds), *The Social Construction of Europe*, London: Sage, pp. 50–64.

CHP (2006) *Tam Üyeliğe Evet, Özel Statüye Hayır: CHP'nin Türkiye – AB İlişkileri Hakkındaki Görüş, Öneri ve Uyarıları* [Yes to full membership, no to special status, CHP's opinion, suggestions and warnings], available at: https://acikerisim.tbmm.gov.tr/handle/11543/2601 (accessed on July 23, 2023).

CHP (2007) *Seçim Beyannamesi: Şimdi Değişim Zamanı ... Şimdi CHP Zamanı* [Election manifesto: it is time for a change, it is time for CHP], Ankara: CHP, available at: https://chp.org.tr/yayin/2007-secim-bildirgesi/Open (accessed on July 23, 2023).

CHP (2010) *Çağdaş Türkiye İçin Değişim, CHP Programı* [Change for a modern Turkey, CHP programme], available at: https://content.chp.org.tr/1d48b01630ef43d9b2edf45d55842cae.pdf (accessed on 10 September 2024).

CHP (2018) *Millet İçin Geliyoruz: Seçim Bildirgesi 2018* [For the nation: 2018 election manifesto], available at: https://chp.org.tr/yayin/2018-secim-bildirgesi/Open (accessed on 1 March 2023).

CHP (2020) *İktidar Kurultayı: Parti Meclisi Çalışma Raporu: 37. Olağan Kurultay, 25–26 Temmuz 2020, Ankara* [Ruling Congress, party assembly working report, 37th Ordinary Congress, 25–26 July 2020, Ankara], available at: https://chp.org.tr/yayin/37-olagan-kurultay-part-mecls-calisma-raporu/Open (accessed on 27 February 2023).

CHP (2022) *İkinci Yüzyıla Çağrı* [Call for the second century], available at: https://chp.org.tr/yayin/kinci-yuzyila-cagri-bulusmasi/Open (accessed on 25 February 2023).

Çınar, A. and Arıkan, B. (2002) 'The Nationalist Action Party: Representing the State, the Nation or the Nationalists?', *Turkish Studies*, 3 (1), pp. 25–40.

Cizre, Ü. and Yeldan, E. (2005) 'The Turkish Encounter with Neo-Liberalism: Economics and Politics in the 2000–2001 Crisis', *Review of International Political Economy*, 12 (3), pp. 387–408.

Cole, M., Radice, H. and Umney, C. (2021) 'The Political Economy of Datafication and Work: A New Digital Taylorism?', in L. Panitch and G. Albo (eds), *Digital Capitalism: New Ways of Living, Socialist Register*, London: Merlin Press, pp. 78–99.

Council of the EU (2018) *Council Conclusions on Enlargement and Stabilisation and Association Process*, available at: www.consilium.europa.eu/media/35863/st10555-en18.pdf (accessed 28 March 2022).

Council of the EU (2019) *Press Release: Turkish Drilling Activities in the Eastern Mediterranean: Council Adapts Conclusions*, 15 July 2019, available at: www.consilium.europa.eu/en/press/press-releases/2019/07/15/turkish-drilling-activities-in-the-eastern-mediterranean-council-adopts-conclusions/ (accessed on 27 July 2023).

Cox, R. W. (1981) 'Social Forces, State and World Orders: Beyond International Relations Theory', *Millennium: Journal of International Studies*, 10 (2), pp. 126–155.

Cox, R. W. (1983) 'Gramsci, Hegemony and International Relations: An Essay in Method', *Millennium: Journal of International Studies*, 12 (2), pp. 162–175.

Cox, R. W. (1987) *Production, Power and World Order: Social Forces in the Making of History*, New York: Columbia University Press.

Crouch, C. (2004) *Post-Democracy*, Cambridge: Polity.

Cumhuriyet (2018) 'İşte Erdoğan'ın Açıkladığı Kabine Listesi' [The Cabinet list announced by Erdoğan], available at: www.cumhuriyet.com.tr/haber/iste-erdoganin-acikladigi-kabine-listesi-1021888 (accessed on 10 May 2023).

Cumhuriyet (2023) 'Deprem Anketlere Yansımaya Başladı: ORC'nin Anketinde Seçim Arifesinde Partilerde Son Durum …' [The earthquake has started to be reflected in the polls: ORC's latest poll on the eve of the elections …], available at: www.cumhuriyet.com.tr/turkiye/deprem-anketlere-yansimaya-basladi-orcnin-anketinde-secim-arifesinde-partilerde-son-durum-2056769 (accessed on 4 March 2023).

Dahlman, C., Mealy, S. and Wermelinger, M. (2016), *Harnessing the Digital Economy for Developing Countries*, OECD Development Centre Working Paper No. 334, Paris: OECD, available at: www.oecd-ilibrary.org/development/harnessing-the-digital-economy-for-developing-countries_4adffb24-en (accessed on 7 January 2022).

Davutoğlu, A. (2008) 'Turkey's Foreign Policy Vision: An Assessment of 2007', *Insight Turkey*, 10 (1), pp. 77–96.

Davutoğlu, A. (2010) 'Turkey's Zero-Problems Foreign Policy', *Foreign Policy*, 20 May, available at: https://foreignpolicy.com/2010/05/20/turkeys-zero-problems-foreign-policy/ (accessed on 4 September 2024).

Derviş, K., Emerson, M., Gros, D. and Ülgen, S. (2004) *The European Transformation of Modern Turkey*, Brussels: Centre for European Policy Studies.

Diez, T., Agnantopoulos, A. and Kaliber, A. (2005), 'File: Turkey, Europeanization and Civil Society', *South European Society and Politics*, 10 (1), pp. 1–15.

Dilemre, H. (2017) 'TÜSİAD Küresel Ticaret: Politikadan Eyleme Konferansı' [TÜSİAD conference on global trade: from politics to action], webinar, available at: www.youtube.com/watch?v=-Uku5SYYaso (accessed 10 November 2022).

DİSK (1996) *Olağanüstü Genel Kurul Çalışma Raporu 1994–1996* [Working report for the extraordinary general assembly], DİSK Yayınları 20, İstanbul: Egemen Matbaacılık.

DİSK (2000a) *Çalışma Raporu 1997–2000: Küresel Saldırıya Karşı Küresel Direniş* [Working report 1997–2000: global struggle against global attack], İstanbul: DİSK Basın Yayın.

DİSK (2000b) *11. Genel Kurul Kararları: Yeni Bir Süreçte Yeniden DİSK* [11th general assembly resolutions: DİSK in a new period], available at: https://disk.org.tr/2006/03/11-genel-kurul-kararlari/ (accessed 10 November 2022).

DİSK (2008) *13. Genel Kurul Kararları, Ayağa Kalkış Çağrısı* [13th General Assembly Resolutions, Call for Uprising], available at: http://www.birlesikmetal.org/kitap/kitap_09/tek/AA-1_Karar_Disk_13GnlKrl.pdf (accessed 28 November 2024).

DİSK (2020) *16. Olağan Genel Kurul: Sonuç Bildirgesi: 2020'lerin DİSK'i, Emeğin Türkiye'si* [16th general assembly conclusions: DİSK in the 2020s and labour's Turkey], available at: https://disk.org.tr/wp-content/uploads/2020/03/YON-BELGE.pdf (accessed 24 December 2022).

Doğa Derneği (2023) *Who We Are*, available at: www.dogadernegi.org/en/who-we-are/ (accessed on 3 June 2023).

DSP (2004) *Türkiye'nin AB Üyeliği Yolunda Ecevit, Kıbrıs ve Helsinki Gerçeği* [Ecevit, Cyprus and reality about Helsinki in Turkey's EU membership process], Ankara: DSP Tantım, Medya, Halkla İlişkiler, Ar-Ge.

Dumenil, G. and Levy, D. (2008) 'Old Theories and New Capitalism: The Actuality of a Marxist Economics', in J. Bidet and S. Kouvelakis (eds), *Critical Companion to Contemporary Marxism*, Leiden: Brill, pp. 95–123.

Duzgun, E. (2022) 'Debating "Uneven and Combined Development": Beyond Ottoman Patrimonialism', *Journal of International Relations and Development*, 25 (2), pp. 297–323.

Eagleton, T. (1996) *The Illusions of Postmodernism*, Oxford: Blackwell.

Ebiçlioğlu, F. (2020) 'Türkiye & Avrupa 5.0: Türkiye-AB ve Yeşil Mutabakat' [Turkey and Europe 5.0: Turkey–EU and Green Deal], webinar, available at: www.youtube.com/watch?v=tS90O76FfrE (accessed on 15 October 2021).

Eralp, N. A. and Eralp, A. (2012) 'What went Wrong in the Turkey–EU Relationship?', in K. Öktem, A. Kadıoğlu and M. Karlı (eds), *Another Empire?: A Decade of Turkey's Foreign Policy under the Justice and Development Party*, İstanbul: Bilgi University Press, pp. 163–183.

Ercan, F. and Oğuz, Ş. (2020) 'Understanding the Recent Rise of Authoritarianism in Turkey in Terms of the Structural Contradictions of the Process of Capital Accumulation', in P. Bedirhanoğlu, Ç. Dölek, F. Hülagü and Ö. Kaygusuz (eds), *Turkey's New State in the Making: Transformations in Legality, Economy and Coercion*, London: Zed Books, pp. 97–117.

Erdoğan, R. T. (2015) 'Cumhurbaşkanı Recep Tayyip Erdoğan Balıkesir Ekonomi Ödülleri 2015 Töreni'nde Konuştu: Ben bu ülkenin anonim şirket gibi yönetilmesini istiyorum' [President Recep Tayyip Erdogan delivered a speech at the 2015 ceremony of Balıkesir Economy Awards: I want this country to be governed like a joint-stock company], CNN Turkey, available at: www.cnnturk.com/video/turkiye/cumhurbaskani-erdogandan-onemli-aciklamalar-11-12-2018 (accessed on 10 May 2023).

Erol, E. (2020) *Tanrıya Uzak Merkeze Yakın: Meksika ve Türkiye'de Çevre Kapitalizminin Tarihsel Sosyolojisi* [Far from God, close to the centre: historical sociology of capitalism on the periphery in Mexico and Turkey], İstanbul: Tarih Vakfı Yurt Yayınları.

Erol, E. (2021) 'Burden or a Saviour at a Time of Economic Crisis? AKP's "Open-Door Migration Policy" and its Impact on Labour Market Restructuring in Turkey', in Ç. E. Şahin and M. E. Erol (eds), *The Condition of the Working Class in Turkey: Labour under Neoliberal Authoritarianism*, London: Pluto, pp. 135–152.

Erol, M. E. (2019) 'State and Labour under AKP Rule in Turkey: An Appraisal', *Journal of Balkan and Near Eastern Studies*, 21 (6), pp. 663–677.

Erol, M. E. (2021) 'Not-so-Strange Bedfellows: Neoliberalism and the AKP in Turkey', in Ç. E. Şahin and M. E. Erol (eds), *The Condition of the Working Class in Turkey: Labour under Neoliberal Authoritarianism*, London: Pluto, pp. 15–37.

Erol, M. E. and Şahin, Ç. E. (2021) 'Introduction', in Ç. E. Şahin and M. E. Erol (eds), *The Condition of the Working Class in Turkey: Labour under Neoliberal Authoritarianism*, London: Pluto, pp. 1–11.

Esen, B. and Gumuscu, S. (2018) 'Building a Competitive Authoritarian Regime: State–Business Relations in the AKP's Turkey', *Journal of Balkan and Near Eastern Studies*, 20 (4), pp. 349–372.

European Commission (1989) *Commission Opinion on Turkey's Request for Accession to the Community*, available at: www.cvce.eu/content/publication/2005/2/4/4cc1acf8-06b2-40c5-bb1e-bb3d4860e7c1/publishable_en.pdf (accessed on 10 September 2024).

European Commission (2018) *Turkey 2018 Report*, available at: https://neighbourhood-enlargement.ec.europa.eu/system/files/2019-05/20180417-turkey-report.pdf (accessed on 25 July 2023).

European Council (1997) *Luxembourg European Council 12 and 13 December 1997: Presidency Conclusions*, available at: www.europarl.europa.eu/summits/lux1_en.htm (accessed on 26 July 2023).

European Council (1999) *Helsinki European Council 10 and 11 December 1999: Presidency Conclusions*, available at: www.europarl.europa.eu/summits/hel1_en.htm (accessed on 26 July 2023).

European Council (2021) *Statement of the Members of the European Council*, 25 March, available at: www.consilium.europa.eu/media/48976/250321-vtc-euco-statement-en.pdf (accessed on 5 March 2022).

European Parliament (2013) *European Parliament Resolution of 13 June 2013 on the Situation in Turkey*, available at: www.europarl.europa.eu/doceo/document/TA-7-2013-0277_EN.html (accessed on 27 July 2023).

European Union (2016) *Shared Vision, Common Action: A Stronger Europe: A Global Strategy for the European Union's Foreign and Security Policy*, n.p.: EU, available at: https://eeas.europa.eu/archives/docs/top_stories/pdf/eugs_review_web.pdf (accessed on 14 October 2021).

European Union (2022) *A Strategic Compass for Security and Defence*, n.p.: EU, available at: www.eeas.europa.eu/sites/default/files/documents/strategic_compass_en3_web.pdf (accessed on 4 April 2022).

Eurostat (2022) *What are the Main Destinations of EU Export of Waste?*, available at: https://ec.europa.eu/eurostat/en/web/products-eurostat-news/-/DDN-20220525-1 (accessed on 5 September 2023).

Federici, S. (2012) *Revolution at Point Zero: Housework, Reproduction, and Feminist Struggle*, Brooklyn, NY: PM Press.

Femia, J. V. (2002) 'The Gramsci Phenomenon: Some Reflections', in J. Martin (ed.), *Antonio Gramsci: Critical Assessments of Leading Political Philosophers*, Vol. IV: *Contemporary Applications*, London and New York: Routledge, pp. 116–131.

Financial Times (2009) 'Economy: Politics Plays Big Part in Reply to Crisis', 8 June, available at: www.ft.com/content/04881032-53c6-11de-be08-00144feabdc0 (accessed on 24 July 2023).

Financial Times (2015) 'Turkey's Foreign Policy of "Precious Loneliness"', 16 November, available at: www.ft.com/content/69662b36-7752-11e5-a95a-27d368e1ddf7 (accessed on 22 July 2023).

Forgacs, D. (1989) 'Gramsci and Marxism in Britain', *New Left Review*, 1 (176), pp. 69–88.

Gehring, A. (2019) *Vom Mythos des starken Staates und der europäischen Integration der Türkei: Über eine Ökonomie an der Peripherie des euro-atlantischen Raumes*, Wiesbaden: Springer.

Gehring, A. (2021) 'Internationalized Class Governance and the AKP's Populism, On Turkey's Integration with the European Union', in E. Babacan, M. Kutun, E. Pınar and Z. Yılmaz (eds), *Regime Change in Turkey: Neoliberal Authoritarianism, Islamism, Hegemony*, London: Routledge, pp. 103–119.

Geras, N. (1987) 'Post-Marxism', *New Left Review*, 1 (163), pp. 40–82.

Germain, R. D. and Kenny, M. (1998) 'Engaging Gramsci, International Relations Theory and the New Gramscians', *Review of International Studies*, 24 (1), pp. 3–21.

Gill, S. (2016) 'Critical Global Political Economy and the Global Organic Crisis', in A. Cafruny, L. S. Talani and G. P. Martin (eds), *The Palgrave Handbook of Critical International Political Economy*, London: Palgrave, pp. 29–48.

Gramsci, A. (1971) *Selections from the Prison Notebooks*, ed. and trans. Q. Hoare and G. Nowell Smith, London: Lawrence and Wishart.

Gramsci, A. (1977) *The Antonio Gramsci Reader: Selections from Political Writings 1910–1920*, ed. Q. Hoare, trans. J. Mathews, London: Lawrence and Wishart.

Guardian (2002) 'Islamic Party Wins Turkish General Elections', 4 November, available at: www.theguardian.com/world/2002/nov/04/2 (accessed on 10 April 2023).

Guardian (2006) 'EU on Collision Course with Ankara over Membership: Brussels takes Unprecedented Step of Partially Suspending Negotiations', 30 November, available at: www.theguardian.com/world/2006/nov/30/turkey.eu (accessed on 15 August 2023).

Guardian (2017) 'Council of Europe Vote Puts Pressure on Turkey over Human Rights', 26 April, available at: www.theguardian.com/world/2017/apr/26/council-of-europe-turkey-human-rights-pace (accessed on 25 July 2023).

Gürakar, E. Ç. (2016) *Politics of Favoritism in Public Procurement in Turkey: Reconstructions of Dependency Networks in the AKP Era*, New York: Palgrave Macmillan.

Gürcan, E. C. and Mete, B. (2017) *Neoliberalism and the Changing Face of Unionism: The Combined and Uneven Development of Class Capacities in Turkey*, Cham: Palgrave.

Güzel, H. (2024) *The Migration of Doctors from Turkey to Germany: What the Numbers Tell Us*, İstanbul: IPC-Mercator Analysis, İstanbul Policy Center, available at: https://ipc.sabanciuniv.edu/Content/Images/CKeditorImages/2024020 1-19022278.pdf (accessed on 14 April 2024).

Haas, E. B. (1958) *The Uniting of Europe: Political, Social and Economic Forces, 1950–1957*, Stanford, CA: Stanford University Press.

Hak-İş (1992) 7. *Olağan Genel Kurul Çalışma Raporu* [7th regular general assembly working paper], Ankara: Ofset Matbaacılık.

Hak-İş (1995) 8. *Olağan Genel Kurul Çalışma Raporu* [8th regular general assembly working paper], Ankara: Alıç Ofset Matbaacılık.

Hak-İş (1999) 9. *Olağan Genel Kurul Faaliyet Raporu* [9th regular general assembly working paper], Ankara: Mina Ajans.

Hall, S. (1987) 'Gramsci and Us', *Marxism Today*, pp. 16–21.

Hardt, M. and Negri, A. (2000) *Empire*, Cambridge, MA: Harvard University Press.

Hardt, M. and Negri, A. (2004) *Multitude: War and Democracy in the Age of Empire*, New York: Penguin Press.

Hardt, M. and Negri, A. (2019) 'Empire, Twenty Years On', *New Left Review*, 2 (20), pp. 67–92.

Hartmann, H. I. (1979) 'The Unhappy Marriage of Marxism and Feminism: Towards a More Progressive Union', *Capital and Class*, 3 (2), pp. 1–33.

Harvey, D. (1989) *The Condition of Postmodernity: An Enquiry into the Origins of Cultural Change*, Cambridge: Blackwell.

Harvey, D. (2015) *Seventeen Contradictions and the End of Capitalism*, Oxford: Oxford University Press.

Heper, M. (1985) *The State Tradition in Turkey*, Walkington: Eothen Press.

Hisarcıklıoğlu, R. (2021), 'AB-Türkiye Yüksek Düzeyli İş Diyaloğu Toplantısı' [Turkey–EU high-level business dialogue meeting], webinar, available at: www.youtube.com/watch?v=CUx1Nv2_eD8 (accessed on 22 December 2022).

Hisarcıklıoğlu, R. (2022) 'EKO İklim, Ekonomi ve İklim Değişikliği Zirvesi' [Summit on EKO climate, economy and climate change], webinar, available at: www.youtube.com/watch?v=dyaSFJwm-Ig (accessed on 22 December 2022).

Hobsbawm, E. J. (1977) 'Gramsci and Political Theory', *Marxism Today*, 21 (7), pp. 205–213.

Hoffman, S. (1966) 'Obstinate or Obsolete: The Fate of the Nation-State and the Case of Western Europe', *Daedalus*, 95 (3), pp. 862–915.

Holman, O. (1996) *Integrating Southern Europe: EC Expansion and the Transnationalization of Spain*, London: Routledge.

Horkheimer, M. and Adorno, T. W. (1973) *Dialectic of Enlightenment: Philosophical Fragments*, Stanford, CA: Stanford University Press.

Howarth, D. (2000) *Discourse*, Buckingham: Open University Press.

Howarth, D. (2013) *Poststructuralism and After: Structure, Subjectivity and After*, London: Palgrave.

Howarth, D., Norval, A. J. and Stavrakakis, Y. (eds) (2000) *Discourse Theory and Political Analysis: Identities, Hegemonies and Social Change*, Manchester: Manchester University Press.

Hürriyet Daily (2016) '"Varsa Yoksa AB" Demeyin, Şanghay 5'lisi Bizi Rahatlatır' [No need to consider EU at all costs, Shanghai Five is good for Turkey], 20 November, available at: www.hurriyet.com.tr/gundem/varsa-yoksa-ab-demeyin-sanhgay-5lisi-bizi-rahatlatir-40282883 (accessed on 17 December 2018).

Hürriyet Daily (2021) 'Turkey to Follow Chinese Economic Growth Strategy: Erdoğan', 3 December, available at: www.hurriyetdailynews.com/turkey-to-follow-chinas-economic-growth-strategy-erdogan-169831 (accessed on 28 June 2022).

IEMF (2022) 'History', available at: www.iemf.org/default.asp?sayfa=sayfa_detay&id=217 (accessed on 17 June 2023).

Irgat, N. (2019) 'Teksif 20. Olağan Genel Kurul', [20th regular general assembly of the Teksif union], available at: www.youtube.com/watch?v=fg8DITk89Ks (accessed on 21 March 2023).

Irgat, N. (2023) 'Teksif 21. Olağan Genel Kurul', [21st regular general assembly of the Teksif union], available at: www.youtube.com/watch?v=xna2vGzSf8k (accessed on 21 March 2023).

İnsel, A. (2003) 'The AKP and Normalizing Democracy in Turkey', *South Atlantic Quarterly*, 102 (2/3), pp. 293–308.

İSO (1995) *Gümrük Birliğinin İmalat Sanayi Sektörü Üzerindeki Etkileri ve Bu Sektörün Rekabet Gücü* [Effects of the customs union on manufacturing industry and the competitiveness of this sector], İstanbul: İSO Yayını.

ITUC (2023), *ITUC Global Rights Index 2023*, available at: www.ituc-csi.org/ituc-global-rights-index-2023 (accessed on 23 July 2023).

İyi Party (2022) *Ekonomik İstikrar ve Kapsayıcı Büyüme için Eylem Planı* [Action plan for economic stability and inclusive growth], Ankara: İyi Party, available at: https://iyiparti.org.tr/storage/img/content/nrzp/ekonomik-istikrar-ve-kapsayici-buyume-icin-eylem-plani-1.pdf (accessed on 7 March 2023).

İyi Party (2023) *Parti Programı* [Party programme], Ankara: İyi Party, available at: https://iyiparti.org.tr/storage/img/doc/iyi-parti-guncel-parti-program.pdf (accessed on 4 March 2023).

Jameson, F. (1991) *Postmodernism, or, the Cultural Logic of Late Capitalism*, London: Verso.

Jessop, B. (2019) 'Authoritarian Neoliberalism: Periodization and Critique', *South Atlantic Quarterly*, 118 (2), pp. 343–361.

Karakaş, C. (2013) 'EU–Turkey: Integration without Full Membership or Membership without Full Integration? A Conceptual Framework for Accession Alternatives', *Journal of Common Market Studies*, 51 (6), pp. 1057–1073.

Karataş, B. (2024) 'Turkey Gains New Wave of Female Mayors after Opposition's Poll Success', 3 April, Reuters, available at: www.reuters.com/world/middle-east/turkey-gains-new-wave-female-mayors-after-oppositions-poll-success-2024-04-03/ (accessed on 16 April 2024).

Kaslowski, S. (2020) 'TÜSİAD 2020 Genel Kurul' [TÜSİAD 2020 general assembly], webinar, available at: www.youtube.com/watch?v=l4BWHCUFiTE (accessed on 20 December 2022).

Kaslowski, S. (2022) 'TÜSİAD 52. Genel Kurulu Toplantısı' [TÜSİAD President of the Board of Directors 2019–2022, TÜSİAD 52nd general assembly], webinar, available at: www.youtube.com/watch?v=vSJxJKxphHc (accessed on 18 December 2022).

Kavlak, P. (2016) 'Türk-İş 22. Olağan Genel Kurulu' [Türk-İş 22nd regular general assembly], available at: www.youtube.com/watch?v=LMvbAuvV7tI (accessed on 23 March 2023).

Kaymakçı, F. (2021) 'AB Türkiye Yüksek Düzeyli İş Diyaloğu Toplantısı' [Turkey–EU high-level business dialogue meeting], webinar, available at: www.youtube.com/watch?v=CUx1Nv2_eD8 (accessed on 22 December 2022).

Keyder, Ç. (1987) *State and Class in Turkey: A Study in Capitalist Development*, London: Verso.

Keyder, Ç. (1996) 'Afterword, The Current Condition of the Popular Classes', in E. J. Goldberg (ed.), *The Social History of Labour in the Middle East*, Boulder, CO: Westview Press, pp. 147–158.

Keyman, E. F. (1999) *Türkiye ve Radikal Demokrasi* [Turkey and radical democracy], İstanbul: Bağlam.

Khan, G. and Wenman, M. (2017) 'The Politics of Poststructuralism Today', *Political Studies Review*, 15 (4), pp. 513–515.

Koç, Y. (1998) *Türkiye İşçi Sınıfı ve Sendikacılık Hareketi Tarihi* [Turkish working class and the history of trade unionism], İstanbul: Kaynak Yayınları.

Koç, Y. (2001) *Türkiye–Avrupa Birliği İlişkileri* [Turkey–European Union relations], Ankara: Türk-İş Eğitim Yayınları 66.

Koç, Y. (2004) *AB Emperyalizmi ve İşçi Sınıfı* [European Union imperialism and the working class], Ankara: Kaynak Yayınları.

Koç, Y. (2006) *Avrupa Sendikacılığı, Enternasyonalizm mi? Çağdaş Misyonerlik mi?* [European trade unionism: internationalism or contemporary missionarism?], Ankara: Kaynak Yayınları.

Kürkçü, E. (2017) 'Kürkçü: Türkiye'nin dış politikası AKP Genel Başkanı'nın hayallerinden ibaret' [Kürkçü: Turkey's foreign policy is composed of dreams of chairman of the AKP], available at: https://hdp.org.tr/tr/kurkcu-turkiye-nin-dis-politikasi-akp-genel-baskani-nin-hayallerinden-ibaret/11392/ (accessed on 25 June 2023).

Kutun, M. (2020) 'The AKP's Move from Depoliticization to Repoliticization in Economic Management', in P. Bedirhanoğlu, Ç. Dölek, F. Hülagü and Ö. Kaygusuz (eds), *Turkey's New State in the Making: Transformations in Legality, Economy and Coercion*, London: Zed Books, pp. 134–151.

Labour and Freedom Alliance (2023) *Emek Ve Özgürlük Ittifaki'nin 14 Mayis Seçim Mutabakat Bildirgesi* [Manifesto of Labour and Freedom Alliance for 14 May elections], available at: https://hdp.org.tr/Images/UserFiles/Documents/Editor/2023/ittifak-14-mayis-secim-mutabakati.pdf (accessed on 25 June 2023).

Laclau, E. (1996) *Emancipation(s)*, London: Verso.

Laclau, E. and Mouffe, C. (1985) *Hegemony and Socialist Strategy: Towards a Radical Democratic Politics*, London: Verso.

Laclau, E. and Mouffe, C. (2002) 'Recasting Marxism, Hegemony and new Political Movements Interview with Ernesto Laclau and Chantal Mouffe', in J. Martin (ed.), *Antonio Gramsci: Critical Assessments of Leading Political Philosophers*, Vol. IV: *Contemporary Applications*, London: Routledge, pp. 135–153.

Lapavitsas, C. (2009) 'Financialised Capitalism: Crisis and Financial Expropriation', *Historical Materialism*, 17 (2), pp. 114–148.

Lapavitsas, C. (2013) *Profiting Without Producing: How Finance Exploits Us All*, London: Verso.

Löwy, M. (2019) 'The Far Right: A Global Phenomenon', International Viewpoint, IV528, 10 January, available at: https://internationalviewpoint.org/spip.php?article5890 (accessed on 23 June 2023).

Macmillan, C. (2009) 'The Application of Neofunctionalism to the Enlargement Process: The Case of Turkey', *Journal of Common Market Studies*, 47 (7), pp. 789–809.

Manisalı, E. (2002) *Türkiye–Avrupa İlişkilerinde Sessiz Darbe* [Silent coup in Turkey–European Union relations], Ankara: Derin Yayınları.

Manisalı, E. (2005) *Türkiye Avrupa Kıskacında* [Turkey in European pincers], Ankara: Derin Yayınları.

Manisalı, E. (2009) *Ortak Pazar'dan Avrupa Birliği'ne* [From the Common Market to the European Union], Ankara: Cumhuriyet Yayınları.

Manners, I. (2002) 'Normative Power Europe: A Contradiction in Terms?', *Journal of Common Market Studies*, 40 (2), pp. 235–258.

Manners, I. and Whitman, R. (2016) 'Another Theory is Possible: Dissident Voices in Theorising Europe', *Journal of Common Market Studies*, 54 (1), pp. 3–18.

Mardin, Ş. (1973) 'Center–Periphery Relations: A Key to Turkish Politics?', *Daedalus*, 102 (1), pp. 169–190.

Marois, T. (2019) 'The Transformation of the State Financial Apparatus in Turkey since 2001', in G. L. Yalman, T. Marois and A. R. Güngen (eds), *The Political Economy of Financial Transformation in Turkey*, London: Routledge, pp. 108–134.

Marx, K. (1852/1934) *The Eighteenth Brumaire of Louis Bonaparte*, Moscow: Progress Publishers.

Marx, K. (1857–1858/1973) *Grundrisse: Foundations of the Critique of Political Economy*, trans. Martin Nicolaus, London: Penguin.

Marx, K. (1867/1990) *Capital*, Vol. 1, intro. Ernest Mandel, trans. Ben Fowkes, London: Penguin.

MESS (1994) *Avrupa Birliği ve Gümrük Birliği* [The European Union and the customs union], İstanbul: MESS Yayını.

MFA (2023) *Türkiye Yüzyili"Nda Milli Diş Politika* [Turkey's entrepreneurial and humanitarian foreign policy], available at: www.mfa.gov.tr/dis-politika-genel.tr.mfa (accessed on 25 April 2023).

MHP (2007) *Seçim Beyannamesi: Milli Duruş ve Kararlılık Belgesi* [Election manifesto: the document of national stance and decisiveness], Ankara: MHP.

Milward, A. S. (1992) *The European Rescue of the Nation-State*, London: Routledge.

Ministry of Foreign Affairs (2022) *Turkey–European Relations*, available at: www.ab.gov.tr/turkey-eu-relations_4_en.html (accessed 5 April 2022).

Moravcsik, A. (1998) *The Choice for Europe: Social Purpose and State Power from Messina to Maastricht*, Ithaca, NY: Cornell University Press.

Moravcsik, A. and Vachudova, M. A. (2003) 'National Interests, State Power and EU Enlargement', *East European Politics and Societies*, 17 (1), pp. 42–57.

Morton, A. D. (2006) 'A Double Reading of Gramsci: Beyond the Logic of Contingency', in A. Bieler and A. D. Morton (eds), *Images of Gramsci: Connections and Contentions in Political Theory and International Relations*, London: Routledge, pp. 45–59.

Morton, A. D. (2007a) *Unravelling Gramsci Hegemony and Passive Revolution in the Global Economy*, London: Pluto Press.

Morton, A. D. (2007b) 'Waiting for Gramsci: State Formation, Passive Revolution and the International', *Millennium*, 35 (3), pp. 597–621.

Morton, A. D. (2010a) 'The Continuum of Passive Revolution', *Capital & Class*, 34 (3), pp. 315–342.

Morton, A. D. (2010b) 'The Geopolitics of Passive Revolution', in A. Anievas (ed.), *Marxism and World Politics: Contesting Global Capitalism*, Abingdon: Routledge, pp. 215–230.

Mouffe, C. (1993) *The Return of the Political*, London: Verso.

Müftüler-Baç, M. (1997) *Turkey's Relations with a Changing Europe*, Manchester: Manchester University Press.

Müftüler-Baç, M. (2005) 'Turkey's Political Reforms and the Impact of the European Union', *South European Society and Politics*, 10 (1), pp. 17–31.

Müftüler-Baç (2017) 'Turkey's Future with the European Union: An Alternative Model of Differentiated Integration', *Turkish Studies*, 18 (3), pp. 416–438.

Müftüler-Baç, M. and Keyman, E. F. (2015) 'Turkey's Unconsolidated Democracy: The Nexus between Democratisation and Majoritarianism in Turkey', in S. Aydın Düzgit, D. Huber, M. Müftüler-Baç, E. F. Keyman, M. Schwarz and N. Tocci (eds), *Global Turkey in Europe III: Democracy, Trade, and the Kurdish Question in Turkey–EU Relations*, Rome: Edizioni Nuova Cultura, pp. 121–129.

Müftüler-Baç, M. and McLaren, L. (2003) 'Enlargement Preferences and Policy-Making in the European Union: Impacts on Turkey', *Journal of European Integration*, 25 (1), pp. 17–30.

Müller, J. W. (2016) *What is Populism?*, Philadelphia, PA: University of Pennsylvania Press.

Munck, R. (2005) 'Neoliberalism and Politics, and the Politics of Neoliberalism', in A. Saad-Filho and D. Johnston (eds), *Neoliberalism: A Critical Reader*, London: Pluto, p. 60–70.

Munck, R. (2016) *Marx 2020: After the Crisis*, London: Zed Books.

MÜSİAD (1995) *Türkiye Ekonomisi* [The Turkish economy], MÜSİAD Araştırma Raporları 12, İstanbul: MÜSİAD.

MÜSİAD (1996) *Pamuk Birliği* [The cotton union], MÜSİAD Araştırma Raporları 19, İstanbul: MÜSİAD.

MÜSİAD (2001) *Türkiye Ekonomisi 2001: 2000 Yılı Değerlendirmesi ve 2001 Yılı Beklentileri* [The Turkish economy 2001: analysis of 2000 and expectations from 2001], MÜSİAD Araştırma Raporları 38, İstanbul: MÜSİAD.

MÜSİAD (2004a) *AB İlerleme Raporu ve AB Müzakere Süreci Konusunda MÜSİAD'ın Görüşleri* [MÜSİAD opinion on the EU regular report and EU accession negotiations], MÜSİAD Cep Kitabı 18, İstanbul: MÜSİAD.

MÜSİAD (2004b) *AB Müzakere Sürecine İlişkin MÜSİAD'ın Değerlendirme ve Önerileri (2)* [MÜSİAD's evaluation and suggestions regarding the EU accession negotiations (2)], MÜSİAD Cep Kitabı 19, İstanbul: MÜSİAD.

MÜSİAD (2005) *Yeni Ekonomik Dönemde KOBİ'ler İçin Rekabet ve Büyüme Stratejileri* [Competition and growth strategies for small and medium-sized enterprises in the new economic system], MÜSİAD Cep Kitabı 20, İstanbul: MÜSİAD.

MÜSİAD (2006) *Türkiye Ekonomisi 2006: İstikrar İçinde Kalkınma Arayışları* [Turkish economy 2006: search for development in stability], MÜSİAD Araştırma Raporları 50, İstanbul: MÜSİAD.

MÜSİAD (2018) *Suriyeli Sığınmacılar ve Türkiye Ekonomisi* [Syrian refugees and the Turkish economy], İstanbul: MÜSİAD, available at: www.musiad.org.tr/icerik/yayin-40/pr-291 (accessed on 17 December 2022).

MÜSİAD (2021) *MUSİAD 10 Maddelik Iklim Manifestosunu Açıkladı* [MÜSİAD announced its 10 articles of climate manifesto], available at: www.iklimhaber.org/musiad-10-maddelik-iklim-manifestosunu-acikladi/ (accessed on 16 December 2022).

MÜSİAD (2022) *Covid-19 Sonrası Döneme Global Bakış Tespit ve Öneriler* [Global perspective: assessment and recommendations for the post-Covid-19 period], available at: www.musiad.org.tr/uploads/yayinlar/arastirma-raporlari/pdf/globalustkuruluCOVIDraporu.pdf (accessed 15 December 2022).

Nas, Ç. (2021) 'Avrupa Yeşil Mutabakatı ve Türkiye' [European Green Deal and Turkey], webinar, available at: www.youtube.com/watch?v=XyOhC7j5uAs (accessed on 14 October 2021).

Nas, Ç. and Özer, Y. (2017) *Turkey and EU Integration: Achievements and Obstacles*, Abingdon: Routledge.

Nation Alliance (2023) *Ortak Politikalar Mutabakat Metni* [Consensus document for common policies], Ankara: Nation Alliance, available at: https://chp.org.tr/yayin/ortak-politikalar-mutabakat-metni/Open (accessed on 2 March 2023).

Nişancıoğlu, K. (2014) 'The Ottoman Origins of Capitalism: Uneven and Combined Development and Eurocentrism', *Review of International Studies*, 40 (2), pp. 325–347.

Nousios, P., Overbeek, H. and Tsolakis, A. (eds) (2012) *Globalisation and European Integration: Critical Approaches to Regional Order and International Relations*, London: Routledge.

OECD (2023) *OECD Data Explorer: Trade Union Density*, available at: https://stats.oecd.org/Index.aspx?DataSetCode=TUD (accessed on 23 July 2023).

Official Gazette (2002) *Resmî Gazete*, No. 24808, 7 July, available at: www.csgb.gov.tr/media/1673/2002_uyesayilari.pdf (accessed on 15 May 2023).

Official Gazette (2010) *Tebliğ*, available at: www.csgb.gov.tr/media/1272/2010_uyesayilari.pdf (accessed on 15 May 2023).

Official Gazette (2021a) *Resmî Gazete*, No. 31553, 30 July, available at: www.csgb.gov.tr/media/83673/2021_temmuz.pdf (accessed on 15 May 2023).

Official Gazette (2021b) *Resmî Gazete*, No. 31529, 2 July, available at: www.csgb.gov.tr/media/81565/2021_uyesayilari.pdf (accessed on 15 May 2023).

Onaran, Ö. (2009) 'Crises and Post-Crises Adjustment in Turkey, Implications for Labour', in Z. Öniş and F. Şenses (eds), *Turkey and the Global Economy: Neo-Liberal Restructuring and Integration in the Post-Crisis Era*, London: Routledge, pp. 243–261.

Önder, N. (1999) 'Integrating with the Global Market: The State and the Crisis of Political Representation: Turkey in the 1980s and 1990s', *International Journal of Political Economy*, 28 (2), pp. 44–84.

Önder, N. (2016) *The Economic Transformation of Turkey: Neoliberalisation and State Intervention*, London: I. B. Tauris.

Öniş, Z. (1987) 'Inflation and Importing Industrialization: An Interpretation of the Turkish Case', *Journal of Economic and Administrative Studies*, 1 (1), pp. 25–43.

Öniş, Z. (2003) 'Domestic Politics, International Norms and Challenges to the State: Turkey–EU Relations in the Post-Helsinki Era', *Turkish Studies*, 4 (1), pp. 9–34.

Öniş, Z. (2007) 'Conservative Globalists Versus Defensive Nationalists: Political Parties and Paradoxes of Europeanization in Turkey', *Journal of Southern Europe and the Balkans*, 9 (3), pp. 247–261.

Öniş, Z. (2009), 'Conservative Globalism at the Crossroads: The Justice and Development Party and the Thorny Path to Democratic Consolidation', *Mediterranean Politics*, 14 (1), pp. 21–40.

Öniş, Z. (2013) 'Sharing Power: Turkey's Democratization Challenge in the Age of the AKP Hegemony', *Insight Turkey*, 15 (2), pp. 103–122.

Öniş, Z. (2015) 'Monopolising the Centre: The AKP and the Uncertain Path of Turkish Democracy', *International Spectator*, 50 (2), pp. 22–41.

Öniş, Z. and Kirkpatrick, C. (1991) 'Turkey', in J. Harrigan, P. Mosley and J. Toye (eds), *Aid and Power*, Vol. I: *The World Bank and Policy-Based Lending*, London: Routledge, pp. 9–37.

Öniş, Z. and Webb, S. B. (1998) 'Turkey: Democratization and Adjustment from Above', in Z. Öniş (ed.), *State and Market: The Political Economy of Turkey in Comparative Perspective*, İstanbul: Boğaziçi University Press, pp. 323–373.

Overbeek, H. (2000) 'Transnational Historical Materialism: Theories of Transnational Class Formation and World Order', in R. Palan (ed.), *Global Political Economy: Contemporary Theories*, London: Routledge, pp. 168–183.

Overbeek, H. (2012) 'Sovereign Debt Crisis in Euroland: Root Causes and Implications for European Integration', *International Spectator*, 47 (1), pp. 30–48.

Özal, T. (1991) *Turkey in Europe and Europe in Turkey*, London: K. Rustem & Brother.

Özbudun, E. (2014) 'AKP at the Crossroads: Erdoğan's Majoritarian Drift', *South European Society and Politics*, 19 (2), pp. 155–167.

Özbudun, E. (2015) 'Turkey's Judiciary and the Drive Toward Competitive Authoritarianism', *International Spectator*, 50 (2), pp. 42–55.

Özden, B. A. (2014) 'The Transformation of Social Welfare and Politics in Turkey: A Successful Convergence of Neoliberalism and Populism', in İ. Akça, A. Bekmen and B. A. Özden (eds), *Turkey Reframed: Constituting Neoliberal Hegemony*, London: Pluto, pp. 482–535.

Özen, Ç. (1998) 'Neo-Functionalism and the Change in the Dynamics of Turkey–EU Relations', *Perceptions: Journal of International Affairs*, 3 (3), pp. 34–57.

Özilhan, T. (2020), 'TÜSİAD 2020 Genel Kurul' [TÜSİAD general assembly 2020], webinar, available at: www.youtube.com/watch?v=l4BWHCUFiTE (accessed on 23 May 2023).

Pakdemirli, B. (2020), 'Tarım ve Gıdada Gelecek 10 Yılda Öne Çıkacak Bazı Konular ve Kavramlar' [Particular topics and concepts which will become pre-eminent regarding agriculture and food in the next decade], available at: www.youtube.com/watch?v=wAHzWDaRNYo (accessed on 26 April 2023).

Pakdemirli, B. (2021a), 'Pandemiye Rağmen Tarım Büyüdü, Tarımsal Hasılada Avrupa'da Lideriz' [Agriculture grew despite the COVID-19 pandemic: Turkey is the leader in Europe in terms of its agricultural production], available at: www.youtube.com/watch?v=iXHVAokbtYo (accessed on 10 September 2024).

Pakdemirli, B. (2021b) 'Tarım Ormanın Geleceği' [The future of agriculture and forestry], webinar, available at: www.youtube.com/watch?v=-ID0X6TK3zo (accessed on 27 April 2023).

Pakdemirli, B. (2022) 'Uludağ Ekonomi Zirvesi' [Uludağ economics summit], webinar, available at: www.youtube.com/watch?v=A-BliKyofBI (accessed on 10 September 2024).

Piketty, T. (2014) *Capital in the Twenty-First Century*, trans. A. Goldhammer, Cambridge, MA: Belknap Press of Harvard University Press.

Polanyi, K. (1944) *The Great Transformation: The Political and Economic Origins of our Time*, Boston, MA: Beacon Press.

Reiners, W. and Turhan, E. (2021) *EU–Turkey Relations: Theories, Institutions and Policies*, Cham: Palgrave.

Robinson, W. I. (2004) *A Theory of Global Capitalism: Production, Class and State in a Transnational World*, Baltimore, MD: Johns Hopkins University Press.

Rodrik, D. (2015), *Premature Deindustrialization, NBER Working Paper Series* 20935, Cambridge, MA: National Bureau of Economic Research, available at: www.nber.org/system/files/working_papers/w20935/w20935.pdf (accessed on 7 January 2022).

Rodrik, D. (2017) *Populism and the Economics of Globalisation*, NBER Working Paper Series 23559, Cambridge, MA: National Bureau of Economic Research, available at: www.nber.org/papers/w23559 (accessed on 28 June 2022).

Rosenberg, J. (2013) 'The "Philosophical Premises" of Uneven and Combined Development', *Review of International Studies*, 39 (3), pp. 569–597.

Rosenberg, J. (2021) 'Results and Prospects: An Introduction to the CRIA Special Issue on UCD', *Cambridge Review of International Affairs*, 34 (2), pp. 146–163.

Rosenberg, J. and Boyle, C. (2019) 'Understanding 2016: China, Brexit and Trump in the History of Uneven and Combined Development', *Journal of Historical Sociology*, 32 (1), pp. 32–58.

Ruggie, J. G. (1982) 'International Regimes, Transactions, and Change: Embedded Liberalism in the Postwar Economic Order', *International Organization*, 36 (2), pp. 379–415.

Rumelili, B. (2008) 'Negotiating Europe: EU–Turkey Relations from an Identity Perspective', *Insight Turkey*, 10 (1), pp. 97–110.

Rumelili, B. (2011) 'Turkey: Identity, Foreign Policy, and Socialization in a Post-Enlargement Europe', *Journal of European Integration*, 33 (2), pp. 235–249.

Ryner, M. and Cafruny, A. (2017) *The European Union and Global Capitalism: Origins, Development, Crisis*, London: Palgrave.

Saad-Filho, A. (2018) 'Privilege Versus Democracy in Brazil', Jacobin, 27 October, available at: https://jacobin.com/2018/10/brazil-election-bolsonaro-haddad-lula-pt-democracy (accessed on 23 June 2023).

Saatçioğlu, B. (2020) 'The European Union's Refugee Crisis and Rising Functionalism in EU–Turkey Relations', *Turkish Studies*, 21 (2), pp. 169–187.

Şahin, Ç. E. and Erol, M. E. (2021) *The Condition of the Working Class in Turkey: Labour under Neoliberal Authoritarianism*, London: Pluto.

Sakallıoğlu, Ü. C. (1992) 'Labour and State in Turkey: 1960–80', *Middle Eastern Studies*, 28 (4), pp. 712–728.

Saval, N. (2016) 'Polanyi in our Times', The Nation, 22 December, available at: www.thenation.com/article/archive/karl-polanyi-in-our-times/ (accessed on 16 July 2023).

Schimmelfennig, F., Engert, S. and Knobel, H. (2006) *International Socialization in Europe: European Organizations, Political Conditionality and Democratic Change*, Basingstoke: Palgrave Macmillan.

Schmitter, P. C. (2005) 'Neo-Neofunctionalism', in A. Wiener and T. Diez (eds), *European Integration Theory*, Oxford: Oxford University Press, pp. 45–74.

Sharma, R. (2021), 'The Billionaire Boom: How the Super-Rich Soaked up Covid Cash', *Financial Times*, 14 May, available at: https://archive.md/eNLqE (accessed on 7 January 2022).

Shields, S. (2003) 'The "Charge of the Right Brigade": Transnational Social Forces and the Neoliberal Configuration of Poland's Transition', *New Political Economy*, 8 (2), pp. 225–244.

Shields, S. (2012) *The International Political Economy of Transition: Neoliberal Hegemony and Eastern Central Europe's Transformation*, London: Routledge.

Sim, S. (2000) *Post-Marxism: An Intellectual History*, London: Routledge.

Tansel, C. B. (ed.) (2017) *States of Discipline: Authoritarian Neoliberalism and the Contested Reproduction of Capitalist Order*, London: Rowman & Littlefield International.

Tansel, C. B. (2018) 'Authoritarian Neoliberalism and Democratic Backsliding in Turkey: Beyond the Narratives of Progress', *South European Society and Politics*, 23 (2), pp. 197–217.

Tekeli, İ. and İlkin, S. (1993a) *Türkiye ve Avrupa Topluluğu: Ulus Devletini Aşma Çabasındaki Avrupa'ya Türkiye'nin Yaklaşımı* [Turkey and the European Union: Turkey's approach to Europe in transcending the nation-state], vol. I, Ankara: Ümit Yayıncılık.

Tekeli, İ. and İlkin, S. (1993b) *Türkiye ve Avrupa Topluluğu: Ulus Devletini Aşma Çabasındaki Avrupa'ya Türkiye'nin Yaklaşımı* [Turkey and the European Community: Turkey's approach to Europe in transcending the nation-state], vol. II, Ankara: Ümit Yayıncılık.

Tekeli, İ. and İlkin, S. (2000) *Türkiye ve Avrupa Birliği 3, Ulus Devletini Aşma Çabasındaki Avrupa'ya Türkiye'nin Yaklaşımı* [Turkey and the European Union: Turkey's Approach to Europe in |Ation-state], vol. III, Ankara: Ümit Yayıncılık.

Therborn, G. (2008) *From Marxism to Post-Marxism?*, London: Verso.

Thomas, P. D. (2009) *The Gramscian Moment: Philosophy, Hegemony and Marxism*, Leiden and Boston, MA: Brill.

TİP (2023) *Devrim Programı* [Programme for revolution], available at: https://tip.org.tr/program/ (accessed on 25 June 2023).

TOBB (2011a) *Başkanların Genel Kurul Konuşmaları 2: Cilt 1953–2010* [Presidential speeches in general assemblies, vol. II: 1953–2010], ed. N. Bozkurt, Ankara: Yorum.

TOBB (2011b) Başkanların Genel Kurul Konuşmaları 3. Cilt [Presidential speeches in general assemblies, vol. III], ed. N. Bozkurt, Ankara: Yorum.

Tocci, N. (2005) 'Europeanization in Turkey: Trigger or Anchor for Reform?', *South European Society and Politics*, 10 (1), pp. 73–83.

Toprak, Z. (1995) *Türkiye'de Ekonomi ve Toplum (1908–1950): Milli İktisat–Milli Burjuvazi* [Economy and society in Turkey (1908–1950): national economy-national bourgeoisie], İstanbul: Tarih Vakfı Yurt Yayınları.

Torfing, J. (1999) *New Theories of Discourse: Laclau, Mouffe and Žižek*, Oxford: Blackwell.

Tormey, S. and Townshend, J. (2006) *Key Thinkers from Critical Theory to Post-Marxism*, London: Sage.

Toscano, A. (2023) *Late Fascism: Race, Capitalism and the Politics of Crisis*, London: Verso.

Tronti, M. (1966) *Operai e Capitale*, Torino: Einaudi.

Trotsky, L. (1906/2007) 'Results and Prospects', in L. Trotsky, *The Permanent Revolution and Results and Prospects*, intro. M. Löwy, London: Socialist Resistance, pp. 24–100.

Trotsky, L. (1928/1957) *The Third International After Lenin*, trans. John G. Wright, New York: Pioneer.

Trotsky, L. (1929/2007) 'The Permanent Revolution', in L. Trotsky, *The Permanent Revolution and Results and Prospects*, intro. M. Löwy, London: Socialist Resistance, pp. 111–256.

Trotsky, L. (1930/2000) *The History of the Russian Revolution*, Marxist Internet Archive, available at: www.marxists.org/archive/trotsky/1930/hrr/ (accessed on 11 September 2024). (accessed on 14 April 2024).

Tüfenkçi, B. (2017), 'TÜSİAD Küresel Ticaret: Politikadan Eyleme Konferansı' [TÜSİAD conference on global trade: from politics to action], webinar, available at: www.youtube.com/watch?v=-Uku5SYYaso (accessed 10 November 2022).

Tuğal, C. (2009) *Passive Revolution: Absorbing the Islamic Challenge to Capitalism*, Stanford, CA: Stanford University Press.

TUIK (2024) *International Migration Statistics 2022*, available at: https://data.tuik.gov.tr/Bulten/Index?p=International-Migration-Statistics-2022-49457&dil=2

Türker, M. (2005) 'Toplumsal Rekabet Ekonomisi ve Sosyal Piyasa Ekonomisi 2' [Social competitive economy and social market economy 2], *Güvercin Dergisi*, 13.

Türkeş, M. (2016), 'Decomposing Neo-Ottoman Hegemony', *Journal of Balkan and Near Eastern Studies*, 18 (3), pp. 191–216.

Türk-İş (2002a), *Belgelerle Türk-İş Tarihi 1963–1980* [The history of Türk-İş in documents 1963–1980], Ankara: Türk-İş Yayınları.

Türk-İş (2002b) *Belgelerle Türk-İş Tarihi 1999–2002* [The history of Türk-İş in documents 1999–2002], Ankara: Türk-İş Yayınları.

Türk-İş (2002c) *Avrupa Birliği Kıbrıs, Ermeni Soykırımı İddiaları, Azınlıklar-Bölücülük, Ege Sorunu, Patrikhane, Heybeliada Ruhban Okulu, IMF Programları Konularında Türkiye'de Ne İstiyor?* [What does the EU want from Turkey regarding Cyprus, allegations of Armenian genocide, minorities-seperatism, Aegean problems, the patriarchate, clergy school in Heybeliada and IMF programmes?], Ankara: Türk-İş Eğitim Yayınları 73.

Türk-İş Editorial (2015) 'Gelişmeler ve Umutlar' [Developments and hopes], 13 March, available at: www.turkis.org.tr/gelismeler-ve-umutlar-2/ (accessed on 21 March, 2023).

Türk-İş Editorial (2016) 'Sabrımızı Zorlamayın' [Don't test our patience], available at: www.turkis.org.tr/sabrimizi-zorlamayin-2/ (accessed on 21 March 2023).

Turkish Youth Study (2023) *Türkiye Gençlik Araştırması* [Turkish youth study], Ankara: Konrad Adenauer Stiftung, available at: www.kas.de/documents/283907/24685727/Turkish+Youth+Study+2023+Executive+Summary.pdf/0bd0a46d-c9ed-959c-5297-20e3a5355530?version=1.1&t=1685717331875 (accessed on 14 April 2024).

TÜSİAD (1996) *Türkiye'nin İhracatında Uzun Vadeli Bir Perspektif ve Öneriler* [A long-term perspective and recommendations concerning Turkey's exports], T/96–1/195, İstanbul: TÜSİAD Yayınları.

TÜSİAD (1997) *Türkiye'de Demokratikleşme Perspektifleri* [Democratisation perspectives in Turkey], T/97–207, İstanbul: TÜSİAD Yayınları.

TÜSİAD (1999) *Avrupa Birliği'ne Tam Üyeliğe Doğru Siyasi Kıstaslar ve Uyum Süreci* [Political conditions and adaption towards full membership of the European Union], T/99–12/276, İstanbul: TÜSİAD Yayınları.

TÜSİAD (2001) *'Perspectives on Democratization in Turkey' and 'EU Copenhagen Political Criteria': Views and Priorities*, T/2001–07/305, İstanbul: TÜSİAD Yayınları.

TÜSİAD (2002) European Union and Turkey: Towards Full Membership, İstanbul: TÜSİAD Yayınları.

TÜSİAD (2008) *Gümrük Birliği Çerçevesinde AB'nin Üçüncü Ülkelerle Yaptığı Serbest Ticaret Anlaşmalarının Avrupa ve Türk İş Dünyasına Etkileri* [Effects of the free trade agreements concluded by the EU with third countries in the context of the customs union on European and Turkish business], T/2008–06/467, İstanbul: TÜSİAD Yayınları.

TÜSİAD (2016) *Industry 4.0 in Turkey as an Imperative for Global Competitiveness: An Emerging Market Perspective*, T/2016–03–576, İstanbul: TÜSİAD Yayınları.

TÜSİAD (2021a) *Yeni Bir Anlayışla Geleceği İnşa: İnsan, Bilim, Kurumlar* [Constructing the future with a new insight: humans, science and institutions], İstanbul: TÜSİAD Yayınları.

TÜSİAD (2021b) *Avrupa Yeşil Mutabakatı, Döngüsel Ekonomi Eylem Planı, Türk İş Dünyasına Neler Getirecek?* [European Green Deal, circular economy action plan, repercussions for Turkish business], T/2021–06/621, İstanbul: TÜSİAD Yayınları.

UNCTAD (2023a) *Gross Domestic Product: Total and Per Capita*, available at: https://unctadstat.unctad.org/datacentre/dataviewer/US.GDPTotal (accessed on 10 September 2024).

UNCTAD (2023b) *FDI Inward Stock, by Region and Economy 1990–2022*, Annex, available at: https://unctad.org/topic/investment/world-investment-report (accessed on 12 August 2023).

UNCTAD (2023c) *FDI Outward Stock, by Region and Economy 1990–2022*, Annex, available at: https://unctad.org/topic/investment/world-investment-report (accessed on 12 August 2023).

UNCTAD (2023d) *World Investment Report 2023*, available at: https://unctad.org/publication/world-investment-report-2023#anchor_download (accessed on 12 August 2023).

UNHCR (2023) *Türkiye Fact Sheet*, available at: www.unhcr.org/tr/wp-content/uploads/sites/14/2023/03/Bi-annual-fact-sheet-2023-02-Turkiye-.pdf (accessed on 24 July 2023).

Uzgel, İ. (2009) 'AKP: Neoliberal Dönüşümün Yeni Aktörü' [AKP: The new actor in neoliberal transformation], in İ. Uzgel and B. Duru (eds), *AKP Kitabı: Bir Dönüşümün Bilançosu* [The book on AKP: balance sheet of a transformation], Ankara: Phoenix, pp. 11–39.

Uzgel, İ. (2020) 'Turkey's Double Movement: Islamists, Neoliberalism and Foreign Policy', in P. Bedirhanoğlu, Ç. Dölek, F. Hülagü and Ö. Kaygusuz (eds), *Turkey's New State in the Making: Transformations in Legality, Economy and Coercion*, London: Zed Books, pp. 64–79.

Uzgören, E. (2018) 'Consolidation of Neoliberalism through Political Islam and its Limits: The Case of Turkey', *METU Studies in Development*, 45 (3), pp. 285–307.

van Apeldoorn, B. (2002) *Transnational Capitalism and the Struggle over European Integration*, London: Routledge.

van Apeldoorn, B. (2013), 'The European Capitalist Class and the Crisis of its Hegemonic Project', *Socialist Register 2014*, Pontypool: Merlin, pp. 189–206.

van Apeldoorn, B., Drahokoupil, J. and Horn, L. (eds) (2009), *Contradictions and Limits of Neoliberal European Governance: From Lisbon to Lisbon*, Basingstoke: Macmillan.

van Apeldoorn, B., Graaff, N. and Overbeek, H. (2012) 'The Reconfiguration of the Global State–Capital Nexus', *Globalisations*, 9 (4), pp. 471–486.

van Apeldoorn, B. and Graaff, N. (2022) 'The State in Global Capitalism Before and After the COVID-19 Crisis', *Contemporary Politics*, 28 (3), pp. 306–327.

van Apeldoorn, B. and Overbeek, H. (2012) 'Introduction: The Life Course of the Neoliberal Project and the Global Crisis', in H. Overbeek and B. van Apeldoorn (eds), *Neoliberalism in Crisis*, Basingstoke: Palgrave, pp. 1–23.

Van der Pijl, K. (1998) *Transnational Classes and International Relations*, London: Routledge.

Van der Pijl, K. (2019) 'A Transnational Class Analysis of the Current Crisis', in B. Jessop and H. Overbeek (eds), *Transnational Capital and Class Fractions: The Amsterdam School Perspective Reconsidered*, London: Routledge, pp. 241–262.

Wenman, M. (2013) *Agonistic Democracy: Constituent Power in the Era of Globalisation*, Cambridge: Cambridge University Press.

Wood, E. M. (1981) 'The Separation of the Economic and the Political in Capitalism', *New Left Review*, 1 (127), pp. 66–95.

Wood, E. M. (1986) *The Retreat from Class: A New 'True' Socialism*, London: Verso.

Wood, E. M. (1990) 'The Uses and Abuses of "Civil Society"', *Socialist Register*, 26, pp. 60–84.

Wood, E. M. (1995) *Democracy Against Capitalism: Renewing Historical Materialism*, Cambridge: Cambridge University Press.

World Bank (2016) *World Development Report 2016: Digital Dividends*, available at: www.worldbank.org/en/publication/wdr2016 (accessed on 7 January 2022).

World Bank (2023) *National Accounts Exports and Imports of Goods and Services to GDP (1981–2020)*, available at: https://data.worldbank.org/indicator/NE.EXP.GNFS.ZS?locations=TR (accessed on 12 August 2023), https://data.worldbank.org/indicator/NE.IMP.GNFS.ZS?locations=TR (accessed on 12 August 2023).

Yalman, G. L. (2009) *Transition to Neoliberalism: The Case of Turkey in the 1980s*, İstanbul: Bilgi University Press.

Yalman, G. L. (2021) 'Crisis in or of Neoliberalism? A Brief Encounter with the Debate on the Authoritarian Turn', in E. Babacan, M. Kutun, E. Pınar and Z.

Yılmaz (eds), *Regime Change in Turkey: Neoliberal Authoritarianism, Islamism and Hegemony*, Abingdon: Routledge, pp. 15–31.

Yalman, G. L. and Göksel, A. (2017) 'Transforming Turkey? Putting Turkey–EU Relations into a Historical Perspective', *Uluslararası İlişkiler*, 14 (56), pp. 23–37.

Yalman, G. L., Marois, T. and Güngen, A. R. (eds) (2018) *The Political Economy of Financial Transformation in Turkey*, London: Routledge.

Yalman, G. L., Marois, T. and Güngen, A. R. (2019) 'Introduction: Debating Financial Transformation in Turkey', in G. L. Yalman, T. Marois and A. R. Güngen (eds), *The Political Economy of Financial Transformation in Turkey*, London: Routledge, pp. 1–23.

Yeldan, E. (2006) 'Neoliberal Global Remedies: From Speculative-Led Growth to IMF-Led Crisis in Turkey', *Review of Radical Political Economics*, 38 (2), pp. 193-213.

Yenel, S. (2020), 'Türkiye & Avrupa 5.0: Türkiye–AB ve Yeşil Mutabakat' [Turkey and Europe 5.0: Turkey–EU and the Green Deal], webinar, available at: www.youtube.com/watch?v=tS90O76FfrE (accessed 15 October 2021).

Yeşilada, B. (2013) *EU–Turkey Relations in the 21st Century*, London: Routledge.

Yıldız, A. (2016) *The European Union's Immigration Policy: Managing Migration in Turkey and Morocco*, London: Palgrave.

Yıldızoğlu, E. (2015), *AKP Siyasal İslam ve Restorasyon* [JDP political Islam and restoration], İstanbul: Tekin Yayın.

Yılmaz, B. (2022) 'İktidar değişirse ne olacak? İyi Partili Bilge Yılmaz tek tek anlattı' [What will happen if the government changes? Bilge Yılmaz from İyi Party explains in detail], webinar, available at: www.youtube.com/watch?v=165qIZtuz0o (accessed on 7 March 2023).

Yılmaz, G. (2016) 'Europeanisation or De-Europeanisation? Media Freedom in Turkey (1999–2015)', *South European Society and Politics*, 21 (1), pp. 147–161.

Yılmaz, H. (2011) 'Euroscepticism in Turkey: Parties, Elites, and Public Opinion', *South European Society and Politics*, 16 (1), pp. 185–208.

Zeytinoğlu, A. (2020), 'Pandemi Sonrası Dönemde Türkiye–AB Ekonomik ve Ticari İlişkileri Semineri' [Seminar on Turkey–EU economic and trade relations after the pandemic], webinar, available at: www.youtube.com/watch?v=CHW3aVJRoQo (accessed 15 October 2021).

Žižek, S. (1999) *The Ticklish Subject: The Absent Centre of Political Ontology*, London: Verso.

Žižek, S. (2000) 'Class Struggle or Postmodernism? Yes, Please!', in J. Butler, E. Laclau and S. Žižek (eds), *Contingency, Hegemony and Universality: Contemporary Dialogues on the Left*, London: Verso, pp. 90–135.

Zürcher, E. J. (2005) *Turkey, A Modern History*, 3rd edn, London: I. B. Tauris.

Index

EU authorised representative for GPSR:
Easy Access System Europe, Mustamäe tee 50,
10621 Tallinn, Estonia
gpsr.requests@easproject.com

www.ingramcontent.com/pod-product-compliance
Lightning Source LLC
LaVergne TN
LVHW050047200525
811683LV00004B/57